A Narrative of War

*From the Beaches of Sicily to the Hitler Line
with the Seaforth Highlanders of Canada
10 July 1943 – 8 June 1944*

A Narrative of War

*From the Beaches of Sicily to the Hitler Line
with the Seaforth Highlanders of Canada
10 July 1943 – 8 June 1944*

Robert L. McDougall

The Golden Dog Press
Ottawa – Canada – 1996

ISBN 0-919614-61-2 (paperback)
vspace1pc

The Publishers and the Author wish to acknowledge with gratitude permission granted to them by the copyright holders to use four maps drawn from the regimental history, *The Seaforth Highlanders of Canada: 1919–1965* (1969) by Reginald H. Roy, *CD., Ph.D., F.R.Hist.S.*

Canadian Cataloguing in Publication Data

McDougall, Robert L., 1918–
  A narrative of war : from the beaches of Sicily to the Hitler Line with the Seaforth Highlanders of Canada, 10 July, 1943 – 8 June 1944

ISBN 0-919614-61-2

  1. McDougall, Robert L., 1918– 2. Canada. Canadian Army. Seaforth Highlanders of Canada–History. 3. World War, 1939–1945–Campaigns–Italy. 4. World War, 1939–1945–Personal narratives, Canadian. I. Title.

D811.M33 1996   940.54'8171   C96-900404-4

Cover design by The Gordon Creative Group of Ottawa.

Text layout by Ch. Thiele, Carleton Production Centre of Nepean.

Printed in Canada by AGMV "l'imprimeur" Inc., of Cap-Saint-Ignace, Québec.

Distributed by:

  Oxford University Press Canada,
  70 Wynford Drive, DON MILLS, Ont., Canada, M3C 1J9.
  Phone: 416-441-2941   *   Fax: 416-444-0427

The Golden Dog Press wishes to express its appreciation to the Canada Council and the Ontario Arts Council for current and past support of its publishing programme.

for

The Lads of Cabar Feidh

Table of Contents

Foreword *una ,, borrowed*

Dear Richard and Ian,

I have thought of you often while working on this book. You are part of its beginnings as a manuscript and its end in publication. The crazy thing about it is that almost thirty-five years lie between.

You will perhaps recognize the book's title, which is borrowed from a piece in a collection of your father's essays published a few years ago under the title of *Totems*. The essay in question was not really an essay but a fragment of a larger work which was the story of the Seaforth Highlanders of Canada in action in Sicily and Italy from the summer of 1943 to the spring of 1944. That narrative (can you stand it?) was itself a fragment of a still larger work never completed. I explained in a prefatory note to the *Totems* piece the circumstances under which the larger work came into being and how it came to be cut short. Let me quote from myself. And as I do, let's think back, my bairns, to our early summers on Savary Island on the west coast of British Columbia. That's where it all started. You, Rich, are ten, Ian is eight, and Christine, bless her heart, is four. The date is about 1960.

> The tent was pitched [so I wrote in the lead-up to the Totems piece] between two fir trees that towered over the beach at Savary Island on the British Columbia coast. I called it my office-tent, and it held comfortably two long working tables and a steamer-trunk full of documents. I was in my early forties, aware for the first time of advancing age and feeling the pressures of supporting a family on a modest income and helping in the care of three children. For three successive summers, for at least three hours a day, my wife [that's your mother, of course] kept the children at bay at the cottage site nearby. She told them father was working. What I was working on was a history of the Seaforth Highlanders of Canada, the regiment with which I had served for almost four years in World War II. It looked like a big job. I was especially reluctant to take it on because my wife was by this time battling cancer. But we talked it over and decided to have a try at it. Regimental pride was part of the picture, and regimental pride is a strangely potent force: together with pride of one's family and pride in one's country, it is perhaps the only pride worth having. Skipping over for the time being the long period of inaction for the Seaforths in England, I began with the assault-landing of the regiment at the southern tip of Sicily on 10 July, 1943. My aim was to write

a lean narrative, as free from speculations and pronouncements as possible. From summer to summer my wife's condition worsened. She died in the fall of 1963. About two hundred and fifty pages in from the Sicily beaches, having finished a section on the dramatic involvement of the Seaforths in the battle for the Liri Valley in Italy, 23 May, 1944, I gave up the project. The official history of the Seaforth Highlanders was taken over by Professor Reginald H. Roy of the University of Victoria and was published in 1969.[1]

So much for the past. The present is my retirement from Carleton University in the summer of 1984 and my turning, in a leisurely way that is the blessing of retirement, to the task of clearing up the paper trail one leaves behind one after nearly forty years of teaching and administration at a university: lecture notes, minutes of meetings, class lists, unpublished articles and the like. And there, looming up towards the end of the trail, was this early and incomplete manuscript of the Seaforth history. What to do with it?

Certainly not throw it out, and that's why I'm addressing these opening words to you. This fragment of a history is the key to an important part of your father's life before you came into the world; and I feel that you should know about it. The particular blessing is that, thanks to the good auspices of Michael Gnarowski and the Golden Dog Press, it is coming to you in the form of a handsome book instead of a shabby manuscript. If of course you want the full story of the Seaforths, you will go to Reg Roy's fine official history, my copy of which in due time I shall pass on to you. But the fragment which I publish here, though intentionally de-personalized, will still have something of my own mark upon it. The other benefit, no less important in its own way, is that my account, abbreviated though it is, nevertheless contains a certain amount of material not present in Professor Roy's official history — the interviews, for example, which I had in 1960 with some of the people involved in the action described.

Back to the personal side of things for a moment, and then I have done. The trouble with a fragment is that it has neither beginning nor end. Well, the rules of this particular game are such that this difficulty cannot be remedied. Whatever virtues the text has must stem from the intensity and colour of the fragment of the story that is told: this is simply a "Narrative of War". I can, however, provide a glimpse of a wider context which will bring the narrator into focus.

[1] *Totems: Essays on the Cultural History of Canada* (Ottawa: Tecumseh Press, 1990), p. 86.

Here are a few key dates and developments which are relevant to the present text. They will at the same time shore up the family records. World War II began in the year I graduated from the University of British Columbia. I took Teacher Training, then taught at Chilliwack Junior-Senior High School while commuting once a week to Vancouver for Canadian Officer Training Corps classes. After further training, this time as Seaforth Reinforcement Officer, at Gordon Head, Victoria, and Currie Barracks, Calgary, I went overseas in July, 1942, and joined the Seaforths in the field in November of that year. Assault training in Scotland followed in the spring of 1943, and in July we made a landing on the southern tip of Sicily as part of the 1st Canadian Division and the British Eighth Army. On the 27th of July, one day short of my 25th birthday, I was wounded just east of Nissoria, which you will find on Map 1 of this volume. I spent the next four months in North Africa, mainly in Algiers, where 95th Canadian General Hospital was located at this stage of the war. By the end of November I was pronounced fit and began hitch-hiking (almost literally) my way back to the regiment. Early in the new year I caught up with the Seaforths again, somewhere near Ortona on the Adriatic I think it was, and I was to remain with the battalion until the end of the war. By that time, of course, the scene for us had shifted from Italy to Europe and VE Day saw us entering Amsterdam to the tumultuous welcome of the Dutch people.

That's about all the framework I can give at the moment for this book, and I think it's all you need. Age and the passage of time having muddied my memory, I have had to rely for much of the hard information in the last paragraph on the letters I sent home during the war to your grandmother in North Vancouver. Your grandfather had died just before my brother and I went overseas, and she was alone. She set great store by our letters. I have in my cupboard a peck of the ones I sent her pretty regularly every week for four years. That's one part of the paper trail I have not dealt with to date. Maybe I'll have time yet for a whack at that pile. Who knows? I hope you enjoy (if that's the word) this book.

Lots of love,

Dad

P.S. In case you're wondering, "Cabar Feidh" is Gaelic for "Stag's Head" — part of the emblem for Seaforth insignia.

Acknowledgements

This fragment of a history of the Seaforth Highlanders of Canada is based primarily on contemporary records of the regiment's part in the campaign fought by the Allies against the Germans (and to a much lesser extent the Italians) in Sicily and Italy between July 1943 and June 1944. Amongst these records, War Diaries of units and formations are a principal source, and the reader who wishes further information on the subject will I am sure receive expert and courteous attention from the Historical Section (G.S.), Army Headquarters, Ottawa. For additional help, the reader might try the History Committee, Seaforth Armoury, Vancouver, B.C. A full and authoritative account of the Canadian participation in the Italian theatre of operations will be found in Lt.-Col. G.W.L. Nicholson's *The Canadians in Italy, 1943–1945* (Ottawa: Queen's Printer, 1956).

The military maps which appear in this volume are reproduced with the kind permission of the Seaforth Highlanders of Canada (Vancouver, B.C.) and Reginald H. Roy, formerly Professor of Military History at the University of Victoria and author of *The Seaforth Highlanders of Canada, 1919–1965* (Vancouver: Evergreen Press, 1969). My thanks go especially to W.F.J. (Wilf) Gildersleeve, formerly Signals Officer with the Seaforths in Italy, for his amiable good services in maintaining my contacts with Vancouver during the course of the present undertaking.

I am grateful to my wife Anne for her love and patience and her practical help in putting this book together.

R.L. McDougall
Ottawa,
January, 1996.

SICILY

10 July 1943 – 6 August 1943

I

Landing at the Pachino Beaches

For the Seaforth Highlanders the Sicilian campaign began early on the morning of the 10th of July at a point seven miles southwest of the Pachino beaches and ended late on the afternoon of the 6th of August at a point just short of Adrano, at the base of Mount Etna, when the 1st Canadian Division was drawn into Army reserve and the pursuit of the Germans to Messina passed to other hands. The time elapsed was 27 days and the distance covered was 125 miles. Opposition on landing was negligible, and the main enemy for almost 70 miles north and west to Piazza Armerina, which was reached on the 17th of July, was a compound of heat, dust, demolitions, an increasingly hilly terrain, and the constant pressure of orders calling for advances over considerable distances without much help from transport. At no time during these early days were the Italian troops to whom the defence of the western and southern parts of the island had been committed a serious obstacle. The remaining 50 to 60 miles, north from Piazza Armerina through Valguarnera and Leonforte, then east through Nissoria, Agira and Regalbuto to Adrano, were a different story. Over this ground, hot and tired beyond belief, the Seaforths fought the stubborn and skilful soldiers of the 15th Panzer Grenadier, 29th Panzer Grenadier and 1st Parachute Divisions. The brigade front was in practice usually the width of a highway or secondary road and the hinterland which dominated it, and the method of advance one of leapfrogging units along a single axis. The spearhead of the battalion was often a company, whose spearhead in turn was usually a platoon or even a section. The campaign cost the Seaforths in total casualties, killed, wounded or missing, 25 officers and 247 other ranks. Six officers and 55 other ranks lost their lives in the four weeks of action.[1]

---

[1]These figures were the highest for the 2nd Brigade, which in turn had by long odds the highest figures for the 1st Canadian Division ("Canadian Operations in Sicily", July–August 1943, C.M.H.Q. Report No. 127, Appendix D, p. 144). High casualty rates are a dubious distinction. In this case I like to think that they were the result of the unusually difficult roles assigned to the battalion in Sicily (and later) and of the great conscientiousness (at times excessive in these early days) of officers and N.C.Os.

By the time the *Circassia* dropped anchor shortly before midnight at her appointed release position off Sugar Beach the loading of the Seaforth serials was already well advanced. Thirty feet above a sea still restless from the afternoon's wind the heavily laden troops stepped from the ship's decks to the boats and moved quietly to their places. Then each boat (10 tons of swinging weight) was dropped as nearly as possible at the right moment to the crest of a wave, where it was freed quickly from the davits and driven away from the dangerous wall of the ship's side. At 1:45, on schedule in spite of the rough seas, the assault serials were reported afloat and circling for the run to the beaches. The boats turned shorewards, forming uncertain lines on the dark swell. The problem now was to put the right boats down in the right places, and naval commanders anxiously checked binnacles and markers against the light from Pachino, which was ablaze from earlier bombing. In most cases direction was found; but in some cases (as at Dieppe, though fortunately without the same serious consequences) it was not. Amongst those who were misplaced that night were the Seaforths, who were supposed to go in on the left of the Patricias but who went in instead on their right.[2]

At 2:45 "A" Company and "C" Company touched down on time and in shallow water, their landing craft having apparently been carried by the swell over the sandbar which had been the subject of such concern the day before. Unmolested on the way in, they encountered little or no opposition on the beaches. The fact that they were slightly misplaced became unimportant. "A" Company on the right, commanded by Capt. S.W. Thomson, blew paths through barbed wire with their Bangalore Torpedoes and moved quickly inland over the low dunes which lay between the beaches and the dry "lake" called Pantano Longarini. "C" Company on the left, commanded by Major J.W. Blair, were held up momentarily when the landing platoons came under light mortar fire which wounded four and killed two.[3] They had also to contend with the confusing pressure of the Patricias on their left. They reorganized without further incident, however, gave way to the Patricias, whose leading elements passed inland,

---

[2]*Ibid.*, pp. 2–3. Similarly, elements of the 1st Brigade, who were supposed to land well to the south on Roger Beach, in fact landed 5000 yards to the north with troops of the Special Service Brigade.

[3]These were the Seaforths' first fatal casualties of the campaign, and therefore the first killed in direct action against the enemy in World War II: K053219 Pte. R.E. Fieldhouse and K052527 Pte. R.H. Hunter.

then themselves turned left towards the causeway at the western end of the salt lakes. By first light both assault companies were in line and moving at a good pace parallel to the shore through vineyards and open fields. Italian soldiers, thinly scattered in outposts, gave up with scarcely a shot being fired. The causeway, an expected strongpoint, was occupied without difficulty, and the companies pushed on to the rising ground beyond.

In the meantime, assured by the success of the first landing, Lt.-Col. Hoffmeister had committed "B" Company, under Capt. F.S. Middleton, and "D" Company, under Capt. E.W. Thomas, in support of the assault and had landed his own headquarters. All had swung left, conforming to the movements of the lead companies, and as dawn came the battalion as a whole was able to consolidate briefly in the area of the causeway before "A" and "C" Company resumed their advance to "Cougar".[4] Contact with 40 and 41 Commando of the Special Service Brigade, who had secured the Seaforths' left flank by an assault nearly four miles up the coast from Sugar Beach, was reported to 2nd Brigade headquarters soon after half-past six. Behind the rifle companies the light-scale vehicles which carried the firepower of the mortars, carriers and anti-tank guns were coming ashore from L.C.Ms.[5] Though these larger craft were stopped (as had been expected) by the sandbar offshore, the battalion lost only two vehicles to deep water. They lost none to enemy fire.

The whole scene had in fact blossomed from the seeds of single as-sault craft isolated by darkness and silence into the grotesquely spreading vine of invasion. Across the peninsula the 51st Highland Division were streaming ashore, and their forward troops were moving swiftly through Pachino. The 1st Brigade of the Canadian division, landing on the right of the Seaforths, had attacked Maucini and the important coastal battery behind it and were ready to push on to the Pachino airfield where they were to join up with British troops. Reserve battalions of the Canadian assault brigades were landing: the Edmontons behind the Seaforths and the Patri-cias, and the 48th Highlanders behind the Royal Canadian Regiment and the Hastings and Prince Edward Regiment. Brigade headquarters, beach control groups, provost sections, and special engineer and maintenance troops were coming ashore. Sherman tanks of the Three Rivers Regiment

---

[4]"Cougar" was the code name of the first objective.

[5]Landing Craft Mechanized. So says W.D., Seaf. of C. But these were one-vehicle craft (50 ft. and ramped) and it seems more likely that the reference would be to L.C.Ts. (Landing Craft Tank). Perhaps Landing Craft Motor?

and self-propelled artillery of the 142nd (British) Field Regiment were ready to leave their ships. The build-up proceeded throughout the sector without serious interference from either Germans or Italians. Up on the causeway it was still possible to feel tense and tired and hot and thirsty. But not lonely. The southern tip of Sicily swarmed with men and vehicles.

A mile beyond the causeway the Seaforths dug in in defensive positions on the sides of the spur which was "Cougar". There they were to stay for the remainder of the day. A brief flurry developed in the morning when a mounted Italian mortar section which the I.O. on patrol observed moving through an orchard on the left flank seemed to threaten the juncture between the Seaforths and the S.S. Brigade.[6] But Canadian heavy mortars (4.2") intervened with a shoot, and (40 and 41 Commando attacking simultaneously) the Italians disappeared. In the afternoon the Navy opened fire on Ispica, and as if in exchange, with the kind of justice the troops came to expect, a handful of mortar bombs and some shells landed on the battalion position. Slit trenches, not taken seriously until now, were quickly dug to regulation depth. That night the Seaforths completed the third and final phase of their assault task by advancing single file in a nightmare march across country two and a half miles along the brigade axis to Ispica, and onto the position whose codename was "Badger".

It was time now for the reserve battalion to be committed, and shortly after midday on the 11th the Edmontons began to close the remaining half-dozen miles to Ispica, which in due time they occupied without opposition. The Seaforths were in fact not to be engaged operationally (that is, as vanguard) for the next few days. One would not dare to say that the battalion rested. They worked hard to reorganize themselves as a land-based unit, they remained alert to the threat of counterattack, and they moved forward. Always they moved forward or were standing by to move forward. That was the pattern.

But as the Germans continued to draw back their outposts through Modica and Ragusa the fists of the division were other units, which in any event struck mostly at air. Late on the afternoon of the 11th, "C" Company, under the second-in-command Capt. B.G. Parker, was dispatched to the coast to occupy Pozzallo, which had fallen earlier to naval bombardment.

---

[6]The Intelligence Officer was Lieut. J.W. Baldwin. The shoot referred to was the result of a chance meeting between an S.S. Bde. officer and an officer of the Sask. L.I. breezing up the road from the beaches farther than he ought in search of game. An interesting early example of flexibility and enterprise.

On the 12th, Major H.P. Bell-Irving, Lieut. A.W. Mercer (the Transport Officer) and Cpl. Davidson of the Signals Platoon played unexpected roles in the taking of Modica while the main body of the battalion trudged uncomfortably but peacefully through the hills to the east of the town. This skirmish in a place supposedly cleared netted seven field, five medium guns and one anti-tank gun, several hundred Italian prisoners, and the commander and staff of the 206th Italian Coastal Division. On the 13th, Capt. Thomson was wounded in a brief exchange with Italian soldiers at a road block beyond Modica; but by late that night the battalion, with the 1st Brigade now in the lead, had advanced another eight miles over dusty secondary roads and mule tracks to a concentration area on the slopes of the hills just east and north of Ragusa. The extreme left flank of the Eighth Army was now halted on the army commander's orders, and the next day General Montgomery himself visited the troops in brigade assembly to tell them what fine chaps they were and how well the battle was going.

The Seaforths were now thirty miles from the beaches. Perhaps prematurely, they had tasted the sweets of victory in their rout of the ineffectual troops of the 206th Coastal Division. They had suffered few casualties, fired few rounds in anger. As battle inoculations go, this had been an easy one. The lessons of Dieppe (such as they were) could scarcely be said to have been put to the test. But officers and men had learned tricks never learned on schemes, and, most important, they had withstood successfully a remarkably severe test of physical endurance.

———————

Extracts from the Diary of Capt. B.G. Parker, 2 i/c "C" Company, dated 9–14 July, 1943.

9 July Wind rising and a choppy sea; not so good for landing. Briefing again and packing. The boys are all in very good heart and confident. I went to Communion at 0730; it meant much. Convoys protected by cruisers and battleships and Spitfires. The wind grew in intensity until 2200 hours and dropped. We started loading at 0015 hours with the second flight.[7]

10 July The great day. The fun really started for me about 0300 hours. Terrific bombardment by our heavy guns. Not much firing seen on shore.

---

[7]Capt. Parker, as 2 i/c of a company, was L.O.B. ("Left Out of Battle") and therefore landed with the second flight of the assault.

Tricky loading landing craft because of heavy swell. Landed wetshod at 0645 hours. Few casualties. Surprise achieved. Saw about 60 prisoners; prisoners and civilians not very perturbed. Dug in in transit area north of the salt lakes. Hot as hell. Very heavy firing about 1600 hours. I move up to "C" Company position, where we come under mortar and artillery fire.[8] See our heavy mortars, self-propelled guns, which silence the enemy. We move off to Phase III. Terrific anti-aircraft barrage when our ships bombed off the beaches that night.

11 July Everyone going to sleep. All completely lost. Lose Blair. Take part of company on, picking up Major Forin, Doug Strain and ten others and guide the lot by the stars.[9] Dig in and sleep two hours. Lots of prisoners. We pull out by truck to take over Pozzallo from the navy. The Germans have just left and the people are starving.

12 July We break open the granary and get bread and macaroni queues going. The people are in terrible condition. General Leese arrives; all going well.[10] We collect many prisoners and put them in the Town Hall. Snipers about.

13 July Up and out by 0700 hours to get bread queues in order. A howling mass of hungry people in the town square, 3000 of them, all in a terrible state; of course they blame Fascism. We arrange distribution of flour and shop to open. Round up 250 prisoners, including 10 officers. Feed them and take them all swimming. Prisoners shipped off by L.C.I.[11]

14 July At midnight we leave Pozzallo by trucks for the battalion, which is north of Modica. We drive through the night, stop before dawn to sleep one hour, then on. Arrive just in time to get ready for march to General Montgomery's inspection of the 2nd Brigade. He seemed very pleased and said all was going nicely and up to date. Canadians had taken 5000 prisoners. The battalion moves off tomorrow, and I am to be left in command of L.O.Bs. Double sentries; Bell-Irving at rear battalion headquarters. Sleep under wall. Have pack horses.

---

[8]This would be "Cougar". See above.

[9]This was the "nightmare march" to "Badger". Forin and Strain were 2 i/c and Adjutant respectively on landing.

[10]Lt.-Gen. Sir Oliver Leese, K.C.G., C.B.E., D.S.O., commander of 30th Corps, of which the 1st Canadian Division was at that time a part.

[11]Landing Craft Infantry.

Extracts from a Personal Narrative by Major H.P. Bell-Irving, dated 17 July, 1943.[12]

As darkness fell on the 9th we began to close the coast, and the sea, which had been very rough, slackened off. It was a fine night, with a bright moon up until midnight. Twenty miles or so off the coast a few aircraft flares were dropped over us and anti-aircraft tracer went up from the peninsula to meet the visitors we were sending over them. A little later I saw the glare of a coast searchlight on the horizon.

The moon had gone down and it was very dark when we manned our craft, which were to take in the second wave of the assault, and with them me, as a sort of acting 2 i/c to the C.O. Only just visible, the dim figures crouched in rows in each craft were a grim reality. ... We reached our anchorage position, stopped, and the command came to lower away. The sea was still fairly rough, but we slipped silently over each wave in turn. Faint outlines of other craft could be seen ahead and astern of us. The glow of a burning aerodrome inland silhouetted the line of the coast more and more clearly as we approached. A searchlight stabbed the darkness towards us, paused and sputtered out. ... Suddenly a stream of red dots issuing from a pillbox on our left announced the beaching of the first wave. Very little firing developed, and a few minutes later we got Jim Blair's success signal and went in to land.[13] A grate, a bump, and down went the door. I was in water, wading ashore. About 15 yards, not very deep, and there it was: Sicily. I could hardly believe it. A lovely sandy beach was bordered with a barbed-wire fence even less formidable than ours in England. We hacked a few holes in the wire and pushed inland to join the leading companies, through neat rows of low bushes which daylight showed to be grapevines. The country we had all memorized from maps and photographs was quite recognizable, but the atmosphere and tropical trees made it all very strange.

The causeway we had expected to fight for was undefended when we got there. The Italian machine-guns were in position and loaded, and

---

[12]Major Bell-Irving, as he himself indicates, landed immediately behind the first assault wave as spare 2 i/c to Lt.-Col. Hoffmeister. In the event of heavy casualties both he and Major Forin might have been required.

[13]W.D., Seaf. of C. of 10 July, 1943, attributes the success signal to "A" Company and Capt. Thomson.

stacks of grenades were laid out around each post. There were signs of a hasty departure. I went back briefly to the beach to help get stores ashore, and I found that a good many Tommy guns had been thrown away on the beach and a good many No. 38 sets.[14] I got a mule cart and collected what I could. . . .

The advance continued according to plan, and in the afternoon we found ourselves in a vineyard on a hill overlooking the beach area.[15] We moved by night to a high position farther inland, and daylight, Sunday, found us there, well established in Sicily. . . . [16] Since then our advance has been very rapid. We passed through deserted Ispica in the moonlight, the first southern town I had ever seen. It is all very beautiful, but too hot and dry to be perfect. The people are indescribably poor. They have no clothes, no shoes, and haven't eaten for days. The Germans have used up everything for the army.

We had a spirited little scrap in Modica, but the people seemed glad to see us when we got into it. They cheer and clap and make a great fuss. I think it is partly relief at losing the Germans, but chiefly an eagerness to cadge cigarettes and a sound instinct as to the side on which their bread is buttered. We didn't stay in Modica, but again dug into a farm in the mountains. I got in some riding on a beautiful charger which I borrowed from an Italian cavalry officer. We have collected quite a string of pack horses and mules from the countryside, but as our vehicles arrive we gradually become independent and too fast for the horses. Ragusa is quite a fascinating place. I went in to try to scrounge some troop trucks, but they had done a good job demobilizing them . . .

-----

[14]Many weapons were put out of order by the sand, which can foul up the bolt action of a T.S.M.G. quicker than anything I know. No. 38 sets were carried (under protest) by Platoon Commanders. They were not generally found to be effective and to the best of my knowledge were not used again at this level in the Mediterranean theatre.

[15]"Cougar".

[16]"Badger".

Letter from K534897 Pte. George Ableson to Mr. John Ableson of 2876 West 5th Ave., Vancouver, B.C., dated 14 July, 1943.[17]

Dear John:

You will have been wondering about the long gap in my letters what was brewing for this outfit to which, as I've told you, I was posted much against my wishes a few months ago. What was brewing and has brewed is an assault on fortress Europe through a cellar trapdoor which is the island of Sicily. We landed in the early hours of the 10th, as you will no doubt have learned by now from the newspapers.

I'm writing this in the shade of a gas-cape slung over the end of my rifle, which I have wedged upright between two stones. I don't think the C.O. would approve of this use of my personal weapon, but he's not around, and Lieut. McLean has gone off to company headquarters to get his orders for the next move. The poor bloody lieutenants run back and forth most of the time looking worried. So does our company commander. It's nice to be a private.

The shade I'm in is not much bigger than my head, and more against light than heat, from which there seems no escape on this sun-drenched island. I'm lying on the side of a hill which slopes down into a kind of valley that I guess we'd call a gulch or draw back home. It's a bit like the country around Ashcroft. If I look over my shoulder I can see a stony slope pretty much the same as this one on the other side of the valley, and beyond the ridge, out of sight, is Ragusa, which I hear the Americans took yesterday. There are very few trees around here, though we have passed through a good deal of orchard and vine country since we left the beaches.

We've had so many orders about what you can't say in letters that I'd have to quit right now if I took them seriously. But Jerry's gone off over the hills to the north, well out of reach of this letter, and I hear the press boys were on Sugar Beach on D-day waiting to photograph Capt. Middleton as he came in with "B" Company, and interviewed him on the spot, so I don't see why I shouldn't have my say. Anyway, the kind of information that interests me, and I think will interest you, is most unsecret. On board

---

[17]This letter, and certain others similarly noted in the pages which follow, is fiction. The historical purist may be dismayed, but I am not since I find myself in the company of the many since Aristotle's time who have believed that fiction is concerned with truth quite as much as history is. I use Mr. Ableson and others to bridge a gap in narrative which I would otherwise be at a loss to know how to span. Most of the material presented through them happened to someone in the battalion in some form; the rest might have happened.

ship I saw an intelligence report Mr. McLean was packing around which contained 41 closely printed pages listing (I remember the exact figure) 21,717 springs to be found on this island, along with their location, yield per second, and so on. I've passed two wells so far, at one of which I filled my water-bottle, adding chlorine to taste; but I didn't stop to check the rate of recovery.

I celebrated my birthday, my 30th, in an assault craft loping over long swells in to the beaches, and that's about as crazy a place to have a birthday as I know. I was seasick, and there was nowhere to be seasick except right in front of you because we were jammed in there like sardines. There were 39 of us, I think it was, in a space that seemed no longer and only a little wider than the corridor from your living room down to the boys' back bedroom. There were two men from the Pioneer Platoon up front, and they and all of us were loaded like packhorses. Someone told us on the way out that this was the best found expedition ever to leave the British Isles. We reckoned they'd put most of what they'd found on the backs of the infantry. Mr. McLean joined us in the dark hole of the Mess Deck just before our serial was called up, and I remember thinking when I saw him against the dim blue light of the companionway that he looked like a Christmas tree. Most of it was from the waist up: web belt, water-bottle, compass, entrenching tool, rolled gas-cape, Verey pistol, map-case, binoculars, Tommy gun, ammunition clips, small pack on the back, radio set strapped on the front of his shoulder, then the whole thing tapering through the steel helmet to the tip of the radio aerial above his head. A German wouldn't need to shoot him; he'd just have to walk up to him, snick him on the nose, and he'd fall over and not be able to get up.

I know I was glad to get out of the narrow door of our craft, glad to be quit of the cold metal, the elevator motion and the bitter stench. I was glad to lie in six inches of water for a minute and feel the sand beneath my fingers, and gladder than I can say that no one was firing at us. I was also glad it was somebody else's job to find out where the hell everyone was and what to do next. The beach was as black as the inside of a sow's belly. Back at Troon, in Scotland, the brass had shat upon us for poor control in platoons and sections, but we didn't do any better on the real thing, and I don't know how we could have, short of painting the men white. After a while I found Mr. McLean in a scallop of the dunes, cussing his 38 set, which he said was no good, and trying to get it off his shoulder, and soon after that it began to get light and we got ourselves organized. It's a good thing there was nothing to fire at because my rifle was full of sand and the bolt jammed solid.

Cpl. Gunther has just been round to say we have to set a guard somewhere up on the ridge, so I'll have to stop. Cpl. Gunther is an American from Texas (don't ask me how he came to join a western Canadian highland regiment) and he says "How yo' all doin', boy?" just like they do in the movies. There's a lot I haven't told you, even of these few days. We had a visit from Monty today, who is lean and hard, has gimlet eyes, and gives off confidence like Lana Turner gives off sex. He told us to break ranks and gather round his car, where he got our heads up with some praise and swaggering talk while he flicked flies with a yak-tail on a thong about his wrist. I have seen nothing of death yet, though I understand two of our boys were killed on the beaches, and I saw our Bren-gunner drill single-shot from the shoulder at 75 yards a bedraggled Italian who emerged from a hut in the path of our advance inland. I don't know when I shall be able to write again. I wouldn't have been able to write this if I hadn't got rested up a little during the 48-hour stay in the town of Pozzallo, where we were sent ("C" Company I mean) to make some sort of order amongst a starving population whose fascist mayor and council had high-tailed it north with the Germans. The boys I've seen from the other companies are bone-weary; they called us Zombies when we came in on trucks from Pozzallo this morning. My love to Martha and the boys.

George

Extracts from the Diary of H/Capt. Roy Durnford, Regimental Chaplain to the Seaforth Highlanders of Canada, dated 10–12 July, 1943.

10 July There was still no news of the whereabouts of the battalion when I returned from brigade headquarters to the beaches. Locke Malkin[18] said he was expecting a message back soon about priorities for some collapsible bicycles and the rum issue, both of which he had ready to load on the sergeant-armourer's truck, and that we might know them.[19] The shoreline

---

[18]Commander of Headquarters Company, at this time in charge of beach loading.

[19]A Seaforth who shall be nameless, now living in Chemainus, B.C., tells me that the rum issue, not unexpectedly, won out. I have the impression that the collapsible bicycles disappeared. My friend in Chemainus points out that there are more ways than one of pedalling a bicycle, depending on how one spells it.

by this time (3 p.m.) was littered along its whole length with stacks of every sort of military equipment and supplies. Trucks were being hauled ashore by every means ingenuity could devise. Some were abandoned and the tops of them were awash about 50 yards from shore. Ships of large tonnage had been driven aground farther east of us, and there they listed one way or another, held fast in sand and rock.

A temporary hospital had been set up by Col. Noble and Major Bailey, the chaplain of the 5th Field Ambulance, was already at work there. It was a building of considerable size, probably the home of some well-to-do landowner. The house was rambling and surrounded by a high stone wall. ... The wounded were being brought in in quite large numbers; already this temporary hospital was far too small for its task. Men were lying about on stretchers in the open. Mosquito netting wherever possible kept the swarms of flies away from the blood-soaked bodies. Steadily they came, some limping in, but most of them in ambulances, jeeps and trucks. They were caked with dirt and blood, and those who were not unconscious looked unutterably weary. My own two boys who had fallen in the first landing had been buried, and I found only a few cases of minor injuries to Seaforths in the hospital.

Italian prisoners were being brought in, and already large numbers were collected in this area. A sorry lot they looked, some with no boots or footwear of any kind. ... I obtained permission to speak to them, and sat down under a big locust tree and handed out some cigarettes. With the little Italian I knew I found out that most of them were glad to be out of the war. They all showed me pictures of their wives, sweethearts and children. A lot of fellow-feeling went back and forth between us. I told them I was Padre to the unit, and they were most impressed by the information. ...

11–12 July ... At 5 o'clock we started out, and we marched all through the evening until night came. Ispica seemed scarcely inhabited when we passed through it. It had been taken early that afternoon by the Edmonton Regiment. But although they had found little opposition, the walls and houses of the town were shattered in many places by the far-reaching guns of the navy; doors and window frames hung at rakish angles, and blood was spattered in the streets. Beyond Ispica, night fell and the moon rose. We were a ghostly procession, marching at well-spaced intervals, half hidden in the pale shadows of the trees, silent and watchful.

Dawn seemed a long time in coming, but eventually, footsore and hungry, we saw the sun rise behind us, lighting up a drab-coloured countryside in a glory not its own. On we went until the exhaustion of this incredibly long test of endurance brought many of our fellows down in their tracks. They lay where they fell. ... With the coming of morning the cool of the night changed to semi-tropical heat. We had spent a night wringing with perspiration, and we could hope for no release from it now. Never had I drunk so much and been so little satisfied. Water-bottles were filled again and again by personnel of the Carrier Platoon, which sometimes ran ahead of us, patrolling the roads, and also covered our rear. ... My feet were masses of blisters, and blisters were developing beneath blisters. They would burst, and the chafing of loose skin on the raw tissue below was excruciating, especially after a ten-minute halt, during which time they became inflamed. I was walking on bleeding feet before it was over, and so were many others. At each halt we would flop down in our tracks. Dust and dirt were of no consequence; we were all dirt and sweat from head to foot anyway. We would stare vacantly at the stars, and, later, as dawn came on, we would cover our faces with our tin hats and smoke during the intervals in silence. Some fell asleep as soon as they touched the ground and began to snore at once. They had to be shaken from deep sleep when the ten minutes were up.

An incident about which I heard the next day is worth recording. One of our Signals corporals, riding his motorcycle at the end of the column, did not realise that we had struck off to the right of the main road at a junction between Ispica and Modica, and he had gone on northward, thinking we had outdistanced him, for he had dallied. He pulled up outside Modica. There, just at the entrance of the town, stood a delegation of Sicilian officials, including the Mayor and some military personnel. They demanded that the corporal accept the surrender of Modica and thus avoid destruction and deaths by shelling. After some bickering the corporal agreed to take one of the delegation on the pillion of his motorcycle for an interview with his commanding officer. The high-ranking representative of the enemy rode behind the corporal. ... I think the matter was passed on to Brigade; I heard nothing more of it.[20]

---

[20]Thus, another story about Modica. There seem to be many truths about Modica since many different men and several different units claim to have had a part in its liberation. See the interview which follows.

*Extract from an interview with Capt. A.W. Mercer, Transport Officer of the
Seaforth Highlanders of Canada, dated 18 July, 1960.*

McDougall: I have an official report, C.M.H.Q. No. 135, which refers to
a ration party arriving unexpectedly in Modica.

Mercer: Yes, that was our ration party. I had been sent back to the
beaches to get our first Compo packs and was returning in a 15 cwt.
truck with a driver and a Patricia sergeant-major we had picked up on the
return trip.[21] We had been told that Modica had been cleared and that the
Seaforths were beyond it. We were entering Modica and had just turned a
corner to go down a hill into the heat of the city when an Italian anti-tank
gun opened fire at point-blank range. The first shot passed between the
driver and me, and cleared off two ration boxes from the top of the truck.
The second shot went through the radiator and the vehicle stopped. The
Patricia sergeant-major was hit and his leg almost severed.

McDougall: Where were they firing from?

Mercer: They were firing from the steps in front of a church.

McDougall: What did you do then?

Mercer: When the vehicle stopped, we scrambled over a wall and tried
to see what was going on. After we had seen the size of the force we
went back to the top of the hill, where we found a Patricia Mortar Platoon
sergeant. On our directions he fired a half-dozen bombs into the town in the
vicinity of this gun. We then found out that Brigadier Vokes was on a lateral
road about a mile to the east, and so we went over and informed him of
the situation. He seemed surprised and disturbed, and he ordered artillery
fire to be brought to bear on Modica. This was done, and I understand
that soon afterwards Brigadier Vokes accepted the surrender of the Italian
commander. We continued on our way in another truck, after taking the
Compo packs from the broken-down vehicle. We found the Seaforths on
the side of a hill to the northeast of Modica, and the troops had their first
square meal since landing.

---

[21]The "Compo pack" was a box of prepared rations (mostly canned) designed to feed 14
men for 24 hours. This issue was for assault or emergency use only and was replaced as
soon as circumstances permitted by the standard British army "dry" rations.

McDougall: The official report mentions that a detachment of the Royal Canadian Regiment's anti-tank platoon got into the town about the same time and under similar circumstances. Do you recall seeing them?

Mercer: No, I don't. Perhaps they came along after we had left.[22]

Extracts from Reports of the German Commander-in-Chief South to the German General Staff, Army, dated 10–15 July, 1943.[23]

10–11 July   O.B.S. has given the following order to the Chief of the German liaison staff at the Headquarters 6th Italian Army: MASS OF HERMANN GÖRING DIVISION IS ORDERED TO DESTROY THE ENEMY WHO HAS ADVANCED TO CALTAGIRONE. BATTLE GROUP SCHMALTZ (NOW AT LENTINI) WILL RETAKE PORT OF SYRACUSE IN IMMEDIATE COUNTERATTACK. . . .

12–13 July   The situation has become more acute. . . . Hermann Göring Division is withdrawing under strong enemy pressure from the Southeast into the area southeast of Caltagirone-Vizzini. . . . The Italian forces in the area under attack are almost a total loss. The German forces at the moment are not sufficiently large to carry out a decisive attack against any one of the enemy bridgeheads. . . .

14–15 July   To relieve pressure on the left flank, mass Hermann Göring Division is being committed to annihilate the paratroops who have descended in the plain of Catania. The centre of the front and battle group Schmaltz have been weakened through this and will not for long be able to resist strong attacks from the South. The western flank is exposed to envelopment, and preparations are being made for retreat to the Etna position. . . . According to reports received up to now, Hermann Göring Division, since 10 July, has suffered the following battle casualties: 30 officers and 600 other ranks. The Division has at the moment 45 tanks ready for action.

---

[22]For a full account of the confusing sequence of events leading up to the final capitulation of Modica see Nicholson, *The Canadians in Italy 1943–1945*, pp. 81–82.

[23]Quoted from Army Headquarters Report No. 14 ("Information from German Sources"), pp. 11–12.

II

The Advance to Leonforte

The German retreat to the "Etna position", contemplated as early as the 14th of July, was to be anything but a rout. It is clear that the original Allied intention, perhaps under prompting from General Montgomery, who must have seen some of the conditions for another breakout like that at El Alamein, had been to strike hard across the Catania plain with 13th Corps, while 30th Corps on the left, and especially the 1st Canadian Division, followed up in something like a flank protection role. The halt of the Canadians near Ragusa on the 14th had in part reflected this intention: the punch was still to go in on the right.[1] But the shrewd if somewhat delayed response to the invasion by the German High Command, who knew well the importance of Catania and the neighbouring Gerbini airfields, resulted in such effective opposition to the Allied thrust up the east coat that the picture changed significantly. The idea of a breakthrough on the right and a swift race to the Straits of Messina gave way to one of a slowly moving pivot around which the left flank of the Eighth Army would wheel through Leonforte, Agira and Regalbuto. An immediate gain to the Allies would be the quick capture of a number of communications centres, Enna most important amongst them, through which the German forces must pass in any withdrawal from the western portion of the island. Since this move would for the moment at least mean a threat to the Germans almost as serious as the one they faced on the Catania front, the fact which the Seaforths had to reckon with was that they would now be obliged not only to advance more rapidly but also to fight harder than had at first been thought likely.

For practical purposes, however, the adjustment was a minor one, and it is doubtful whether the men of the battalion were aware at the

---

[1]In a letter to General Simmonds dated 10 June 43, General Leese wrote: "The Allied plan after landing . . . is for the Americans to form a firm base on the West covering the aerodromes, and for 13 Corps to drive on relentlessly in order to seize Syracuse, Augusta and Catania with the least possible delay. From these bases the Eighth Army will strike with its right in order to secure crossings over the Straits. The general conception is thus to hold on the left and strike on the right." Quoted in C.M.H.Q. Report No. 126, p. 61.

time of a change in the divisional role. Division, briefly in the minds of privates during the planning of invasion, had become again another world. Everything seemed to be going well and according to plan, as indeed within reason it was. There could be no mistaking the fact that the arc of American penetration extending inland from Gela on the western coast was deep enough to be touching the Canadian axis in the centre, and the morning situation report on the 14th showed the 5th (British) Division in Augusta and commando and airborne landings under way in the Lentini area and at the mouth of the Simeto River. What was immediately clear was that the Seaforths would not lie long on the hills near Ragusa. Late on the night of the 14th, while the 1st Brigade were setting out from Girratana, northeast of Ragusa, to clear through to Vizzini, a Seaforth column of men and vehicles followed a tortuous route down a mule path (quickly christened "The Devil's Causeway") to Ragusa itself, where it picked up the secondary road north through Chiaramonte and Licodia to Grammichele. Ahead lay a marathon march-to-contact, virtually without respite, of over thirty miles.

The engagement in store for the battalion, its first in World War II, was the assault on Leonforte.[2] But as a prelude to this engagement it was to experience between Valguarnera and Leonforte its baptism of fire at the hands of an enemy that meant business. Regiments of the 1st and 3rd Brigades had had to fight hard to take Valguarnera on the 17th and 18th, and the division was now unmistakably in German territory. Early on the morning of the 19th, having been assigned the lead in what was for the moment a single divisional axis of advance, the Seaforths passed through the 48th Highlanders in Valguarnera. Two miles beyond the town, in relatively open upland country, they came under enemy fire.

The situation was a classic of its kind. Bridges south of Valguarnera were blown, and the battalion was advancing without benefit of supporting arms. Rounding the shoulder of a low spur that lay at right angles to their line of march, "A" Company (now commanded by Capt. F.W.I. Merritt) found itself entering a piece of ground which was like a large saucer tilted slightly to the west. Though the company was under last-minute orders to deploy up to the rim of the high ground to the right, it had scarcely begun this movement when it was hit by a heavy concentration of mortar and machine-gun fire. The killing ground was there, the leading elements of

---

[2]In military talk an engagement is in scale and intensity something between a skirmish and a battle.

the battalion had been pinned down, the tail had gone to ground. Before counter-measures could be taken (and this was to be several hours later) the small enemy force had withdrawn, having successfully held up the advance of a division for the better part of a day. "A" Company suffered 18 casualties, including one platoon commander (Lieut. E.G. Begg) wounded.[3] The complement to this baptism took place the following morning a mile and a half up the road when "B" and "C" Company were caught in similar circumstances by a German rearguard and spent an uncomfortable day being mortared and shelled on the forward slope of a hill. The two occasions, as was certainly intended, imposed caution on the battalion; they also taught it the rudiments of discipline under fire.

The taking of Leonforte was not primarily a Seaforth affair since in the end the decisive tasks in the three days of fighting for the town were assigned to the Edmontons and the Patricias and duly carried out by them. The part played by the battalion was nevertheless operationally important and, as many will testify, memorable. The paradox of the situation is indicated by the fact that the official army history has very little to say about the Seaforths at Leonforte, while at the same time recording that Seaforth casualties for the engagement, listed as 76 officers and men, including 28 killed, were the highest in the 2nd Brigade.[4]

The route taken by the Seaforths out of Valguarnera reflected General Simmonds' decision (on advice from above) to by-pass Enna, which was expected to fall unopposed to the Americans, and to concentrate his main force against Leonforte and Assoro. The division would then wheel sharply right to follow the succession of ridges over which Highway No. 121 passed to the base of Mount Etna. Late on the night of the 20th, the Seaforths were an attenuated file at the head of the brigade column plodding in bright moonlight up the long gradient to Leonforte. The immediate left flank was open; the right flank was well secured by the 1st Brigade, which had been directed against Assoro, and, farther east, by the 231st (Malta) Brigade, which had been directed against Agira. The town the battalion was approaching was perched high on the shoulder of a hill, at a height

---

[3] It was a day of valour, and recognition for valour, for the Medical Section. For their work in caring for the wounded on the open hillside the M.O., Capt. W.K. (Ken) MacDonald received the M.C., and L/Cpl. R.R. Story and Pte. McBride the M.M. Both Capt. MacDonald and Cpl. Story were killed in action later in the Sicilian campaign.

[4] See Nicholson, *The Canadians*, pp. 107–10. Patricias' casualties were 21 killed and 40 wounded; Edmontons' were 7 killed and 17 wounded.

of 2000 feet above sea level; it had a population of 20,000 (no doubt now mostly decamped) and it was plainly an important link in the lateral communications system of the island. Surprisingly, the word was that it would be undefended, or at worst only lightly held.[5]

"C" Company, serving as vanguard to the battalion, came in sight of Leonforte at first light. The road they were following ran around the left edge of a piece of high and craggy ground on the near side of a deep gully, swung right to find an easy gradient down to a crossing over a dried-up water course, then swung left again in a long rise to the town. The bridge at the bottom of the slope was of course blown, and the leading section of the company was fired upon as it came into view. The men deployed quickly to the high ground on the right, which looked as if it would provide the cover of a reverse slope but which in fact, as they were to learn to their cost, was exposed to observation and plunging fire from the top of a high line of bluffs above and to the right of Leonforte. Major Forin (who happened at the time to be travelling with the head of the battalion column) went forward with the company officers to the meagre shelter of some rocks and bushes on the lip of the rise.[6] The assessment was brief. Perhaps under the smart of the delay imposed on the battalion in the preceding days by small German forces, it was decided that two platoons should be pushed immediately into the town. No. 12 Platoon (R.A. Wilson) and No. 13 Platoon (R.L. McDougall) were given the job and were soon on their way down into the valley. They were in full view of the enemy, and they ran as if their lives depended on it, as indeed they did. But they were not fast enough. As they crossed the stream-bed and began to climb the far slope they were hit by defensive fire. Within moments, despite fire-support from No. 14 Platoon and elements of "B" Company on the ridge behind, the force was scattered and lost to use. Part of No. 13 Platoon, under the platoon officer, climbed to the left shoulder of the Leonforte escarpment under the walls of the town; but here, later in the day, they were shot up by Allied artillery, which by this time had begun preparations for another

---

[5]Corroborated independently in several personal accounts, but not reflected in official documents. The view that a place was undefended or only lightly held became common, and I record an example of it here for this reason. It doubtless developed as a result of wishful thinking or from a desire (often misplaced) on the part of commanders to cheer up their subordinates in the absence of positive information about the enemy.

[6]Major Forin's place, as 2 i/c battalion, would be to the rear. But 2 i/cs liked to freelance, and were often extraordinarily useful in this role.

phase of the attack. They dropped down the precipitous sides of the valley to the west and made their way back to the battalion carrying their wounded on improvised stretchers.

"B" Company had in the meantime taken up the probe which "C" Company had forfeited. "C" Company had suffered a number of casualties; principally, however, it was simply a dispersed force and therefore out of the game for the moment. But after a fighting patrol of 22 men from "B" Company had followed the same course as the platoons of "C" Company with the same results, it became clear that the remaining strength of the battalion would have to be conserved for a set-piece attack. Company commanders, commanders of supporting arms and signals personnel gathered at battalion headquarters for orders. They received their orders, but they did not carry them out; for as the group dispersed the battalion was faced with sudden and perverse disaster: a salvo of 9-inch shells, fired short by Allied guns, burst in a tight pattern around the headquarters position.[7] Four persons were killed, including the Adjutant (D.H. Strain), the Pioneer Platoon Officer (J.H. Budd) and one signaller (G.J. Carmichael), and half-a-dozen others were severely wounded, including one company commander. With the C.O. himself suffering shock from the concussion of the blasts, the nerve centre of the battalion was badly damaged.

Although Hoffmeister reported immediately to Brigade his willingness to carry out the attack planned for that night, Brigadier Vokes ordered the Seaforths to stand down and transferred their role to the Edmonton Regiment. Thus it was that the Seaforths' share in the part of the engagement still to be fought became secondary. They were not to be inactive, however. They continued to occupy the high ground fronting Leonforte (now called "Bloody Hill") where they stood up to murderous fire from across the valley and hit back with their mortars and whatever other weapons they could muster. Moreover, when the Edmonton's attack went in on the night of the 21st they supplied a composite company of 100 men under Major H.P. Bell-Irving in a cut-off role designed to block the rear exit from Leonforte. This patrol, because of the darkness and the distance to be travelled over strange and difficult country, was not exactly a textbook success. It was a confused patrol and only a fraction of it seems to have

---

[7]Some say one shell only, but the consensus says several. Only the moment's hysteria blamed the artillery for this kind of misfortune. It was easy to be off a fraction in laying out a gun, and especially where there had to be some measure of reliance on Italian maps, which could be quite unreliable.

reached the objective. But confused as it was, it aroused confusion also in the enemy, who showed signs of alarm at having one hostile force in his midst (the Edmontons) and another at his rear.

By noon on the 22nd the situation in Leonforte was still uncertain. The bulk of the Seaforth composite company had returned to the battalion positions. In the meantime, however, the Engineers had been working without respite in the open to establish a crossing at the blown bridge, and at two o'clock, their work completed, a force of Patricias made a dramatic dash into the town in the wake of a troop of Shermans and themselves riding on the quads of the 90th Battery's anti-tank guns. Patricias and the isolated elements of the Edmontons still in Leonforte joined forces. After a hard fight the balance tipped decisively against the Germans and the town was reported cleared at 5:30 that evening.

Still in position on "Bloody Hill", where the slit trenches had grown deeper by the hour, the Seaforths were to continue for some time yet on the alert as reports of threatened counterattacks came in and the German airforce made a show of strength (low-level bombing and strafing by single planes) against the troops of the 2nd Brigade spread out on the hills around Leonforte. But the battle had moved on, and the 1st Brigade, passing through the 2nd and wheeling right, was engaging the enemy towards Nissoria. On the 23rd the battalion marched two miles across the hills to the town of Assoro, which had been taken on the preceding day in a brilliant action by the Hastings and Prince Edward Regiment. There it went into 48-hour rest.

Extract from a Letter Written by General B.L. Montgomery (Commander, Eighth Army) to General Oliver Leese (Commander, 30th Corps) dated 15 July, 1943.[8]

... So operations are a bit slow and sticky on the right, and all indications are that enemy troops are moving eastwards from Caltagirone-Enna area and across the plan of Catania. He is trying desperately to hold us off from getting to the airfields about Catania.

As we are held temporarily on the right, it is now all the more important to swing hard with our left; so push on with all speed to Caltagirone, and then to Valguarnera-Enna-Leonforte. Drive the Canadians hard.

---

[8]Quoted in Nicholson, *The Canadians*, p. 92.

Letter from Major J.D. Forin to Mrs. Forin, dated at Piazza Armerina, 17 July 1943.

Dearest Vivian:

We are just out of Piazza Armerina, in the heart of Sicily, in a hazelnut grove which is cool and which has a clear-running stream coursing through it. We have had a hard two-days' march and little sleep. The whole battalion came through the above place at 5 o'clock this morning — the Germans having left after a shelling — and came on here to take up a position. We have rested most of the day, and in that time have all shaved and bathed in the stream, and eaten and slept — all fundamentals. Other Canadian troops have gone on through today, and our big guns set up nearby are shelling positions much farther along. Many hundreds of Italians lined the streets in Piazza Armerina, really a squalid city, fully of hungry people, but with a huge domed church set on a pinnacle in its centre, and they clapped and cheered as we came through. One can't however depend on any exhibition such as this — they huzza by day and snipe by night. The nights are moonlit, which makes it interesting and easy going. The aromas one smells at night are strong — some pleasant from trees and bushes, some unpleasant from other causes. Today, just after landing here, an Italian woman had a baby in a nearby farmhouse, and our M.O., Capt. MacDonald, delivered it. He has done all sorts of such things for civilians. Almost all our troops able to do any scrounging have Italian pistols and weapons now. I am not loading myself up with any such. I am now just starting in to eat the evening meal, and it is very good. I am well. Will you drop my family a line? I haven't had time, and I don't expect to be able to write in the next few days. All love to you and the babes.

Douglas

Extracts from the Diary of H/Capt. Roy Durnford, Chaplain to the Seaforth Highlanders of Canada, dated 19 July, 1943.

Word came back that "A" Company was trapped in a valley just ahead, and the doctor and I were called forward to help with the wounded and dying. We were spotted on the way and our Red Cross truck was mortared —

whether intentionally or not I don't know. Sitting where I was on the top of the truck, I had a good view and watched tensely as vicious bursts of flame and clouds of dust, dirt and rock flew into the air to the right and left of us. It seemed ages before we got to the scene of the battle proper, though actually it was only five minutes by my watch.

We proceeded into the valley on foot, leaving the truck on the road. Wounded were being brought out, and I attended the dying. Boys I had known well were among the victims, torn and bleeding beyond all hope of recovery. Mortar bombs continued to drop steadily and with nerve-wracking nearness. The worst experience under these conditions is that of listening to the "fluff-fluff" of the oncoming bomb and wondering where it is going to land; the sound is something like the beat of the wings of a large bird flying just over one's head. One ducks automatically, but quite uselessly of course, because it's too late by then. ... In the hills off to our front we could hear the enemy mortars fire, and we could count the seconds which elapsed before the bomb landed in our valley.

It was an anxious time for us all. But to the dying it meant nothing. They were calm, bravely facing the end. Some were able to speak, but in most cases they were unconscious, having received morphine earlier from our first-aid men. We dug graves out of sun-baked and rock-like soil, and over this task we sweated for hours until the last man was laid down in his blanket. It was a tragic afternoon for me.

We got all the wounded out and finally got out ourselves. In the midst of the tragedy it was a great joy to me to be on hand when wounded men looked up and smiled at their padre with a cheerful greeting. Yet that night, when I lay down to rest for a couple of hours, I could not get the faces of those lads out of my mind. I saw them vividly: pale faces and bloody, with a faraway look in their eyes. The scene came back to me: the feverish manner in which we picked and hacked at the flint-like ground, fissured widely in tropical heat; the pouring sweat under a pitiless sun; the tender lifting of those poor bodies and the gathering at the graves of men stripped to the waist and leaning on their picks and shovels. "I am the resurrection and the life, saith the Lord; he that believeth in me, though he were dead, yet shall he live. ... " The words had never possessed a note of greater triumph for me. Bare-headed and bowed, the boys listened to the words of the burial service with tears in their eyes. It was an unforgettable moment snatched out of the din and confusion of a bloody conflict. ... We had reversed the rifles which belonged to the fallen, and removing the bolts from their sockets we planted the weapons deep into the soil at the head of each grave. I could see them all now: heaps of earth, helmets containing my written records of the lads below placed at the foot of the mounds, and the butt-ends of the rifles starkly standing in rows. There we had left them who only a few hours before had been cheerfully active and full of the zest of life. They had fought in this first brush with the Germans an unequal fight, but they had died well. . . .

Extract from an Interview with Brigadier H.P. Bell-Irving dated 19 July, 1960, at Vancouver, B.C.

McDougall: I need some information about the 100-man composite patrol which you took into Leonforte on the night of the 21st of July. I've read you the passages from the War Diary.

Bell-Irving: Yes. There was a single exit road behind Leonforte, and a volunteer composite company of Seaforths based on "B" Company, under my command, was sent around to hold this road and block the exit of the Germans while the Edmontons attacked into the town. This patrol was not successful in so far as the headquarters group got split up, and the patrol mixed up in getting started; and the troops were so tired that in the climb up the hill at the back quite a number of them went to sleep.

McDougall: It was dark now, was it?

Bell-Irving: I rather think it was quite black dark, though there may have been a moon earlier. Well, we arrived at the back entrance to Leonforte with very few troops.

McDougall: How did you get round to the back? By skirting the town to the left?

Bell-Irving: Yes. We got around to a big wall, and we got over and in with not much more than a good-sized platoon. I remember Dunc Manson was there.[9] We took up a position astride this road, in a seal position, and the noise of battle came closer to us. It became evident that the Edmonton attack had not been successful because there were Edmontons being driven back upon the seal, and the Germans appeared to have the upper hand. I

---

[9]Lieut. J.D. Manson, "B" Company.

can remember being in there and feeling that the town was not going to be taken.

McDougall: Were you in the town at all, or out in the back of it?

Bell-Irving: We were in the northeast corner of the town, on the road leading out. Anyway, my idea at the time was that we're here, and we'd better stay. I thought we might find something relatively strong that we could hold, and stay there until somebody caught up. There were German tanks in the street, and I can remember lying in the ditch with a tank right alongside me, and another firing along the ditch with tracer. There was tracer all over the place. We tried to throw grenades into the tanks, but it was quite hopeless. We evacuated out of the town along the road, and we found a big house which looked like something we might hold. I left the troops I had with me in some woods beside the road and Dunc Manson in charge. I don't remember who went with me, but I went into the big house, which was clear, and when I came out a tank on the road right in front of me fired. I ran, the tank chased me, and we got split up. Eventually I made my way back to the battalion with one corporal of the Edmontons I had picked up on the way. I had taken a composite company of Seaforths into my first battle, and I'd come out with one Edmonton. I wished to God I'd been killed, I was so ashamed of myself. I thought those I'd left behind had been killed. But they got home alright, and I think took prisoners on the way. I credit Dunc Manson with doing a splendid job.

Extract from an Interview with Pte. G.A. Reid, dated 23 July, 1960, at North Vancouver, B.C.

McDougall: We've had a look at the sequence of events up to the 21st of July. Can you go on from there?

Reid: We went on a patrol up a goat trail that night, around behind Leonforte. I can remember walking until I couldn't feel my knees. I don't know what happened to the company commander, but we just went on.

McDougall: Who was in command then?

Reid: I believe a sergeant. We got up behind Leonforte, and Major Bell-Irving was there. How he got there I don't know, but he started firing a Verey pistol. Well, there was armoured cars or something up in the back, Jerry's armoured cars, and they started just going round in a circle and firing out, and they chopped up the countryside quite a bit. The whole company, or whatever it was, scattered, and there were 16 of us left. The senior man was a lance-corporal that had volunteered from Support Company, and he said, well, what do you think we'll do? And I said, well, our job originally was to take this little hill and try to get just as many Jerries as we could when they started shelling for the Edmonton attack, you see. So we set out after this hill. We were going through a nut orchard, or an olive orchard, I don't remember which, when we saw the hill, and we were just making for it . . .

McDougall: It's night time?

Reid: At night — another bright moonlight night. And we kind of stopped to look it over, not having anybody that really knew what they were doing; and they said, well, do you think that's it? And this lance-corporal said, Gee I don't know; and he said, what do you think, George? And I said, well, it's the only one, you know . . .

McDougall: Is it your impression that you were pretty well round behind the town now?

Reid: We're up on the hill, and there's a bit of a flat piece. So we made to take this little knoll and set up our guns; and just then I heard a click.

McDougall: A Schmeisser being cocked?

Reid: Yes, I guess. And I figured either somebody's just shot at us and they misfired or they're going to. So I yelled "Down!", and everybody just ducked. They fired right over our heads. Jerry had beat us to it. So I said, let's get them before they get us. I had a Bren gun. I didn't hear anything, and I was just going to start spraying and attack, you see, and I said, "Come on, let's go!" But nobody answered, and I looked around and I was all by myself. So there was my chance to get the M.M.

McDougall: But you weren't in the mood that night?

Reid: No. Anyway, I yelled and fired my Bren at them, where they seemed to be behind some trees. And just then they threw these potato-mashers[10] and rolled me over with the concussion. I was just getting out

---

[10]The German stick-grenade.

of the daze when they threw a few more at me and rolled me the other way. I figured they were going to get me sooner or later, so I fired right at the top of the hill and made a run behind the first tree I could find.

McDougall: You had tracer? You could see where you were firing?

Reid: Oh yes.

McDougall: How was the tracer arranged? One in four?

Reid: One in five. So anyway, I got behind this tree and I changed mags and gave them another burst. Then I ran behind another tree and started withdrawing. I emptied my last mag and took off. You know how the hills were in that country, they're all terraced. Well, I took about two steps on each terrace, I think, and I was down at the bottom of the hill. I got burnt on the inside of my arm from a Jerry bullet.

———————

Letter from K534897 Pte. George Ableson to Mr. John Ableson of 2876 West 5th Ave., Vancouver, B.C., dated at Assoro, 24 July, 1943.[11]

Dear John:

I've seen a lot since I wrote you last, by which I mean a lot of blood-letting and the kind of butchery that goes with war. I wouldn't exactly say I'm happy in the service. But I get along, and so do most of the boys I see around me. We're so tired it's like a terrible sickness. The C.O. and the officers expect plenty of us (tempers are thin) and the surprising thing is that we seem to have quite a bit to give. Why should a team of medics, in a volunteer army and for the dollar or two a day they earn, go out to do a job on a hillside with bullets and bombs hot on their tails as the hounds of hell? The funny thing is they weren't ordered out, they were ordered to stay back until the situation had cleared a little. That was down the road a piece. It's true I've seen some of our boys running the wrong way in a funk (the story is that a handful of them ran right back past brigade headquarters a few days ago, and there was hell to pay for that), and I've seen Padre Durnford dishing out tea and cigarettes and whatever else a padre has to give to men whose bodies and eyes were stiff from shell-shock. But the general picture is different, and, if you like the idea of a race of bloody heroes, better. Perhaps the western frontiers have bred a rugged people.

———————

[11]Fiction: see note p. 11.

29

I saw my first dead four or five days ago as we wound our way up a hill into Valguarnera. I think they were Hasty Ps, and they lay, eight or ten of them, like dark shadows on a road whitened by moonlight. I thought at first they were asleep, because I'd seen us sprawled out like that, just dropping anywhere from sheer exhaustion. But the black stains and the smell were not those of sleeping men. The next day we had our own dead and wounded, though I saw little on that occasion since it was "A" Company ahead of us that was hit, and I spent most of the day holed up waiting for orders. Ever squash your foot down on the head of a column of ants? That was the battalion.

The day after that again, I was closer to it. We were spread out on the forward slope of a hill, bald as the palm of your hand, when we were shelled and mortared. The reverse slope just a hundred yards behind us looked like a much better place to be, and I heard Lieut. McLean yell to Sgt. Mottl that we ought to go back. But Sgt. Mottl (and I thought this was funny at the time, like an echo from the Crimean War) sang out, "You can't go back, sir, without orders," and I guess the orders never came because we just dug in where we lay and stayed there the rest of the day. The man in the slitty next to me got a packet from an 88 mm. gun as he was sitting on the edge of his hole during what he thought was a lull in the shelling. Yip-whang, just like that. No trajectory, no warning. It took out most of the side of his neck and he was still looking surprised, though there was another kind of look coming into his eyes too, when I got to him. Another shell, yip-whang, landed on the lip of Lieut. McLean's slitty while he was in it, and he came out covered with dirt and I think one eardrum blown because he's been deaf as a post ever since.

Then there was Leonforte. I thought when I began this letter I was going to give you a stiff-lipped account of death in war. But I don't know. As I sit here on one of the terraces that climb the heights of Assoro, the smell of food drifts along from where the boys are cooking up a meal, and I think more about the things of life than about the things of death. The point is one reaches saturation very quickly, and after that one dead or badly messed up person is much like another. I think I was filled up yesterday morning when I went with the Padre and some others up onto the ridge we occupied in front of Leonforte to bury seven men from "B" Company who had been lying up there in the blistering sun for the past three days. They had had a direct hit in a kind of catacombs arrangement open at the top and surrounded by three low walls. We worked for an hour and a half in five-minute relays, which was all any of us could stand at a time. We all of us threw up at one time or another that morning.

Leonforte fell in the sense that the Germans didn't seem to want to give it up but had to, and that's the first time it's happened that way since we landed. But just who took the place and how, I don't really know. I know I didn't have much of a hand in it, though it's true I fired my rifle for the first time at the enemy. I mean to say I fired it at the cliff-tops opposite us where the enemy were supposed to be. A nice impersonal 20 rounds or so, like shooting on a range except that there was heavy stuff dropping all around us. Afterwards there was a great deal of coming and going of patrols, and prisoners drifting in, and all the milling about of troops of every kind that we are becoming accustomed to, but as far as our platoon was concerned we never got off the hill in front of the town. We lent a hand in whatever way we could, and I remember at one point helping the Mortar Platoon shift ammunition. Lieut. Harley, who is tall and very English and has a grin like the Cheshire cat's, looked really happy. He had all the brigade mortars under command, and he said he was having a beautiful shoot. On our first day on the hill our own artillery dropped some shells meant for the Germans on BHQ. I believe it was quite a mess. You could feel the pulse of the battalion go down.

The call has gone out for chow. Having fed for the past two weeks on hard-tack, bully-beef, figs and tomatoes, we are now on a diet so rich it makes you belch to look at it. This is what is called the Compo Ration, and it comes in wooden cases small enough for a man to heft fairly easily. In the cases are soups, stews, puddings, biscuits, chocolate bars, tins of candies, salt, tea, jam, margarine, cheese, fish, fruit and vegetables. All tinned or dried. The tea is mixed with sugar and dried milk and makes a good brew. But the richness of the food is cloying after the spartan days behind us. We feel bloated, and the path to the latrine has become a well-worn trail in the past 24 hours.

Yours,

George

31

A Narrative of War

Letter from Major J.D. Forin to Mrs. Forin, dated at Assoro, 24 July, 1943.

My dearest Vivian:

Another note. . . . I have just sent off a wire, which should reach you soon — probably much sooner than the two letters I have written you from Sicily thus far.

Bill Harris, one of our ex-company commanders,[12] came up with reinforcements today, and brought with him a bottle of lime juice, which we attacked avidly. We have had nothing of such since our arrival, and it was very good.

We are still in rest, and the gunfire of battle is facing eastward towards Mount Etna, which can be plainly seen from the high ground above this town. We had some hard fighting for Leonforte, but finally won the place. There was a quite large force of Germans against us from what they choose to call a "crack" German division. A lot of them won't fight again. The days have been stifling and we've had to be out in the sun digging and working. Doug Strain, our Adjutant, and Lieut. Budd were killed, and Bill Merritt quite badly wounded at Leonforte; how I got off is beyond me, as I was beside them. The men in the battalion have done marvellously — just as finely as we knew they would. Three of them brought in 21 prisoners two nights ago, and a little later one man brought in 7.

We sent a truck out into the country this morning with the Mayor of Assoro and collected about 1 1/2 tons of wheat, which went to the local grist mill to be made into macaroni and allotted to the locals, who are in desperate need.

Bert Hoffmeister is sitting in the same room, writing also. It has been a nice lazy day for all of us — quite a change after the last ten. Harold Newing, our Sally Ann[13] representative, has just come up to the unit with cold lemonade and hot tea. He will visit the companies in turn and dispense his wares. He is just now being driven off in my jeep . These jeeps are most useful vehicles in this kind of country — they hold well to the rough roads, make way on trails not passable to ordinary vehicles, and are light on petrol. . . . Loads of love to you all.

Douglas

---

[12]Soon to command "B" Company.
[13]Salvation Army.

32

Extracts from Reports of the German Commander-in-Chief South to the German General Staff, Army, 23 July, 1943.[14]

On 22 July Leonforte was taken by the enemy. From report of XIV Panzer Corps to O.B.S. at 1530 hours: Enemy threatens to separate the regiments of 15 Panzer Grenadier Division. ... Only available reserve (consisting of one platoon) has been committed. ... Considerable casualties. ... Considerable loss of vehicles, especially at 3 Battalion Grenadier Regiment 15, owing to continuous attacks by fighter-bombers, artillery and low-level aircraft. ... 1st Heavy Field Howitzer Battery total loss through bombing. ... 15 Panzer Grenadier Division withdrew in general line Campofelice-Gangi-Regalbuto. ...

---

[14]Quoted in Army Headquarters Report No. 14 ("Information from German Sources"), p. 13.

III

Through "Grizzly" to Agira

On the 17th of July General Patton had flown to Algiers to complain to General Alexander about the unspectacular role assigned to American troops in the western part of the island and to show him in a draft plan how readily his Seventh Army could swallow up Palermo and, in the Patton manner, roll eastward to Messina. On the same day General Hans Hube had transferred the headquarters of the 14th Panzer Corp to Sicily and had established it on the northern slopes of Mount Etna, east of Randazzo.[1] By the 23rd both commanders could be reasonably content with their missions. Palermo had fallen on the 22nd, and on the following day General Bradley's 2nd (U.S.) Corps, which had been moving north from Enna on the left of the Canadians, had taken Petralia and had swung right almost ninety degrees to form a new front between Leonforte and the north coast. Hube, for his part, having reinforced and reorganized his positions,[2] controlled by this time a firm and compact front which ran in an arc from San Stéfano in the north, through Nissoria and Catenanuova, to Catania on the east coast. At his back an able young Colonel by the name of Baade (whose skill the Seaforths were to admire later when he commanded a division in front of Ortona) was preparing the Messina area for a smooth evacuation of German forces from the island. The 11,540 prisoners reported taken by the Americans behind Bradley's front on the 25th included, Hube knew, very few Germans.

General Montgomery's plan for the Eighth Army remained unchanged. Army initiative would continue to lie with the Canadians, who would drive eastward while the remainder of 30th Corps, and 13th Corps on the Catania plains, maintained pressure northward. Reading the orders of higher formations, one has the impression that what was contemplated was a single speedy advance of the 1st Canadian Division from Leonforte to Aderno.[3] In fact, it was to take several false starts and a week of confused

---

[1] See Nicholson, *The Canadians*, pp. 113 and 115.

[2] German reinforcements since D-day included the 1st Parachute Division and the 29th Panzer Grenadier Division.

[3] Renamed in modern times "Adrano", but appearing on maps used by the Seaforths in the form "Aderno".

and costly fighting for the Canadians to reach Agira, which lay eight miles east of Leonforte and only about one-third of the distance to the Corps objective at the base of Mount Etna.

The heights of Assoro, and especially the ramparts of a ruined castle immediately above the rest positions which the Seaforths occupied on the 23rd, commanded a magnificent panorama of the ground to be fought for.[4] The dominant feature, extending from foreground to middle distance, was a spine of relatively high land crossed by three ridges over which Highway No. 121 passed eastward through the village of Nissoria to Agira. The road twisted occasionally to meet the gradients of the ridges, and the ridges themselves were notched, so that in each case prominent hills or cols lay north and south of the road. To the right of the spine the land fell away to the valley of the Dittaino River, to the left to the valley of the Salso. Beyond Agira (dead ground to the observer at Assoro) it fell to the confluences of the Salso with the Troina and the Simeto Rivers, then rose again to Aderno. Agira looked like a disproportionately large cone, and remarkably close in the hard clear light, and, almost directly behind it, Mount Etna rose against the backdrop of the sky.

As the 1st Canadian Division continued its thrust without intermission beyond Leonforte, the news reaching the headquarters of the Seaforths[5] was, as usual, fragmentary. Such as it was, it was not reassuring. The 1st Brigade was known to be in action on the right flank of the division where it was to join forces with the 231st (Malta) Brigade, temporarily under General Simmonds' command, in exercising pressure from the south on Agira. The 2nd Brigade was in reserve. The 1st Brigade (so it had been said) would attack on the 23rd through to Agira. In the detailed plan the Royal Canadian Regiment would pass through the 48th Highlanders when the latter had secured a firm base at the junction of Highway No. 117 with Highway No. 121 just beyond Leonforte.

But soon there were disquieting rumours from the front: the 48th Highlanders had been hit hard almost at their start line, the R.C.R. had been stood down, and reconnaissance cars of the 4th Princess Louise Dragoon Guards probing forward to Nissoria had been turned back by heavy mortar fire at the outskirts to the village. The next day, the 24th, brought news of a set-piece attack, and this information was confirmed

---

[4] I think there is a Charles Comfort painting of the site and the view. The ruined castle became a spectator's box for formation commanders and important visitors.

[5] Hereafter referred to as BHQ.

later in the day by the appearance of Kittyhawk fighter-bombers strafing the road towards Agira, and by the sound of such a whistling rush of shells over the Assoro positions in the direction of Nissoria as the Seaforths had never heard until then.[6] Late that night, however, the ominous reports again came back: the Royal Canadian Regiment had been badly hurt and Nissoria was not yet taken. On the 25th the story was the same again, the victims this time the Hastings and Prince Edward Regiment. The stories were perhaps distorted and exaggerated in the minds of anxious men, but they were right enough in essential facts. The 1st Brigade and most of "A" Squadron of the Three Rivers tanks, a considerable force, had spent itself in bloody fights which had still not extended the Allied line beyond Nissoria.[7] It was in fact the ridge three-quarters of a mile beyond the town that was the stumbling block. On this ridge, one to each hill astride the road, were an estimated two companies of Panzer Grenadiers.[8] They were well dug in, well supplied and well supported by mortars and guns. They would be hard to dislodge. The heartening development of the 25th, clutched at despite its total absence of relevance to the immediate situation, was the news of Mussolini's resignation and of the impending dissolution of the Fascist Party in Italy.

Early on the morning of the 26th Lt.-Col. Hoffmeister attended a conference at brigade headquarters at which he learned that the 2nd Brigade would relieve the 1st that night. The Patricias were to take the heavily contested ridge beyond Nissoria, now given the code-name "Lion", and were then to press on to take a second ridge a mile or so farther east, whose code-name would be "Tiger". The Seaforths were to pass through the Patricias on "Tiger" and proceed to secure the report line "Grizzly", comprising two features this time of very marked prominence lying north and south of the road and about 1000 yards short of Agira. Back in his own headquarters in the Mayor's house in Assoro, the C.O. put the battalion on half-hour's notice to move. The cooks prepared a good hot meal and an issue of haversack lunches. Newly arrived reinforcements were posted to the companies. By ten o'clock the battalion was in position close behind

---

[6]The barrage was fired by three field regiments R.C.A., an S.P. and field regiment R.A., and two medium regiments R.A. The Germans found this kind of concentration shattering, as indeed it was.

[7]The three battalions of 1st Brigade had lost (killed, wounded and missing) close to 200 men in the two days of fighting. See Nicholson, *The Canadians*, p. 126.

[8]C.M.H.Q. Report No. 135, p. 40 (mimeographed).

the Patricias under the arc of an Allied barrage and on the receiving end of shelling prompted by the new attack on "Lion".

When it came to be the Seaforths' turn, as it did a few hours before first light on the 27th, there was to be little choice of tactics. There seldom was, even in this most fluid type of warfare. "Lion" was assumed to be clear, whatever the situation at "Tiger". But, as soon became apparent, "Lion" was not clear, and so it seemed unlikely that the Patricias had taken "Tiger". Lt.-Col. Tweedsmuir, whose Hastings and Prince Edward Regiment had had bitter experience of this ground two nights before, was to supply the classic description for attack under these circumstances: "The only thing," he wrote, "[is] to get as far as possible in the darkness and hope for the best."[9] The two leading companies of the Seaforths, "A" Company on the left of the road and "C" Company on the right, filed out from Nissoria and proceeded to get as far as possible in the darkness, hoping for the best.

The success which opened the way to Agira lay with "A" Company, and more especially, it seems fair to say, with its commander Major H.P. Bell-Irving, who was to be at his venturesome best that day and well and truly earn the first D.S.O. awarded to the battalion in World War II.[10] "C" Company's No. 13 Platoon, committed to the right flank of "Lion" on the south side of the road, ran immediately into stiff opposition from machine-gun emplacements located just beyond the wooded crest of the hill. By the time this fire-fight was over, first-light was at hand and the company, disorganized further by fire from enemy tanks and mortars, had for the moment lost its chance to get forward. "A" Company on the left was also opposed on "Lion", but "A" Company pressed on, and, precisely in its pressing on, saved the day. It followed (not despising the means) a donkey trail which promised good direction into enemy territory and with the approach of dawn found itself at the base of a low hill, which it climbed and occupied against no more than token resistance. The hill, Major Bell-Irving was pleased to discover in daylight, was the left shoulder of "Tiger". From the highway which dropped down the hill on the far side of "Tiger" a German Mark IV tank contested briefly the arrival of the Seaforths on the position. But Canadian Shermans, now securely on "Lion", were firing effectively on

---

[9]Nicholson, *The Canadians*, pp. 124–25.

[10]Lt.-Col. Hoffmeister was also awarded a D.S.O. for his contribution to the same day's action.

"Tiger",[11] and the dreadful attrition of the continuous Canadian attack of the past few days had all but liquidated the 300 to 400 German infantrymen whose responsibility it had been to hold this ground. By noon on the 27th the Seaforths and elements of the Patricias were consolidated on the second leg of the thrust to Agira. It was time now for "Grizzly", which unfortunately had been occupied that night by fresh troops comprising the entire 1st Battalion of the 15th Panzer Grenadier Regiment.[12]

Wisely, there was no delay on the part of the 2nd Brigade. While Canadian firepower of all kinds took a heavy toll of retreating enemy remnants in the dip of ground dominated by "Tiger", the C.O. issued new orders. "A" Company's objective was to be the right or south end of "Grizzly" feature, named on battalion maps Mount Fronte and easily identifiable by its flat or "square" top. "D" Company, attacking to the left of the main road, was to capture a walled cemetery on the crest of a hill which together with another hill half a mile further north made up the left or north end of the same feature. "C" Company was to support "A" Company and "B" Company was to support "D" Company. One squadron of tanks was assigned to each side of the axis-road, and F.O.Os. (Forward Observation Officers)[13] of the artillery were to move with each forward company in order to provide fire support by observation in addition to the usual prearranged concentration.

"A" Company left "Tiger" at two o'clock and advanced rapidly to first contact, which occurred in a vehicle park a short distance forward beside the main road. The enemy withdrew, however, without being pressed, and the advance was resumed to a hill nearly a mile forward which opposed the main objective. Here No. 8 Platoon, leading the company, came under plunging fire from the flat top of "Grizzly" (south).[14] Committed promptly to a fire-support role by the company commander, the platoon

---

[11]Some of the effectiveness was tragically misdirected. One of Major Bell-Irving's platoon officers was killed by fire from our own tanks when the Shermans failed to identify the Seaforths on "Tiger".

[12]See Nicholson, *The Canadians*, p. 131.

[13]The F.O.Os. were equipped with carriers, or rode on occasion in tanks, and their 22 sets were a useful extra link to brigade in an emergency.

[14]No. 8 Platoon was commanded by Lieut. J.L. Harling, who at this point and later on the flat top of "Grizzly" was to give Major Bell-Irving the kind of support that cheers the heart of a company commander. Lieut. Harling was put in for what looked like an unquestionable M.C. for his work on "Grizzly", but the award was for some reason not approved by the reviewing authorities.

made excellent use of the cover afforded by terraced vineyards and orchards traversed by sunken tracks to infiltrate to the base of the hill they now called simply "Grizzly", where they engaged the enemy in a vigorous action. In the meantime, Major Bell-Irving had taken No. 7 Platoon and No. 9 Platoon[15] on a wide flanking movement to the right which brought them eventually to the base of the extreme south end of the hill. Here, as Major Bell-Irving had hoped, they found a rise of ground to the heights above so steep and narrow that the Germans had not troubled to cover it with fire. A handful of men quickly carried the top and established a firm footing for the company on the southern end of the plateau. They took thirteen prisoners without much difficulty, though in the face of increasing harassment from mortar fire as the Germans showed themselves sensitive to the danger at their backs. It was now almost five o'clock in the afternoon.

The securing of the remainder of "Grizzly" occupied the best efforts of the Seaforths for the next twelve hours. The plateau extending north from "A" Company's base on its south rim was traversed diagonally by a rocky ridge whose left and most distant end was marked by a farmhouse and outbuildings. The land on the near side of the ridge sloped gently upward from the Seaforths' positions: it was covered with olive trees but no underbrush. The land on the far side of the ridge, which it soon became clear the Germans were prepared to defend bitterly from the northern rim of the plateau, was an open meadow perhaps 150 yards in length. Since "A" Company had by this time been attacking almost continuously for sixteen hours, Major Bell-Irving decided to rest his troops and conserve their badly wasted resources by exploiting no further forward than the ridge line that night. Combining the remnants of No. 8 Platoon (now back with the company from its fire support role) and No. 9 Platoon into a single force of 21 men under Lieut. Harling, he sent them to occupy the house on the left. At this point the company signallers got through to BHQ on the No. 18 set, and the company commander was able to give a brief account of the situation to the Adjutant.[16] Mortar fire, he was told, would be brought down on the north end of the plateau if "A" Company would for the moment stay back from the ridge. "A" Company complied, the mortar

---

[15]Commanded by sergeants; both platoon officers (A.L. Robinson and M. Wilson) had become casualties in the course of the day's fighting.

[16]The work of men of the Signals Platoon, now and later, was outstanding; for his remarkable services on the 28th of July Cpl. D. Meade, "A" Company signaller, was awarded the M.M. The new Adjutant, succeeding Capt. Strain, was Capt. J.H. Gowan.

fire came down — and, disconcertingly, an Allied artillery concentration which blanketed the entire plateau for thirty minutes but in the event caused no casualties to the Seaforths. The company then took up its positions, and the situation was stable at nightfall under intermittent fire from German mortars and rifle grenades.

It was an uneasy night for a handful of weary men. Cpl. F.W. Terry, who was a company stalwart and had distinguished himself often that day, had been killed by a sniper at dusk, and this loss piled on top of the many other losses sustained since "Lion" had taxed the spirit of the company. Ammunition was running low, and the wireless set, having lasted long enough to carry a final call to BHQ for supplies and reinforcements, had faded out completely. Lieut. Harling's force was in the house to the left but had not succeeded in exploiting beyond it. Midnight brought a flurry of fire as the enemy probed the ridge line. Then at five o'clock, as the pale wash of first light spread over the plateau, the expected counter-attack came in: advancing infantry supported by a vicious "stonk".[17] Lieut. Harling's force bore the brunt of the attack, withstood it, then turned it back.

The counter-attack became a rout for the Germans because of the timely arrival on the flat top of "Grizzly" shortly after five o'clock of No. 14 Platoon of "C" Company. In the course of the 24-hour advance from Nissoria, men of all companies of the Seaforths had had jobs to do, and some had done their jobs well and others (some men of "A" Company included) not so well. But components of success and failure within a single battalion in battle make up a mixed equation. It would be "B" Company's or "C" Company's or "D" Company's turn to win another day, but not this day of the taking of "Grizzly". "D" Company's attack on the walled cemetery on the north side of the main road had been stopped by fire well short of its objective, and the C.O., accepting this fact and the need to conserve his resources to reinforce the success by this time promised on his right, had drawn the company into reserve. "B" Company and "C" Company, both vulnerable to enemy defensive fire in the difficult role of support to the attacking companies, had been badly cut up and dispersed in the low ground between "Lion" and "Grizzly". Yet one platoon of "C"

---

[17]The "stonk", in the context of the German defensive system, was an intensive concentration of shell and mortar fire — in fact of all available fire, including machine-gun and grenade. The Germans in Sicily and Italy did not have anything like the amount of artillery at the disposal of the Allies; but they did a good deal to restore the balance by using what firepower they had in restricted, hence heavy and effective, concentrations.

Company, led by Lieut. J.F. McLean and sent on a flanking movement to the right and in the general direction of "Grizzly", had persisted in its mission throughout that hot afternoon of the 27th and on into the night. It had often lost its way, it had run out of water, and it had dropped half its strength in stragglers. But these men persevered, and at dawn on the 28th they climbed by the same steep route that "A" Company had taken to the top of the "Grizzly" feature, where they appeared to Major Bell-Irving as welcome as the sun itself. They quickly joined Lieut. Harling's force in clearing the Germans from the north rim of the plateau.

In the meantime the Edmonton Regiment, capping four days of excellent work on the left flank of the 2nd Brigade, had taken the walled cemetery and the hill to the left of it which was the northern limit of "Grizzly". The Patricias entered Agira on the afternoon of the 28th and cleared it against only sporadic opposition. On the 29th, BHQ of the Seaforths, which had been kept well forward throughout the preceding action, moved up to the base of Mount Fronte. On the afternoon of the 29th it rained. Rain being something new in the experience of the Seaforths in Sicily, the five-hour downpour was duly recorded in the unit War Diary. Battle casualties suffered by the battalion in the advance from "Lion" to "Grizzly", both inclusive, were 3 officers and 45 other ranks.[18] Casualties suffered by the 1st Canadian Regiment in the eight-mile advance from Leonforte to Agira were 438 all ranks.[19]

Extract of Letter from Major J.D. Forin to Mrs. Forin, dated 27 July, 1943.

... The word is that we get no letters from England for another fortnight or so. We hear the news occasionally, though when the unit is engaged in battle there is no time for listening. Various news summaries come in to us daily. Bert Hoffmeister is well; John Gowan is filling in the Adjutant's job since Doug Strain was killed. We include in our transport now several big Italian vehicles from German hands. These are useful, as our scale of vehicles on landing was below that allowed to us in War

---

[18] K.I.A. and D.O.W. were 2 and 9.

[19] Agira was counted, in Army Records, a battle, and, subsequently, a battle-honour for the Seaforths.

Establishment.[20] We are also collecting some mules and horses for the carriage of heavy gear across country. The mules make strange half-crying sounds when tethered; if we overload them, they sit down and refuse to budge. . . .

Extracts from the Diary of Capt. B.G. Parker, 2 i/c "C" Company, dated 27–29 July, 1943.

27 July Back with L.O.Bs. again, who have strict orders not to meddle forward.[21] See plenty of signs of Jerry at shelled red house just beyond Nissoria. Don Newson lands right on top of me in one dive. Tank battle 200 yards ahead. Many German dead and some of our own along the road. Five Sherman tanks burnt out, also some German tanks and 88 mm. guns. Shelled most of the day. Lie up. Have cramps and vomiting. . . .

28 July In the morning went up with Locke Malkin to forward BHQ.[22] Due to wrong map reference we stop near cemetery and get well and truly shelled. Drive on to Agira and discover it had not yet been taken. Get out in double quick time with shells rather close. Return to Nissoria and "F" Echelon.[23] Sleep in gully, wrapping puttees round middle for warmth. Just lie down and sleep. Tremendous bombardment over our heads that night, with multiple-mortars replying. Like express trains coming. "General" Moore, on horse, with spurs, chaps and balmoral, rides through.[24]

---

[20]War Establishment laid down the standard composition for battalions and formations in terms of men, equipment and vehicles. Seaforth of C. were on "Assault Scale", which was a much reduced W.E., until the close of the Sicilian campaign.

[21]2 i/cs had shown an unwillingness to be left out of battle, and there had been some casualties among them. Hence the "strict orders".

[22]In action, BHQ was split into "Forward" or "Tac" (for "tactical") BHQ and "Rear" BHQ. Forward BHQ comprised the C.O., perhaps the I.O., signals personnel, and such other representatives of supporting arms or sub-units as the occasion demanded. The composition was flexible and the trick was to get this command part of BHQ as far forward as possible without unnecessary risk of having it knocked out.

[23]This was the "fighting" echelon of the battalion, usually located at or near Rear BHQ. Chief components were the vehicles of Support Company not engaged in action.

[24]Foreshadowing the formation, at Agira, of the Scout Platoon. The "General" was K52776 Pte. D. Moore of the Intelligence Section.

29 July Great thunderstorm with heavy rain for two hours.[25] The first rain we have had here, and it freshens things up wonderfully. Edmontons in cemetery to the left and battalion up on hills to the right. Corporal Storey killed. Don Newson wounded in the head. Actually see shell in the air before it lands 25 yards away.

Extracts from a Student Lecture given in England 10 April, 1944, by Lt.-Col. H.P. Bell-Irving.

... The first surprise of our assault on "Grizzly" gained a salient through the trees on the left, including the house and thirteen prisoners, but only a narrow ledge on the right since German machine-guns were still firing from the rocky ridge. A heavy fire-fight went on for some time. The Germans used a great deal of ammunition, including rifle grenades which burst in the trees with lots of noise, but with very little effect. I took a corporal with me round the rocks to the right to have a look at this rather dubious flank. As we climbed on to the top of the plateau the corporal was killed by a sniper at 100 yards.[26] This was the only fatal casualty in the "Grizzly" attack. I hope you will understand me in the right way — because I'm well aware that a man was killed, and in this case a particularly fine one — when I say that the incident does bring out the advantage of officers and men being dressed and equipped exactly alike in battle.

... An interesting administrative point cropped up before it got dark that night. Our water discipline was bad, and the men drank all their water far too soon. In front of the house, in the open, was a well. The main German defences, north of the meadow, had the well completely covered. Several attempts to reach it were immediately beaten off, until the company medical corporal, with a German prisoner, went out unarmed, got some water, and was allowed to get away with it.

Darkness brought comparative quiet until midnight. Then a shower of mortar bombs came down, followed by an orgy of Spandau fire.[27] The

---

[25]Seaf. W.D. says five hours. I have made no attempt to resolve minor discrepancies such as this one. Reports of a single circumstance vary; we know that, but it is useful to be reminded of the fact.

[26]K52631 A/Cpl. F.W. Terry, M.M. An excellent soldier.

[27]The Spandau was a standard German automatic weapon with a very fast rate of fire. The rate of the Bren gun was much slower — hence not only more economical but also (as Bell-Irving suggests) somehow less hysterical to the ear.

occasional "bang-bang-bang" of the Bren gun, in reply, somehow gave us a feeling of superiority over the Germans. In a few minutes it all petered out and lapsed into silence. Ammunition was very low and the company was getting tired. Our fire discipline was excellent.

At five o'clock in the morning the attack really came in. Heavy fire was followed by yelling Germans running across the open. They can't have been very keen because they threw most of their stick bombs too soon and they burst on their side of the ridge. My only subaltern, six-foot-six in height, stood straight up in front of them singing a wild song and throwing grenades as hard as he could. His twenty men followed his example, and a shower of mills grenades finished off the counter-attack. The arrival of a very determined young officer from "C" Company with a handful of men enabled us to take the offensive, and within fifteen minutes "Grizzly" was clear.

Extract from an Interview with Major J.F. McLean, dated 7 July, 1960.

McDougall: This is about the attack on "Grizzly"?

McLean: Yes. As I remember, we started out from "Tiger" about four or five o'clock in the afternoon. We were to support "A" Company onto "Grizzly" from the right, but somehow our platoon got separated from the company and we found ourselves on our own and eventually on top of a hill which I thought might be our objective. Jack McLeod was No. 2 on the 2" Mortar,[28] and he came up when we were having a rest, and he said, these are not the instructions you gave us when we started up, we're on the wrong hill. I said, this looks like the right hill to me. But we got the map out, and all of us had a look at it and decided that McLeod was right and we were on the wrong hill.

McDougall: What next?

McLean: Well, we went on, heading as best we could for the next hill. But this was very bad country, vineyard country with terraced steps, and after we'd been at it most of the night, as it seemed, I decided about three

---

[28]Infantry close-support weapon, issued to platoons, firing H.E. (high explosive) and smoke bombs. It was an awkward piece to carry, had rather limited usefulness, and was frequently mislaid.

in the morning to hell with this, we're all going to be so dead on our feet by the time we get there we'll be no use to anybody. So I ordered an hour and a half rest. It was so pitch black that we kept falling down all the time. Then we woke, and in the half-light just before dawn there was "Grizzly" right in front of us. And so we climbed the steep bluff, and who'd we find at the top but Budge Bell-Irving. He was glad to see us because he was just about out of ammunition and water and everything. We hadn't had anything to drink for hours ourselves, and our lips were all kind of stuck together. I guess you know the rest. We joined up with Jim Harling and cleared the top.

McDougall: I've heard there's a story that comes a little later about the Padre.

McLean: That was the afternoon of the day we captured the hill. We still hadn't any water. We were very conscious of dust flying around because as soon as you put up dust Jerry put mortars into it. Suddenly we saw a car coming along the road underneath the hill, with dust flying out in all directions. We were very much annoyed and ran down to see who it was — and of course it was Roy Durnford. He wanted to know if he could be of any help to us. So we said, the best help you can be for us is to go back very, very slowly and don't raise any dust. Well, he said, there's nothing you want, then? We said, nothing that he had that we wanted; the only thing we were missing was water. And he said, all right, I'll go back. Away he went in a cloud of dust again, and Jerry started to fire immediately. Not more than half an hour later, by gosh, more dust, and I was properly annoyed this time and went down the hill ready to shout at him. It was the Padre again, all right, and what do you think he had but three Jerry-cans[29] of water.

McDougall: So you forgave him?

McLean: Yes, we did.

---

[29]The "Jerry-can" was, as I recall, a five-gallon container which was Allied equipment but modelled after a German prototype — hence the name.

Letter from K534897 Pte. G. Ableson to Mr. John Ableson of 2876 West 5th Ave., Vancouver, B.C., dated 28 July, 1943.[30]

Dear John:

Just a note to let you know that I got a piece of shrapnel in my leg yesterday and am now at one of our advanced clearing stations a few miles behind the front. I suppose there's no harm in telling you it's Leonforte, and it's funny to see even the little I saw of it coming in on a jeep, this time from the inside rather than from the outside, where we were a few days ago. The wound is a slight one and I may get right back up to the battalion. On the other hand, I may not, because I'm told that once the evacuation system has started to swallow you it can't or won't stop until you've gone right down the gullet — maybe even farther. A fellow with a sore finger can find himself in North Africa, next thing he knows.[31] I'll try to keep you posted.

Padre Durnford has been in, very happy because he's now the proud owner of a 1930 Fiat which nobody else wanted because they couldn't get it started. I asked him how he got it going, and he said, well, you know, a little prayer goes a long way. He's quite a man. Leonforte is far from peaceful; they hit the hospital with heavy shelling this morning. Not pleasant.

I hope you can read this. It starts out as a letter-size sheet with me, but I think it's then photostatted and ends up about 3" by 4".[32] My writing pad is with my large pack, and God knows when that will catch up with me.

Yours,

George

---

[30]Fiction: see note p. 11.

[31]Evacuation throughout most of the Sicilian campaign was to North Africa, where British hospitals, pending the establishment of Canadian hospitals in Sicily, had remained in service after the close of the Tunisian campaign.

[32]An early form of air-letter, issued to Canadian troops in Sicily.

Extracts from Reports of the German Commander-in-Chief South to the German General Staff, Army, 29 July, 1943.[33]

The enemy (1 U.S., 1 Canadian Infantry Division) exerts pressure on our forces withdrawing to straighten the front-line after local breakthroughs. . . . Strong enemy pressure on 15 Panzer Grenadier Division continues. Local penetrations . . . . Nicosia was lost in the afternoon.[34] Strong fighting for Agira continues (1 Canadian Infantry Division). Street battles in the town. . . .

---

[33]Quoted in Army Headquarters Report No. 14 ("Information from German Sources"), p. 14.

[34]Nicosia, about eight miles to the north of Nissoria, was an important point on the American axis of advance eastward towards Mount Etna.

IV

The Aderno Front

The success of the Seaforths before Agira was to be climaxed one week later in the valleys of the Salso and Troina rivers twelve miles to the east when they joined forces with two squadrons of the Three Rivers Regiment to fight an engagement which General Simmonds later agreed was a model of infantry cooperation with tanks.[1] In the meantime they enjoyed four days of rest on "Grizzly" and licked their wounds. But of course the division did not rest since its role in operation "Hardgate", which was the code-name for the entire Allied offensive against Aderno, called for a sustained thrust of the Canadians to the east. The 231st (Malta) Brigade, still under Canadian command, was able with the fall of Agira to complete its mission of cutting the main road behind the town. It now turned right and made for Regalbuto over ground very similar to that which the Seaforths had covered between Nissoria and "Grizzly". To the south the 3rd Brigade continued eastward along the line of the Dittaino River towards Catenanuova, where, having contacted the left flank of the 51st Highland Division, they turned north to secure the southern approaches to Regalbuto. On the 1st of August, General Montgomery inserted between the 3rd Brigade and the 51st Highland Division a fresh formation whose extra weight could be counted on to accelerate the destruction of the German forces in Sicily. This was the 78th (British) Division, newly arrived from North Africa. The advance of the 78th from Centuripe northeast to Aderno between the 3rd and 7th of August would coincide with the thrust of the 2nd Brigade down the valley of the Salso to the junction of the Salso and Simeto rivers. To the north, Americans of the Seventh Army fought towards the town of Troina, which they would take against bitter opposition on the morning of the 6th. Back on Highway No. 121, still the main axis east for the Canadians, the 1st Brigade on the 31st of July began to relieve the hard-pressed 231st (Malta) Division on the outskirts of Regalbuto.

For the Seaforths drawn together on "Grizzly" there was occasional shelling to put up with and the usual number of what were politely called

---

[1] See Nicholson, *The Canadians*, p. 160.

"rest-area tasks" to be carried out. Two of these tasks stand out from the list of the merely routine. One was the recommissioning (as it might be called) of the Seaforth Pipe Band, whose personnel had landed in Sicily as infantrymen attached to companies, but which stood ready to sound the pipes and drums in traditional ceremonies as soon as occasion allowed.[2] Agira was such an occasion, the first of many to follow, and on the 31st of July, and again on the 1st of August, the Pipe Band played in the town square to the heart's content of the battalion and to the amazement, and in some cases the dismay, of the Italian civilians who gathered to listen.[3] The second important task was the creation of a Scout Platoon by the expedient of adding 30 volunteers drawn from the rifle companies to the strength of the existing Intelligence Section. The Intelligence Section, eight in number, would continue with its customary work; the new recruits were to be mounted and would, as required, patrol singly or in groups in advance of the forward companies.[4] Given the type of warfare experienced thus far, the battalion plainly needed the most sensitive means it could devise for purposes of probe and reconnaissance.

As the creating of the Scout Platoon indicates, the respite at Agira was amongst other things an occasion for the Seaforths to ask themselves as honestly as they might what they had done well and what they had done badly since the landing of the 10th of July. The accounting covered the range of subjects made familiar by countless schemes in England: communications, control by night, the siting of weapons, the advance under an artillery barrage, the attack with tanks in support, and so on. Only the imperatives of a game played for keeps were new, though it is true that the force of these imperatives was sufficient to clarify remarkably the meaning of such words as "leadership" and such phrases as "the confusion of battle", which until now had been mere textbook abstractions. There were some new postings to be made. But the time for hindsight and for

---

[2]There was no W.E. for the Pipes and Drums. At least so I think, though the W.E. which became effective 15 August, 1944, shows a handwritten addendum on Sheet 2 of 1 Sergeant-piper and 5 Pipers. Band policy was to some extent clarified at Agira when it was agreed that pipers and drummers should be maintained as a Regimental band. They would play on every possible occasion, and would at other times make themselves useful in a variety of ways.

[3]Retreat was beaten by brigade order and Brigadier Vokes attended.

[4]The Scout Platoon was initially under the command of Lieut. A.W. Gray; the platoon sergeant was G.K. McKee. The Scout Platoon did not long remain mounted; the use of horses, for a variety of reasons, became impractical.

adjustment to lessons learned was short. The nature of the action in which the Seaforths would next be involved was already taking shape.

The key to this future action was the lie of the land between Regalbuto and Aderno and the willingness of Canadian commanders to make imaginative use of it. It was, in a word, tank country. Some of it was not, and part of the advance would have to be accomplished by the familiar goat-like means of infantry scaling heights unassailable by vehicles of any kind. Such country lay to the north of the Salso where a succession of steep crags stretched eastward like the knuckles of gnarled fingers. Three of these craggy features were clear to the eye from the hill-top at Agira: Hill 736 and Mount Rivisotto, which together straddled the entrance of the Troina River and the Troina-Aderno road into the valley of the Salso, and Mount Seggio, which was the precipitous west bank of the Simeto River three miles above its junction with the Salso in front of Aderno.[5] But the valley of the Salso was wide, and between the main river bed (dry at this time of year) and the heights to the north the land was rolling in its course east, and especially in its later reaches where the valleys of the Salso, Troina and Simeto became one. It was open land, dry and barren except for occasional olive trees and a scattering of scrub oaks. Highway No. 121 from Regalbuto to Aderno followed for the most part the southern slopes of the valley of the Salso. It had been accepted, for want of better, as the route of advance for the Canadian division since Leonforte. There was now a reasonable alternative. The decision was made to abandon the road.

On the 2nd of August, which was the day the 48th Highlanders entered Regalbuto, the Edmonton Regiment began the deployment of the 2nd Brigade into the country north of Highway No. 121. The four rifle companies, their support to come up later by mule train, followed the course of the Salso River as it swung away from Regalbuto to the northeast, then, as the river turned right again, maintained their original bearing in a strike across rough and rising ground towards Hill 736, which they were required to take. The attack on Hill 736, however, was not successful on the 2nd. It went in again late the following night, this time (a fact of consequence to the Seaforths) directed initially against a crag about one mile south of Hill 736 called Point 344.[6] The taking of the intermediate objective by the Edmontons was still being contested by a handful of Germans at first light on the 4th.

---

[5]Hills unnamed on maps were named in army usage according to their heights in metres.

[6]Identification of targets, as of objectives, was difficult in this country. Fire-orders to the artillery became jokes: "Fire on M.G. post at small crag immediate to the left of big crag".

50

The Seaforths left "Grizzly" a little before eight o'clock on the evening of the 3rd and about four hours before the Edmontons launched their second attack towards Hill 736. The battalion objective was a "rocky crag", not otherwise identified, which lay midway between Hill 736 and the Troina River. The companies were lifted forward by T.C.Vs., [7] and the route was Highway No. 121 into Regalbuto, then left onto a narrow country road which ran northeast from the town to a point where the railway, passing from Regalbuto to Carcaci, bridged the Salso River. Debussing just short of the river, "C" Company led the way across the dry bed and turned right along the tracks. The remainder of the battalion followed, and in the small hours of the morning the Seaforths came abreast of the Edmontons, whose battle for Point 344 they could read obscurely in the sounds of gunfire to their left.

About an hour before dawn Hoffmeister decided he was at a point immediately south of the Seaforths' objective. He therefore faced the battalion north (as it were) and, as daylight came, saw what it must contend with: a high rugged hill, topped on the left by a rocky crag which seemed to go straight up to the clouds.[8] On the right side of the hill, he noted, the slope was less formidable and was studded here and there with olive trees. Directly to the left of BHQ the bed of the Salso River wound uphill until it passed out of sight in the hills north of Agira; still further left the cart-track from Regalbuto to the river crossing showed itself occasionally through breaks in the intervening ground. To the right the valley of the Salso wound down through more hills to the Catania plains. Behind, a mile across the valley, was yet another range of hills. These, with the taking of Regalbuto, were in Allied hands.

Having set up BHQ and the R.A.P.[9] in a red house approached by a long avenue of trees, Hoffmeister sent "A" Company on the right and "D" Company on the left against the "rocky crag".[10] "B" Company was at this time out of contact on the extreme left flank, where it had been

---

[7]Troop Carrying Vehicles.

[8]W.D., Seaf. of C., 4 August, 1943. Here as elsewhere I draw on the phrasing of the official battalion record.

[9]Regimental Aid Post.

[10]A red house marked by a long avenue of trees may seem an unwise choice for a headquarters. But since one was perpetually in a state of being over-looked by the enemy in Sicily, and later in Italy, the important consideration was to have cover from fire (for command personnel and the No. 22 set), and this protection the Italian *casa* admirably provided.

committed just before daylight to investigate the situation on Point 344, from which fire was being directed against the Seaforths. As it turned out, this company was to join with the Edmontons later in clearing the forward slopes of Point 344 in the direction of Hill 736.[11] "C" Company, which had first experienced the interference from the left, was regrouping and would soon be in reserve behind BHQ.

In the white light and growing heat of early morning, Major Bell-Irving took "A" Company in a wide circuit to the right, where the ground favoured an approach to the crag. Here the company quickly won an advantage and pressed it home by splitting into sections which independently searched the rocky abutments and drove the enemy from their machine-gun and sniper posts. The only company at this point still in touch with BHQ by No. 18 set, they were able to support their attack in its later stages with directed fire from four Shermans newly arrived at the red house below. "D" Company, faced with precipitous cliffs on the left, was unable to close with the defenders. By nine o'clock the battalion was able to report to brigade: "We have captured objective except for western tip".[12] The C.O. then went forward to discuss the situation with his company commanders.

The situation, despite the reported success, was by no means secure, and Hoffmeister stayed forward for the remainder of the day to give what help he could in stabilizing it. By noon he had consolidated "D" Company with "A" Company on the right flank, where success was promised, and had redirected the strength of the combined companies against the western parapets of the "rocky crag". Supporting fire from the artillery and the medium machine-guns of the Saskatchewan Light Infantry was now available on call at BHQ but was of little use since observers below were unable to distinguish friend from enemy. It was for the infantry still to decide the issue, and this they did in hot and bitter fighting throughout the afternoon. At four o'clock the Seaforths reported the entire objective in their hands. There remained, as usual, the question of whether or not the Germans would challenge the loss of their position. As night came on it became apparent that they were still very much interested in this one, and the C.O. was concerned.

Though the C.O. was concerned, he was now obliged to shift his attention to the brigade action developing eastward along the Salso. "B"

---

[11]There was a problem of identification for a time which led to an exchange of fire between Edmontons and Seaforths.

[12]W.D., Seaf. of C., 4 August, 1943.

Company, sent on a roving mission at two o'clock that afternoon to re-
connoitre a crossing for tanks near the river junction two miles farther
down the valley, had in the end found themselves unopposed on the far
side of the Troina River and with a foothold beyond on high ground which
had been assigned to the Patricias as an objective and which, indeed, the
Patricias subsequently occupied. A two-mile stretch to the Troina road
was therefore now available for rapid exploitation towards Aderno. It was
the cue General Simmonds had been waiting for. In a message despatched
to Brigadier Vokes on the evening of the 4th, he urged that "a quick blow
... be struck in the undulating country north of the river which will carry
you right up to the western bank of River Simeto".[13] The striking force
which would deliver this blow would be made up of tanks, reconnaissance
vehicles, self-propelled artillery, anti-tank guns and a battalion of infantry.
It would be commanded by Lt.-Col. E.G. Booth, the C.O. of the Three
Rivers Tank Regiment. What was hoped for was less the winning of a
patch of ground than "a good mix-up in open country".[14]

At six o'clock on the evening of the 4th, the Intelligence officer of the
Seaforths[15] had gone to brigade headquarters to get information on recent
developments. He returned at eight o'clock with orders for the battalion
to move off eastward at six o'clock the following morning as the infantry
component of "Booth Force".[16] Hoffmeister was notified and came down
from the rocky outposts above to meet with his company commanders in
the red house shortly after midnight. Booth joined them there, and by three
o'clock in the morning plans were set for the next day's operations. "A"
Company and "D" Company had of course to be withdrawn from the hill.
The position being sensitive, however, the C.O. ordered Major Bell-Irving
to leave a platoon behind to hold it until further notice. No. 7 Platoon took
on this task, which it fulfilled with distinction against repeated harassment
over the next twenty-four hours. The enemy which the Seaforths faced
here, and on the following day on the far side of the Troina, were crack
troops of the German 3rd Parachute Regiment.

---

[13]Quoted in Nicholson, *The Canadians*, p. 159.

[14]*Ibid.*

[15]Now Lieut. J.J. Conway.

[16]Brigadier Vokes appears to have anticipated General Simmonds' orders. Vokes writes:
"This letter arrived after 2300 hrs 4 Aug 43. Almost identical orders had already been issued
by me and arrangements were already under way." See Nicholson, *The Canadians*, p. 159.
Some sort of "accelerated action" had been anticipated by all commanders following the
fall of Regalbuto.

"Booth Force" formed up on the west bank of the Troina less than six hours after its final orders had been issued (which was good time for preparations as complex as these) and by half-past eight on the 5th it had crossed the dry river bed and turned right to begin its sweep through the vineyards and orchards which lay between the Troina road and the river courses to the west.[17] "C" Company and "A" Company, by this time mounted on the backs of two troops of Shermans, soon outdistanced the rest of the infantry but were held effectively in control by Hoffmeister, who rode with the tank commander and had at his side an extra wireless set netted in to his companies. A mile down the valley, thus far unmolested, the infantry dismounted from the tanks and swung left to cross the Troina road and make for the long spur which dominated the Simeto River beyond, the road from Aderno to Bronte, and Aderno itself. "C" Company led the way, and the German resistance, carefully held in check until now, stiffened suddenly against the forward platoons. But there was no loss of momentum. The tanks fired over the heads of the infantry at targets as they appeared or were pointed out to them by the men on the ground, then followed the company in its advance and shot it onto its objective. By a quarter past eleven four tanks were hull-down on the crest and a scattering of infantry had spilled over onto the far slope of the spur.[18]

But the ridge was a long one and firmly held, and the battle had not yet reached its peak. The nerve centre of the battalion was divided between Hoffmeister's post with Booth on the one hand, and a forward BHQ on the other, which the Adjutant had established just below the top of the near slope of the hill. Command was flexible under these circumstances, and in a smooth exchange of information and orders "A" Company was quickly committed to support "C" Company by an attack on the right flank of the feature. At half-past three, "D" Company, under the command of Capt. E.W. Thomas, crossed the Troina road and set off to match "A" Company's right flanking movement with a drive to the left. Though the whole length of the slope on the Salso side was being shelled, mortared, and shot up

---

[17]Most of the evidence I have reviewed suggests that the Troina road was *not* used for the advance. The official army account, however, declares unequivocally that "the little force rolled briskly down the road to Carcaci." See Nicholson, *The Canadians*, p. 160. But see also above, same page: "From this start line the whole force was to strike eastward at 6:00 a.m. through the vineyards and orchards between the Salso River and the Troina road."

[18]It was on this premature thrust over the crest of the hill that Major Blair, commander of "C" Company, was taken prisoner.

by fire from machine-gun posts on the ridge still manned by the enemy, cooperation between all arms, and especially between tanks and infantry, was again excellent, and by shortly after four o'clock the Seaforths were able to report the objective taken and secure. Eleven men had been killed and 32 wounded in the course of the day's fighting.[19]

The part played by the Seaforths on the 5th of August was a small but most worthy contribution to a memorable day for the Allies in Sicily. On the Aderno front, the 2nd Battalion London Irish Rifles (of the 78th Division) occupied Carcaci that day, and with the Seaforths pressing towards the lower reaches of the Simeto and the Edmonton Regiment victorious that afternoon on Hill 736 and that night besieging Mount Revisotto across the Troina, the few German survivors of this onslaught broke off contact and made their way by twos and threes northwards along the Aderno-Bronte road.[20] To the north, Troina fell to the Americans on the 5th; to the south, Catania fell to the British. The campaign was clearly in its final phase. And for this final phase the 1st Canadian Division would not be required. On the 6th it discharged its last obligations to 30th Corps by sending the Patricias unopposed onto Mount Seggio and the 3rd Brigade unopposed across the Simeto River. Late that night the Seaforths were drawn back to the area of the crossing over the Salso near Regalbuto, and three days later, on the 10th, they were on their way by transport to Militello. There they would rest. This time, really rest.

Extract from a Student Lecture Given in England 10 April, 1944, by Lt.-Col. H.P. Bell-Irving.

... In order to cover the ground in half an hour, this story of the taking of "Grizzly" has of necessity been sketchy. I hope some small lessons will have come out of it. There is one big lesson which I want to rub in, perhaps at the risk of disagreeing with the textbooks.

You have heard in this course from very able champions of armour and guns. I want to make a point for infantry. It has been written that infantry

---

[19]Amongst those whose death was felt most that day was the M.O., Capt. W.K. Mac-Donald. He was killed tending the wounded on the exposed slopes of the spur. Lieut. F.C. Hall was killed on the same position; and Capt. G.N. Money of the Anti-Tank Platoon was taken prisoner when he turned left instead of right at the crossing of the Troina.

[20]See Nicholson, *The Canadians*, p. 164.

reached their lowest ebb in the last war. They lost their manoeuvrability completely, being pinned down by massed machine-guns. The artillery had to take on the machine-guns, then the infantry advanced and took over. This short history of "A" Company does, at a low level, illustrate something of what infantry can do in infantry country such as our battalion faced in front of Agira. The performance of the company depended entirely on freedom of manoeuvre, freedom of time, and the delegation of initiative to subordinate commanders. It seems clear that Western Europe will provide at least some country more like Sicily than North Africa. If that is so, I suggest that you give the infantryman his head, make some F.O.Os. walk, and let the guns support the infantry's need of the moment.

Extract from an Account of the Seaforth Pipes and Drums Given by Pipe Major E. Esson, dated 16 February, 1945.

... When the battalion is in action, the pipers and drummers are available for a variety of duties which include such jobs as inducing Italian mules to take an interest in the winning of the war and leading them forward to BHQ, where their services are needed for crossing country that is too much even for a jeep. Assisting in the battalion bakery is another outlet for the bandsman's versatility, as is also the operating of a tailor and a barber shop, where in the former even such major tasks as the turning of a kilt can be accomplished, and where in the latter Piper Campbell satisfies all comers except those who want hair grown where there isn't any. In the early days of the Sicilian campaign, of course, members of the Pipe Band soldiered with the companies and helped to build the fine record of the battalion. It was after the battle for Agira that band policy was changed to conform with that of other highland regiments in this "battle-dress" war.[21] This meant that we were able to get the pipers and drummers off the company rolls and maintain them as a Regimental Band. From then on they were used on every possible occasion to keep alive the spark of highland traditions — playing "Johnny Cope" at sun-up, piping the various company areas, beating Retreat several times weekly when circumstances permitted. ... I recall especially the Retreat in Agira. The band that day

---

[21]The decision made at the beginning of World War II to put highland regiments into battle-dress remained a sore point with traditionalists. Highlanders had worn the kilt in and out of action in World War I.

was scattered over the length and breadth of liberated Sicily in search of mules required for the next action. When Major Forin passed on to me the brigade order for Retreat a scant two hours before the time set for the ceremony, not a bandsman could be found. But somehow they were rounded up and scrubbed and kilted, and we kept our appointment. That Retreat was broadcast by way of the B.B.C. to the Commonwealth while the town was still within range of German guns. . . .

––––––––––

Letter from K53729 Pte. W.P. McCrosky to Mrs. Mabel McCrosky of 26 Dalgleish Rd., Glasgow, Scotland, dated 1 August, 1943.[22]

Dear Mabel:

How are you darling, I sure miss you. I am O.K. but have had some pretty close shaves. It is hot where we are, I got a thirst as long as your arm and they don't give us no beer in this man's army. Darling I wish you and me could go down to the Beacon Arms and have a pint or two. I just been to church service. You know me, I don't go much for that sort of thing but I went down even though I didn't have to. We helped the Padre build a kind of stone altar in an olive orchard near Corporal Terry's grave. I guess you may remember Corporal Terry, I brought him round to your house one day on our last leave. He got killed a couple of days ago. We got oranges and grapes galore around here, darling, I'd sure like to be able to send you some. You should see the funny little lizards running over the rocks and hiding in the cactus plants. Must go and wash my shirt now. I'd sure like some socks, darling, if you can knit some. We get an issue every so often from Quarters but the pair I have are all matted like, so they pretty near stand up by themselves. I sure hope a letter comes from you soon. Be good, darling, and don't take any bad nickels as we used to say back home.

Love and kisses,

Jim

––––––––––

––––––––––

[22]Fiction: see note p. 11.

Letter from Major J.D. Forin to Mrs. Forin, dated near Agira, 2 August, 1943.

My dearest Vivian:

It is now about 7:30 p.m., cool and quiet, with the sun barely showing, as it goes down, through the trees. It has been another hot day. We were to have moved out tonight, but at the last moment the move was stood over till first thing tomorrow morning. Today I had a hot bath — not, mind you, from a bath-tub, but from my wash-basin. We get pretty dirty. My batman has managed to get a couple of armfuls of straw to make the ground, which is dried and hard, softer under my sleeping-bag. I sleep under a mosquito net, in my clothes of course, and hardly need more covering. There are lots of flies by day, persistent and dirty, and mosquitoes by night, and the mosquitoes are in some cases malarial so one must fend them off. We take malarial pills four days a week, yellow and bitter things they are, and have given up our shorts for long trousers to keep the mosquitoes from our knees and legs. Davie Blackburn[23] tumbled from his motorbike yesterday and is going about with a bandaged arm. The filled-in craters on the roads are hazardous for motorcycles. Locke Malkin has just brought along a handful of ripe almonds which we will get into in a minute or so. Last evening we had a church service here — sang a couple of hymns and heard a short sermon and a prayer or so. Today we have had for our meals some sweet little tomatoes and some cucumbers which grow to great dimensions in these parts. We also bought some "fresh" eggs, but they didn't taste very good. This evening a travelling Italian barber, a mere boy, quick and adept at his trade, cut my hair along with that of a number of others. The M.O. is treating some sores on my arm which came from infection from the fetid soil while I was engaged either digging trenches or getting under cover. Jack Conway has just come in to BHQ, where he is taking over Intelligence Officer duties; he is one of two surviving subalterns with whom we landed. Could you have a picture of yourself and the Babes taken and send me a miniature? Hoping this finds all well.

All my love,

Douglas

---

[23]Captain W.D. Blackburn, Support Company Commander.

THE ADERNO FRONT

Extract from an Interview with Major-General B.M. Hoffmeister, dated 25 July, 1960, at Vancouver, B.C.

McDougall: Could we talk about "Booth Force"?

Hoffmeister: When I went up to see Budge Bell-Irving on the rocky crags above the Salso, I had no knowledge of "Booth Force" whatsoever. It was while I was up there that I got a signal from brigade calling me to an "O" Group[24] down in the valley. So I struggled down the hill. I remember two fellows coming with me, and they really had to help me down. I was tired and I was sick with the tummy-bug that hit so many of us, and I was just so miserable. I think the "O" Group was set for two in the morning. We were finished shortly before three, and as I remember we had to be in the assembly area several miles away by six o'clock the same morning. The big problem was to withdraw the Seaforths committed up on the heights.

McDougall: You were to marry up with tanks at the Troina River?

Hoffmeister: That's right. Well, we were assembled in the dry stream-bed at the appointed time, but the tanks were late in getting in because of a bridging failure. We were obliged to stay down there for protection, and we were eaten alive by mosquitoes. There was a lot of malaria showed up at Militello as a result.[25]

McDougall: According to Budge Bell-Irving, he had to leave No. 7 Platoon up on the hill where you had spoken to him, and they stayed there for 48 hours.

Hoffmeister: That's right, and leaving them there worried me tremendously because I didn't know whether that platoon could hold out. I remember having quite a row with brigade later on about the relief of that platoon. Brigade wanted us to continue to hold that particular position, and there we were having to go on to another show.

McDougall: The War Diary of the 12th Armoured Regiment pays tribute to this group. Apparently a troop of tanks managed to get up there somehow, and with this platoon they stuck it out.

---

[24]An "orders group", comprising company commanders, commanders of supporting arms, signals personnel, etc.

[25]Troops were issued Mepracin tablets against malaria (see Major Forin's letter above) but the dosage was not easily maintained in battle.

Hoffmeister: They did a wonderful job. I felt the Germans regarded that position as being of some tactical importance, and I was worried that they would mount a full-scale attack on it. . . . But let me get back to "Booth Force". This was in fact the first real infantry-cum-tank show that we had had. We married up company for company, and we rode on the tanks forward into the battle area. I established myself with Booth's tank and rode right with him the whole way.

McDougall: Did you take your own link with you?

Hoffmeister: Yes. Booth and I worked closely together. Every now and then I would leave him when it was obvious we were going to be stationary for a while and go to my own HQ to satisfy myself that everything was all right there. As a matter of fact, my own HQ was moving up very much on the same axis under the Adjutant, John Gowan. There was no danger of my being out of touch with the battle as it was being reported to my own HQ; I had a No. 18 set in Booth's tank netted in to my companies. The whole thing was tied in extremely well.

McDougall: The troops rode right into contact on the tanks?

Hoffmeister: That's right. We were going through an area that had quite a few olive trees on it, and there was a fair amount of cover. The troops stayed on the tanks for a surprisingly long time. We were all delighted to do so because we were pretty tired. Then as soon as we came under heavy fire we left the tanks, and from there on it was a straight support role with specific squadrons supporting specific companies. The whole thing was referred to later as a textbook piece of infantry-cum-tank cooperation. It was watched by Sir Winston Churchill from the high ground to the south.

McDougall: Centuripe?

Hoffmeister: Yes. I had lunch a few months ago at George Drew's home in London, and I found myself sitting next to Sir Winston. He had a very clear recollection of watching this tank battle from the high ground and of sending a signal afterwards congratulating the people concerned. . . .

THE ADERNO FRONT

Extracts from the Diary of H/Capt. Roy Durnford, Regimental Chaplain to the Seaforth Highlanders of Canada, dated 3–6 August, 1943.

... Major Forin told me that I must not go forward with my vehicle since only "essential" vehicles were to move. I forgot all about this order, however, for on the 3rd I took my car back to base to be repaired, and when I returned on the 4th to find the battalion had pulled out the night before I set out in search of it. I left my batman and the car with the 5th Field Ambulance at the entrance to Regalbuto and went up the line by ambulance.

We were heavily shelled as we entered the Salso valley. In fact the ambulance could go no farther because of impassable roads and demolished bridges. So having said good-bye to my driver I got on a dispatch-rider's motorbike and rode pillion over railway ties until I was a mass of bruises. We went about a mile (or so it seemed) by this railway route, which was the only one available, and then cut across country until we came to our advanced first-aid post. Here I got the directions I needed and went on by foot to the high and precipitous ridges on which our companies were engaged. I found the colonel with Budge Bell-Irving. The colonel was plainly sick but carrying on, and there were many dead to bury.[26] I began at once. The ground was like iron. The Germans must have seen me for they dropped mortars all around until I was forced off the pitch. In the end we succeeded in burying only one body before nightfall. I had a bite to eat, my first meal since breakfast, and tried to get some sleep. But soon the shelling began — quite big pieces regularly spaced at intervals of twenty yards along the length of the ridge. After about an hour it was quiet again and we could hear a German patrol making its way up the slope below us. I don't know whether they thought we had gone or had all been killed, but they were talking quite casually as they came. The boys gave them a few bursts of fire, and they disappeared in a hurry.

---

[26] I should perhaps insert at this point Padre Durnford's note on burial procedures. "It was agreed among us," he says in his diary, "that where the services of the Padre could not reasonably be expected within a short time, the officer to whose company the fallen were attached would perform this service himself. But in most cases I was on hand soon enough to do the job that belonged to my office. Graves would be dug, and rough crosses, made on the spot, would be erected. The details of the fallen soldiers would be placed in writing in tins at the foot of the crosses and under their steel helmets. Later, these lads would be re-interred by the Graves Registration Commission in some cemetery established for Canadian soldiers. Meantime, the fullest particulars would be forwarded to the authorities concerned, together with the soldiers' effects and the location of the graves."

The next day, which was the 5th, I went back to find my car. The bridge was still unrepaired and we had to use the railway lines again. The 5th Field Ambulance, together with my car, had moved, but I found them both eventually in Regalbuto, and all was well. I had a quick meal and returned to the valley of the Salso. We had not gone far when we were shelled, and the road police ordered us back, car and all. At brigade headquarters, where I slept that night, I heard that the M.O. of the Seaforths had been killed. It was hard to believe since I had been away from him only a few hours.

The following morning, very early, I went back up the line to find at BHQ that it was all too true about the M.O. My friend Frank Hall had been killed, too, and four others. We set out for our forward areas. I found Kenneth MacDonald lying where he had fallen, which was much further forward than an M.O. should be. I buried him in an orange grove amidst his own first-aid staff, who had insisted on digging his grave and carrying his body to it. They wept there for the loss of a gallant soldier. . . .

Extract from an Interview with Major-General Hoffmeister, dated 25 July, 1960, at Vancouver, B.C.

. . . I know of no braver man in my experience than Ken MacDonald. He was one to whom war was just the most dreadful thing anyone could contemplate. He hated every bit of it. He hated the idea of the suffering, the maiming of men, and before he went into action I'm sure he had to fight a battle with himself. I got to know him very well. I think the kind of courage he required to do the job he did was of the highest order. He was an extremely sensitive man. On the day he was killed he had gone forward into an area really contrary to my orders, because I had checked him on two or three previous occasions when I felt he had gone forward too far. Medical officers, especially good ones like Ken, were hard to replace. But I couldn't stop him; when men were suffering he went out to them. . . .

Extracts from the Diary of Capt. B.G. Parker, 2 i/c "C" Company, dated 5–6 August, 1943.

5 August We hear at "F" Echelon that the battalion has had a good engagement in cooperation with the tanks. German soldier found dead on the field had some of Major Blair's effects on him, so we assume Jim has been taken prisoner. Sgt. Poole has been killed, and nine others wounded. Hear that Cpl. DeRuiter did an excellent job storming a post with No. 13 Platoon. Lieutenants McLean and Wilson both evacuated and C.S.M. Black has taken over the company.

6 August Rejoin the company and take over command. Have touch of fever and feel like death warmed up, having been on the move all night with the ration truck from "F" Echelon. We reorganize on the hill in front of Aderno. Carleton Yorks[27] are to take over from us at ten o'clock tonight. Note that officers killed since the landing include Doug Strain, Jim Budd, Frank Hall, Art French (who died of wounds down the line), Marriott Wilson, and Ken MacDonald. Wounded, including three treated for shock, are Thomson, Begg, Hyndman, McBride, Dickie Wilson, McLean, McDougall, Scott, Newson, Baldwin, Cameron, Church and Middleton. Blair and Money are missing, believed P.O.W. A heavy toll. Many good privates and N.C.Os. gone too, of course, but proportionately less than in the case of officers.

Extracts from Reports of the German Commander-in-Chief South to the German General Staff, Army, 6–10 August, 1943.

6 August The complete lack of reserves in 29 Panzer Grenadier Division sector aggravates the situation in the extreme. ... If correction of the situation in the sector of 15 Panzer Grenadier Division is not possible, Corps Commander will withdraw the division to the shortened "Hube" position.[28]

---

[27]The Carleton and York Regiment of the 3rd Canadian Infantry Brigade.

[28]General Hans Hube had transferred the headquarters of 14 Panzer Corps to Sicily on 17 July in order to establish a bridgehead position to screen the withdrawal of German troops from the island.

8 August Sharp enemy pressure on withdrawing troops of 29 Panzer Grenadier Division with penetrations into the withdrawing units at Fratelo. . . . [29]

10 August The evacuation of Sicily has started according to plan.

---

[29]On the north coast, where a seaborne "hook" had been made that day behind enemy lines.

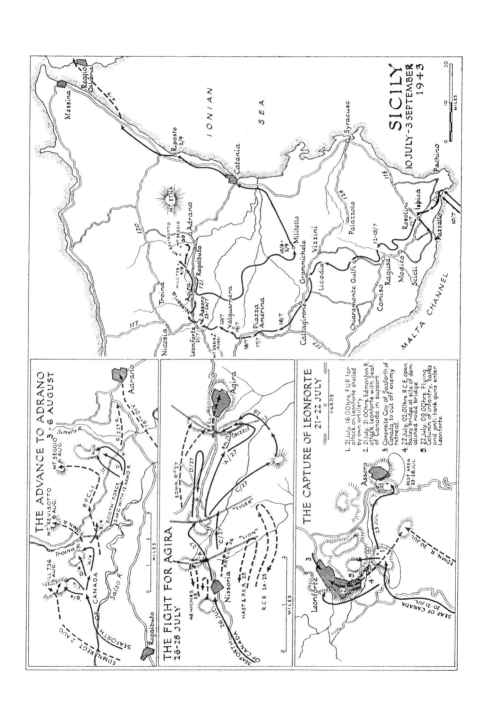

THE ADVANCE TO ADRANO
3-6 AUGUST

THE FIGHT FOR AGIRA
26-28 JULY

THE CAPTURE OF LEONFORTE
21-22 JULY

1. 21 July, 16.00hrs. FUP for attack on Leonforte shelled by own artillery.
2. 21 July, 21.00hrs. Edmonton R. attack Leonforte with Seaf. of Canada in support.
3. Composite Coy of Seaforth of Canada, to cut off enemy retreat.
4. 22 July, 02.00hrs. R.C.E. open Sd'dery bridge at site of demolished road bridge.
5. 22 July, 09.00hrs. Flying Column of infantry, tanks and anti-tank guns enter Leonforte.

SICILY
10 JULY–3 SEPTEMBER
1943

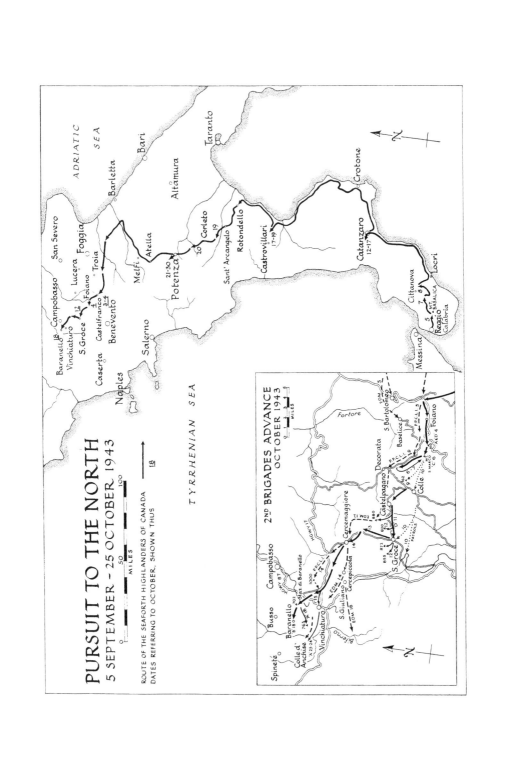

PURSUIT TO THE NORTH
5 SEPTEMBER – 25 OCTOBER 1943

MILES
0   50   100

ROUTE OF THE SEAFORTH HIGHLANDERS OF CANADA
DATES REFERRING TO OCTOBER, SHOWN THUS   18

TYRRHENIAN SEA

ADRIATIC SEA

Naples
Salerno
Caserta
Benevento
Castelfranco 3·4
S. Groce 4
Vinchiaturo 12
Baranello 8
Campobasso
San Severo
Lucera
Foggia
Foiano
Troia
Barletta
Bari
Altamura
Taranto
Atella
Melfi
Potenza 21·30
Corleto 20
Sant' Arcangelo 19
Rotondello
Castrovillari 17·19
Catanzaro 12·17
Crotone
Cittanova 8
Locri
BASILICA 7
ST. 6
Reggio 5
Calabria
Messina

2ND BRIGADES ADVANCE
OCTOBER 1943

MILES
0   1   2   3

Spinete
Busso
Campobasso
Colle d'Anchisa
Baranello B·180
Sisti di Baranello
1000
203
HWY 87
765
X·13-2·7
Vinchiaturo
Biferno
S. Giuliano
Cercepiccola
PPCLI
EDM·14
EDM·18
Decorata
Cercemaggiore
852
855
880
902
S. Groce
12·7
Castelpagano
PPCLI·9
PPCLI·10
PPCLI·13
GOLLO
EDM·5
S. Bartolomeo
Basilice
EDM 4 Foiano
Fortore
PATROLS
PATROLS
HWY 17
13
14
15

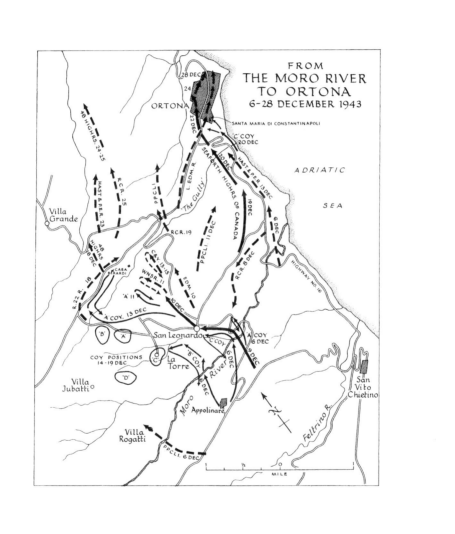

FROM
THE MORO RIVER
TO ORTONA
6-28 DECEMBER 1943

ORTONA

SANTA MARIA DI CONSTANTINAPOLI

'C' COY
20 DEC

ADRIATIC

SEA

48 HIGHRS. 24-25

HAST & PER. 25

RCR. 25

HAST & PER. 23

PPCLI

L.EDM.R.

SEAFORTH HIGHRS OF CANADA

19 DEC

6 DEC

Villa
Grande

RCR.19

The Gully

PPCLI. 11 DEC

HIGHWAY NO.16

48
HIGHRS
8 DEC

CASA
BERARDI

C'COY 13-15

EDM. 10

RCR. 8 DEC

R.22.R. 15

WNSR. 11

'A' 11

10 DEC

'A' COY. 13 DEC

San Leonardo

'B'

'A'

'C' COY.

'A' COY
6 DEC

COY POSITIONS
14-19 DEC

'C'

La
Torre

'B' COY
6 DEC

Moro River

9 DEC

San
Vito
Chietino

Villa
Jubatti

'D'

Appolinare

N

Villa
Rogatti

PPCLI. 6 DEC

Feltrino R.

½

MILE

THE HITLER LINE, 23 MAY 1944

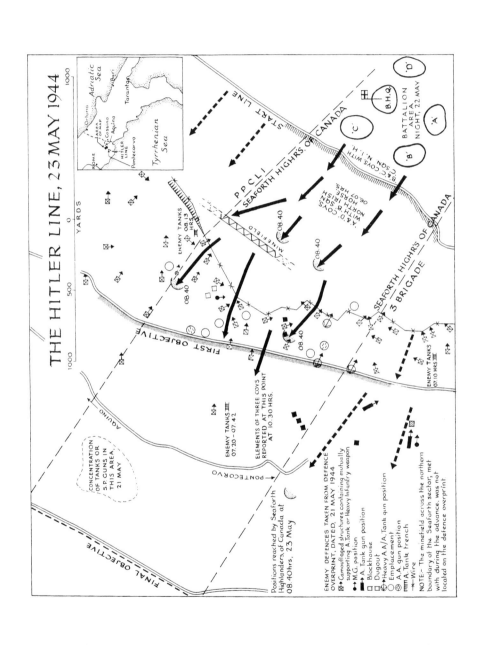

Adriatic Sea
Bari
Taranto
Ortona
AREA OF MAP
Cassino
Aquino
HITLER LINE
Pontecorvo
ROME
Tyrrhenian Sea

YARDS
1000   500   0   500   1000

START LINE

PPCLI
SEAFORTH HIGHR'S OF CANADA
'B' 'C' COYS WITH PPCLI
'A' 'D' COYS WITH NORTH IRISH HORSE 0607 HRS.
MINEFIELD
08.40
08.13 HRS.
ENEMY TANKS 07.20 - 07.42

FIRST OBJECTIVE
08.40
08.40
08.40

SEAFORTH HIGHR'S OF CANADA
3 BRIGADE
ENEMY TANKS 07.10 HRS

BATTALION AREA, NIGHT, 22 MAY
'D'
B.H.Q.
'C'
'A'
'B'

AQUINO
CONCENTRATION OF TANKS OR S P GUNS IN THIS AREA, 21 MAY
PONTECORVO
ELEMENTS OF THREE COYS REPORTED AT THIS POINT AT 10.30 HRS.

FINAL OBJECTIVE

Positions reached by Seaforth Highlanders of Canada at 08 40hrs, 23 May

ENEMY DEFENCES TAKEN FROM DEFENCE OVERPRINT, DATED, 21 MAY 1944
⊠ Camouflaged structures containing mutually supporting A.Tank or Heavy Infantry weapon
● M.G. position
A. Tank gun position
■ Blockhouse
□ Dugout
⊕ Heavy AA/A.Tank gun position
Emplacement
⊙ A.A. gun position
▥ A.Tank trench
✕ Wire

NOTE:- The minefield across the northern boundary of the Seaforth sector, met with during the advance, was not located on the defence overprint

SOUTHERN ITALY

4 September 1943 – 18 October 1943

I

The Pursuit Up "The Boot"

The encampment near Militello lay on the southwest fringe of Sicily's Catania plain and some 50 miles behind the spearhead of battle from which the Seaforths had been withdrawn on the 6th of August. There were gentle slopes rising westward to the spine of high ground along which the battalion had passed on its climb from the beaches to Leonforte, there were trees for shade, and (this was a pleasant surprise after the dry beds of the Salso and Troina rivers) there were streams running through the company positions. The troops enjoyed the beauty and peacefulness of the setting for three weeks, and they called the place "Happy Valley". During these three weeks, Churchill and Roosevelt and their Chiefs of Staff met at Quebec to make decisions of far-reaching importance to the conduct of the war, American and Canadian forces occupied Kiska, and the Russians, now on the offensive over a 450-mile front, recaptured Kharkov. In the northeast corner of Sicily the Americans and the British, fighting against stiff resistance almost to the last day, took Messina on the 17th. In the same period both German and Allied commanders reappraised the situation as they saw it in the Mediterranean theatre of war. The conclusions they reached are the context for what the Seaforths were to do and suffer in the months to come.

For the Germans the invasion of Sicily meant a second front, but probably not the second front which would in the final analysis be opened against them. They were especially vulnerable, as it seemed, in the Balkans, in the south of France, and of course in the west where they faced England across the Straits of Dover.[1] In the meantime the Russian front, where German troops had been newly thrown on the defensive, was a grave threat which could be met only by exorbitant commitments of men and materials. Yet Italy was not to be lightly given up. Rommel, it is true, when the loss of Sicily became inevitable, advocated a quick withdrawal of German forces

---

[1]Nicholson notes that the Balkans had received priority in reinforcements as early as May, 1943, when the German garrison there had been increased from seven to thirteen divisions. The cover-plan for "Husky" was to this extent successful. See Nicholson, *The Canadians*, p. 194.

to the northern parts of Italy as part of a wider plan to prevent the dissipation of German strength on overextended fronts; but Kesselring opposed him, and Kesselring's view, which was also Hitler's view, prevailed: "the war must be kept as far as possible from the heart of Europe, and thereby from the borders of Germany."[2] Accordingly, as Hube withdrew the remnants of his four divisions and their equipment from Sicily between the 10th and the 15th of August, the German reinforcement of the Italian peninsula, begun much earlier, continued at an accelerated rate. By the time the evacuation was completed there were close to twenty German divisions in Italy. Six of these, constituting the German 10th Army under the command of Col.-Gen. Heinrich v. Vietinghoff, were concentrated south of Rome.[3]

Hitler placed the "centre of gravity" for the defence of southern Italy in the Naples-Salerno area, and neither Kesselring nor Vietinghoff saw any good reason to disagree with him. This was on the assumption that southern Italy was attacked. As late as the 22nd of August Vietinghoff thought that an attack so directed was to be regarded "only as a secondary possibility"; it seemed to him much more likely that the Allies would go after bigger game in Sardinia and Corsica, which would in turn lead them to central or northern Italy and perhaps even southern France.[4] But if they were to come south of Rome, it must surely be assumed that their main blow would be aimed directly at Naples. The alternative, more obvious tactically, of an assault across the Straits of Messina to Reggio Calabria did not seem to the Germans to have much to recommend it: the terrain stretching north and east into Calabria was extremely mountainous, a hazard even to infantry, and there were few military objectives that an invader would be likely to covet south of Naples and the Foggia airfields. By the end of August Vietinghoff had completed the disposition of his forces. The Italians, whose ultimate defection had been anticipated for some time, had no place in the German scheme of defence.[5] Three German divisions

---

[2]From a High Command situation report dated 25 July, 1943, quoted in Nicholson, *The Canadians*, p. 195. Rommel was at this time Commander-in-Chief in the north of Italy, Kesselring Commander-in-Chief in the south. On the difference in views between Rommel and Kesselring, see A.H.Q. Report No. 18, fn., p. 2 (mimeographed).

[3]Nicholson, *The Canadians*, pp. 195–96.

[4]A.H.Q. Report No. 18, pp. 4–5 (mimeographed).

[5]Theoretically, the Italian 7th Army, with headquarters at Potenza, was responsible for a part of the defence of southern Italy; the 211th Coastal Division in particular, reinforced by a battalion of Blackshirts and a battalion of paratroopers, was to hold the most southerly tip of Calabria with the vague assurance that German troops in a counterattack role would

(Hube's 14th Corps) were grouped around Naples; at their backs, though not under Vietinghoff's command, were two further divisions concentrated near Rome against political contingencies expected to arise with the capitulation of Italy. To the south the responsibilities of the 76th Corps, with two divisions under command, reached deep into Calabria. But these responsibilities were limited: elements drawn down into the Aspromonte to cover the withdrawal of 14th Corps from Sicily would move north again on contact with the enemy, and no serious stand was contemplated beyond the Castrovillari region almost 150 miles from the Reggio beaches. The Naples-Salerno area would remain the "centre of gravity".

As the Seaforths shook themselves down in "Happy Valley" during the second week of August, a rumour made the rounds of the companies that the battalion would be back in England by Christmas. It was the variant of a familiar myth about "going home", and it was to be heard often again in the months to come and in the end laughed at. But the story may at this time have had a peculiar relation to a set of facts. For the necessity of compromise which had attended the birth of "Husky" was a necessity still in the Allied planning of what should follow the successful conclusion of the campaign in Sicily. Throughout, the Americans had remained suspicious of the development of operations in the Mediterranean theatre, and it had been with difficulty only that Churchill had made his point at Casablanca in May, 1943, that useful employment of some kind should be found locally for the troops engaged in "Husky" at the close of their main assignment.[6] The compromise did not obscure the fact that the second front would go in in the west in 1944; no one was to forget that. Landings in northern Italy were therefore out of the question as sequels to the landings in Sicily; and even in the case of lesser undertakings set farther to the south the principle of economy of means would be increasingly a check upon the imaginations of the planners. Under these conditions the obvious, which was a thrust by the Eighth Army across the straits to the toe of the boot with only limited immediate objectives, became attractive. Then, when success in the Sicilian campaign and the fall of Mussolini on the 25th of July lent encouragement, the more daring alternative of an assault northward across the Tyrrhenian Sea could be considered. By mid-August both plans were

come to their aid in the event of invasion. Only the Blackshirts and the paratroopers were at all effective. "On balance," writes one historian, "the Italians at that time were probably of help to none and a hindrance to all." A.H.Q. Report No. 18, fn., p. 7 (mimeographed).

[6]See Nicholson, *The Canadians*, pp. 182–83.

firm; Operation "Baytown" would be directed against Reggio between the 1st and the 4th of September, and Operation "Avalanche" would be directed against Salerno (the most promising objective within range of existing fighter-cover) on the 9th. The conditions of limitation, however, remained, and the Canadians might well have been sent back to England at the end of August, as indeed a variety of other Allied troops were. It is important to recognize that in staying they stayed to participate in a restricted and in all respects less than top-priority campaign.[7]

While their future was being laid out for them elsewhere by other hands, the Seaforths went about their business. "It must be remembered," writes an anonymous veteran of the campaign in Sicily, "that when a battalion is 'in rest' everyone from the Corps commander down is thinking of things for the members of the unit to do and so many people become attached elsewhere that few commanders actually command their war establishment".[8] The troops rose at dawn, worked from seven to ten in the morning, rested in the heat of the afternoon, and worked again in the evening. There were lectures to give and to attend, kit and clothing deficiencies to be made up, reinforcements to be posted, pay parades to be mustered, snipers and scouts to be trained, company exercises to be carried out in daylight and in darkness. Some men went on course, some took part in a series of visits to a station of the 79th Group (Kittyhawk) of the United States Air Force, where they learned about the work of fighter-bombers, and many rode off in all directions to meet the rash of needs which higher formations develop when they are out of the line. The Pipes and Drums practised, and selected teams in the companies trained for a divisional Sports Day set for the end of August. Drivers picked up the battalion's full-scale vehicles at Catania and brought them home to roost. Ceremony had its place. On the 15th the Seaforths held a service of commemoration at which Lieut. R.F. Perrett read the role of honour for Sicily, and Pipe-Major Esson played a lament for the dead. On the 13th Brigadier Vokes inspected the battalion area, and on the 20th Generals Montgomery and Simmonds stopped by to address the troops. Two days later the men laid out their kit and stood

---

[7]A dispatch written by General Alexander at the time noted that in the operations now to be undertaken "the Mediterranean theatre would no longer receive the first priority of resources and its operations would become preparatory and subsidiary to the great invasion based on the United Kingdom." Quoted in Nicholson, *The Canadians*, p. 180.

[8]From a mimeographed document in my possession entitled "Infantry Battalion" and marked SECRET. Unsigned and no date.

to attention for a brief visit by General A.G.L. McNaughton. Then, on the 25th, the fulfilment of plans laid for some time, 18 officers and 200 other ranks left for Catania to join with the 2nd, 5th and 6th battalions of the Imperial Seaforths in a memorable reunion.[9] The beating of Massed Retreat by 41 pipers and 22 drummers in the great Sports Stadium of the city was beautiful and stirring. Celebrations went on into the night. On the 28th the Seaforths took the crown in brigade sports from the Edmonton Regiment and the Patricias, and on the 29th, which was a Sunday, there was a compulsory church parade at which Padre Durnford delivered an electrifying sermon on the soldiers' habit of fouling the name of Christ. August was quite a month. September was to be quite a month too, though in a different way.

The story of the Seaforths in battle takes a long leap from the valley of the Salso and Simeto rivers, where the battalion broke off contact with the Germans on the 5th of August, to a piece of high ground more than one third of the way up the length of Italy called Hill 1007, where on the 6th of October it once again engaged the enemy in earnest. In between lay, in August, the rest-period near Militello, and, in September (following the crossing to mainland Italy), a foot-destroying, soul-numbing advance over more than two hundred miles of country, mostly mountainous, stretching north from the beaches at Reggio. In August the majority of unit casualties were caused by malaria and venereal disease; in September they were attributable to bad feet or sheer exhaustion.

It seems unnecessary to chronicle in detail the gruelling test of the September days, most of which were lived through by members of the battalion in a haze of weariness and hunger. The Germans did not defend the beaches opposite Messina, and they made, as planned, no serious stand south of Castrovillari. And when the 14th Corps failed to dislodge the Americans and the British from the bridgehead at Salerno between the 9th and the 15th, the German forces to the south drew back still farther to conform with the movement of the hinge which must now swing north upon Naples. The Seaforths crossed the Straits of Messina on infantry landing ships on the 4th of September in the wake of the 1st and 3rd Brigades, who had landed unopposed on the 3rd and who were already, on the morning of the 4th, both well ahead of their schedule of advance. The companies marched all that day and the next, three thousand feet straight up, as it seemed, over twisting dusty roads into the Aspromonte. On the

---

[9] A similar reunion had taken place in France towards the close of World War I.

evening of the 6th they were in Delianuova, whence they passed, early on the 7th, through Santa Christina, picking up the road again beyond the town and skirting the northern fringe of the Mastrogiovanni Plateau. Five miles farther on they turned left to follow a donkey track along a high ridge (steep landfall on either side to the sea) to Highway No. 111 near Cittanova. The 2nd Brigade now led the division on its main axis up the mountainous centre of the Calabrian peninsula. On the right flank the 3rd Brigade was already abreast, and more than abreast, in a mobile exploitation of the east-coast road whose success would make possible in the next phase of the advance the abandonment of the central route. On the left flank the 5th (British) Division had passed through Gioia Tauro, at the west end of the Cittanova lateral, on the 6th of September and was on its way to join up with a fresh landing of the 231st (Malta) Brigade twenty-five miles to the north. It was noon on the 8th, and the Seaforths rifle companies had advanced on foot approximately 65 miles over rugged country in less than four days.[10]

On the evening of the 8th the Allies announced the capitulation of Italy; on the morning of the 9th the Allied 5th Army landed at Salerno, and later the same day elements of the 1st (British) Airborne Division were put ashore unopposed at Taranto on the heel of the boot from cruisers of the Mediterranean fleet.[11] For the Seaforths the pattern of movement changed and quickened. T.C.Vs., now available where jeeps and motorcycles alone had supported the advance to date, were placed at the disposal of the battalion. On the 10th, with the Allied Fifth Army obviously face to face with difficult odds at Salerno, General Alexander made clear to General Montgomery the "utmost importance" of his maintaining pressure on the Germans from the south; and General Montgomery, though not to be pushed to a schedule he thought inconsistent with the administrative requirements of his own army, took measures to comply.[12] On the 12th, when forward elements of the 1st Division were already patrolling 100

[10]The figure is impressive only in terms of obstacles surmounted: the heat, the gradients, the uncertainty of the route, hunger, darkness, and broken sleep.

[11]A measure of 2nd class priorities in this theatre of operations: the 1st Airborne lacked sufficient aircraft to put it down in the manner to which it was accustomed. Assault landing craft were likewise unavailable.

[12]Montgomery liked to intimate later that he had saved the Fifth Army's bacon at Salerno by a spectacular advance from Reggio. Kesselring thought the advance from the south "very cautious". Nicholson concludes that the Fifth Army won its own battle at Salerno — though the withdrawal of German forces from the bridgehead area after their counterattacks had

miles to the north, the Seaforths were brought forward in a single day-long lift through Locri on the east coast and up the east-coast road to Catanzaro. Then, after a pause of four days during which supply troops of the division worked desperately to cope with over-extended communications (and, as it happened, the battle of Salerno reached and safely passed its crisis), three bold moves brought the battalion within the sound of gunfire again. On the 17th it was lifted by trucks 130 miles up the coast to a divisional concentration area between Cassana and Castrovillari. On the 19th the bulk of it was lifted by infantry landing ships 50 miles farther up the coast to Nova Siri Station, then by trucks again inland and north another 50 miles to Corleto. And finally, on the 21st it was lifted another 25 miles to Potenza, and five miles beyond the city to the northwest, where it took up defensive positions. On the road inland to Potenza the Seaforths had been preceded by the 3rd Brigade's "Boforce" (a flying column commanded by the West Nova Scotia's Lt.-Col. Bogert) which had to contest possession of Potenza with Germans of the 1st Parachute Division. As the men of the companies settled down in the new area they could hear the rumbling of guns in the distance. Fourteen days and perhaps 400 miles by road and track from the Reggio beaches they were approaching contact with the enemy.

But there was to be no serious fighting for any of the units of the 1st Division for some days yet, and least of all for the Seaforths who were to sit tight on the high ground northeast of Potenza for a full week. The truth was that by the 21st the administrative problems of most of General Montgomery's formations had become so acute that neither the 1st Division in the centre of Italy, nor the 5th (British) Division immediately to the left between the Canadians and the army at Salerno, could contemplate a major move forward before the 1st of October.[13] The Allied line was now secure across the entire width of the boot; but the troops who had established the eastern half of it from Potenza, in the heart of the southern Apennines, to Bari on the Adriatic coast, were for the moment immobilized. Fortunately, elements of the 78th (British) Division and of the 4th (British) Armoured Brigade were precisely at this moment ready to land at Bari. Landed at Bari on the 22nd, these forces quickly secured Foggia and the Foggia

---

failed was undoubtedly hastened by the approach of the Eighth Army from the south. See Nicholson, *The Canadians*, p. 218 ff.

[13]The Eighth Army, during the early stages of operations in Italy, consumed supplies at the rate of 2000 tons per day. The opening of Bari (about the 19th of September) and Naples (on the 1st of October) helped to remedy the difficult situation.

plains against only light resistance from the Germans, who had in any event already decided to make their next main stand farther north and closer to the line of the lateral road from Termoli to Naples, where the mountains again became their friends. And so the Seaforths got out their large packs, enjoyed visits from a unit of the Mobile Baths (British) and contributed a major share to the victory of the 2nd Brigade at a divisional Sports Day held in Potenza on the 29th. The Patricias had patrolled north 25 miles to Atella and Melfi between the 22me and the 27th, and the Royal 22me had been sent the same distance east against Spinazzola on the 24th. But the fringe of contact had passed quickly on, and when the Seaforths received orders to move again on the 30th their destination was an assembly area over 100 miles away, to the north and west of the Foggia plain.

———————————

Letter from Major J.D. Forin to Mrs. Forin, dated at "Happy Valley" (near Militello), 14 August, 1943.

My dearest Vivian:

We have moved into a rest area about 80 miles by road south of the point I last wrote you from. I took out a recce[14] party a day or so before we moved in and located the place in the larger area in which we had to find our site. Most of the countryside held sun-baked hills, but by following our noses we finally came on a lovely valley green with orchards and gardens, and with fresh, clean, cold streams flowing in good volume into it from several directions. The streams supply three cisterns which hold enough water for swimming, about 7 feet deep and 15 to 20 feet square. Spots like this are likely to be malaria-ridden, but so far we have seen very few mosquitoes.Everyone who visits us speaks of it as a "Garden of Eden", and that it is. The few officers of BHQ who eat together — the C.O., Gowan the Adjutant, myself, Keith Murdoch (now a Captain and Intelligence officer), the Padre, the Paymaster and the Auxiliary Services Officer[15] — have our meals from tables set up in the shade of some huge apple trees. Our batmen have scrounged, in addition to the tables, a few ramshackle chairs so that we don't have to sit on the ground or on our bedrolls. These

---

[14] Always "recce", never "reconnaissance".

[15] The Paymaster was Capt. G.F. Williamson; the Auxiliary Services Officer ("Sally Ann") was Supervisor H.E. Newing.

latter, incidentally, we have up with us for the first time.[16] It made me feel about twice as hot on opening mine to find my greatcoat and battle-dress *AND* winter underwear there. I spoke to an English-speaking Italian farmer soon after we came here to get him to set some compensation for our taking vegetables and fruits, and we hope some chickens, from the neighbouring farms. This particular farmer used to live in Boston, and there are a number of Sicilians with similar histories of time spent in the U.S.A. Why they ever came back here is beyond explanation. Today at lunch two Italians came around to our table with a pair of chickens, very much alive, which they wanted to swap for a pair of boots. Many of these people have no boots or shoes of any kind but go about with feet done up in pieces of rubber tires or bandages made from old strips of cloth. Our communication with the outside world is almost non-existent. Towns are at a distance and out of bounds, and in any event there is not much to be found in them. No newspapers, though there is word of a big mail in today, which we all hope is true. Yesterday the Padre and the Auxiliary Services Officer went down to Syracuse to bring back some kit-bags and make some purchases for the battalion. The Padre was disappointed in the city, describing it as stucco-fronted and dirty — that is, what was left of it. We are well off where we are. The Pipe Band plays Reveille at five-thirty in the cool morning half-light and Retreat at seven o'clock in the evening. The evenings are lovely — an almost full moon, very cool, blue fleckless sky and quiet. From our headquarters I can see the supply vehicles of British and American Divisions making by road towards Messina. They go along, leaving great columns of dust behind them, down on a plain which we overlook from our hill-side position.

We have almost 100% new company and platoon officers now. Re-inforcements are satisfactory on all counts, however, and we are training them up while we have the chance. Haven't heard from you yet, and as you can guess am *very* anxious to get your letters. Try airmail — it is getting through. You needn't worry about me for at least a fortnight. All love to the three of you. Ever,

Douglas

---

[16]Other ranks' equivalent of the bedroll (and usually made available at the same time) was the kit-bag, which contained spare boots, shoe brushes, clothes brush, woollen gloves, spare shirt, trousers and underwear, canvas shoes, two towels, etc. Officers' bedrolls contained similar items, and anything else that could be got in. Some were very heavy.

Extracts from a Letter Written by Lieut. W.H. Melhuish to his Family in Vancouver, B.C., dated at "Happy Valley", 19 August, 1943.

Dear Family:

Well, I finally got back to the Regiment after a three-weeks lapse, and you can bet I was glad to get some mail, my first in nearly two months. We are situated in a valley, and what a blessing, for it is irrigated and we have running water, and even, too, small pools for swimming. I'll tell you more about the place later. Thank goodness the flies are not as bad here as they were at Syracuse, where I spent several days waiting to come back up the line. We used to have to wave our food from side to side to keep them off, and you could count 30 or 40 clustered together in places. I remember a chap sitting next to me at lunch one day getting thoroughly browned off with flies attacking his food and suddenly clapping his hand over a piece of meat left on his plate and shouting wildly, "All right, damn you, *I'll* eat that!" He was in a real state about it, and I've felt the same myself. . . .

If you got my last two letters (Nos. 64 and 65) you will know what ailed Willie. But just in case you didn't and are worrying, it was only a plain old sprained ankle. After spending about a week in hospital I was discharged to a newly opened Canadian "rest camp" nearby, where I found Don Newson, Dunc Manson, Rusty Martin and Al Robinson, and where we all proceeded to sit around, sleep, eat, swim, read, loaf and generally do nothing. The view from the camp atop the cliffs was good, and in the distance we could see Augusta, quite an important port. The camp itself was a former German Meteorological Station. I was there about three days and then was sent to the Canadian Base Reinforcement Unit a few miles away to await a posting to the battalion. It was quite a wait, and at one stage Borden Cameron and I set off on our own in search of the Seaforths, though without success. Excuse, please, if I am repeating myself, but letters can get lost, and since the official word you'll get of me will probably be that I've been "wounded in action", I want to make sure you know I'm all right. . . .

I enclose a few more trophies of the chase, being some unused Italian stamps, a few more postcards, and a German newspaper clipping picked up in the hills relating to the Dieppe raid of August, 1942. Will try to write a more interesting letter next time. Much love to you both,

Bill

Extracts from an Official Account of the Seaforth Reunion at Catania, 25 August, 1943.[17]

... As the afternoon wore on, convoys of Seaforths converged on Catania from all directions. At 4:00 p.m. the Pipes and Drums assembled in an area near the Park, and at 4:30 they were led out the gate by the Drum Major of the 5th Battalion. It was a never-to-be-forgotten sight, that kilted phalanx of 63 bandsmen swinging through streets lined with Italians agape with wonder and admiration and with Seaforths from all the battalions. Into the huge stadium they marched to take up their positions before thousands who had arrived early to watch the spectacle. Despite differences in drill and drum beating that had had to be rectified in only one rehearsal, the Massed Retreat, which began promptly at 5:00 p.m., was excellent. It was recorded for re-broadcast later to the world. ...

In the evening, Officers and Sergeants were the guests of the 6th Battalion at their headquarters in Misterbianco, a few miles west of Catania. The Officers' Mess was a large house, the property of an Italian baron, set in spacious gardens and having a rectangular forecourt suitable for the pipes, and a large balcony where there was ample room for spectators. The Sergeants' Mess opened on a long rectangular terrace with a wall around it and pillars at the corners. It was an ideal setting for a party.

Following cocktails (champagne) and a sumptuous buffet supper came the formalities of the occasion. Lt.-Col. Ainslie, C.O. of the 6th Battalion, in an excellent address reminded the gathering that there was a precedent for the present occasion in a reunion of Seaforth battalions held in 1918 immediately after the end of World War I. On that earlier occasion the C.O. of the Seaforth Highlanders of Canada had said that the gathering was unique and would probably not be repeated. But, said Lt.-Col. Ainslie, it had been repeated, and though he could scarcely wish for another war to provide the occasion for a third meeting of the clans, he hoped that another reunion would be possible before the close of the present conflict. The C.O. of the Seaforth Highlanders of Canada, Lt.-Col. B.M. Hoffmeister, then made a most fitting and appealing speech, such as to reach the hearts of all Seaforths assembled. He said that in speaking to them he felt rather like a junior member of a firm addressing a Board of Directors. He said how proud they all were to be Seaforths and how they had always done and would always do their utmost to conform with all regimental customs

---

[17]W.D., Seaf. of C., August, 1943. Appendix 8.

and traditions. When they had set sail from England, they had hoped for meetings in the days ahead with other Seaforths; but they had never dreamed of the possibility of a reunion of the four battalions. They were delighted and greatly honoured to be present.

After the Canadian toast to the 2nd, 5th and 6th Battalions, the Pipe Majors of both the Seaforth Highlanders of Canada and the 5th Battalion played "Pibrochaide". Pipe Major Esson of the Canadian Seaforths then gave the regimental Gaelic toast. . . .

Extract from a Letter Written by Lieut. W.H. Melhuish to his Family in Vancouver, B.C., dated 26 August, 1943.

. . . 6:00 p.m. Am recovering from my first social binge on the island. It was the occasion of our battalion getting together with the three Imperial battalions of the Eighth Army — an event without parallel in regimental history, though two battalions did, I believe, get together in France in 1918. The splendid spectacle of the massed bands took place in the modern sports stadium in Catania. Then the lucky officers, only a limited number, made the trip to the 6th Battalion Mess on the Etna road. A lovely place, and what a time we had! I started out with four glasses of Italian champagne, and the proceedings turned quite rosy! The buffet supper they gave us, though probably no more than an extra good one in Canada, was stupendous, and the variety amazing for the island. We finished up sleeping on couches or chairs, on the verandah or anywhere, and came back the 40 miles or so to "Happy Valley" early (but not bright) the next morning. The Imperials were not at all stand-offish, far from it, and I felt very pleased to have been at the gathering. . . .

Extracts from a Letter Written by Pte. G. Ableson to Mr. John Ableson of 2876 West 5th Ave., Vancouver, B.C., dated at "Happy Valley", 29 August, 1943.[18]

. . . Coming back to the battalion is coming home. It's not a matter of seeing one's pals again, not entirely at any rate. You know I was never the

---

[18]Fiction: see note p. 11.

chummy sort, and besides, most of the few I knew reasonably well are off-stage in hospital or lying in shallow graves. There are of course familiar faces. Colonel Hoffie and Major Forin are still here, as is also "C" Company's tireless little organizer Capt. Nip Parker, whose Parker Construction Company has set up in this happy valley the most ingenious installation of home-made showers imaginable. Then there are the permanent staffers, as we call them, real characters most of them and fast becoming the durable core of the battalion: the Padre, for example, "Pay" Williamson, "Postie" Sinclair, Pipe Major Esson, and (to take another at random) the battalion sanitary corporal, Leo Greig.[19] But it's not quite a matter of familiar faces either. It's just your bounded world, that's all, with its well defined relationships, its things expected of you and not expected of you, its own ways of doing things, its mystique, its cohesive spirit, what you will. You know when you leave it, and you know when you come back. Inside, there are the companies and the platoons, but all Cuidich'ns:[20] outside, there are the near neighbours in the Brigade, the Edmontons and the Patricias in that order, but beyond these nothing to which or to whom one really belongs. Not even Monty has been able to sell us on the importance of "belonging" to the Eighth Army. You don't come home to an army, to a corps, to a division, or to a brigade. You don't even come home to a platoon or a company. You come home to a battalion. I find that interesting.

... This being Sunday, I managed a walk in the afternoon up into the hills, where I saw a dozen partridge, a wren, something that looked like a flicker, and a goldfinch. Not exactly the Canadian varieties, but recognizable. On the way down I was caught in a crashing thunderstorm and returned to find the camp nearly washed out. My bedding now hangs above me in an apple tree, to catch the evening sun. We had a memorable battalion church parade this morning, one of the laid-on kind, and it became memorable when the Padre stood up and said as loud and clear as you please, "The title of my sermon this morning is 'Jesus Fucking Christ' ". Well, there was a moment's silence, followed by a few nervous titters, then the boys just listened, no mistake. It was about blasphemy, of course, and the Padre made a good case for our cleaning up our language. What effect this will have in practice, I don't know; most of the men lace their talk

---

[19]"Pay" is the Paymaster, Captain G.F. Williamson; "Postie" is the Postal Sergeant, K52834 Sgt. William Sinclair.

[20]From the Gaelic of the regimental motto: "Cuidich'n Righ" (in English, "Help the King").

with cuss words as naturally as they take air into their lungs, and perhaps as inoffensively. . . .

The word is passed from R.S.M. Ireland that a recce party left for parts unknown this morning, so I expect we shall be leaving here within the next few days. The odds right now are 2 to 1 in favour of England by Christmas. The old story. It's Italy first, for sure. If you're down at the Armoury and want to talk sports, you can say that the Seaforths won the brigade championships yesterday hands down — 53 points for us, 38 for the Edmontons, 25 for the Patricias, 3 for the Sask. L.I.[21] I say "us", but they got no help from me. Corporal Cameron was the star, winning the 440, the 880 and the mile. Also Nichols and Hammond. Somebody may know the names. The prize cup was made from a German shell case, nicely polished. . . .

Extracts from the Diary of H/Capt. Roy Durnford, Regimental Chaplain to the Seaforth Highlanders of Canada, dated in Italy, 4–8 September, 1943.

4 September Dawn at sea: lilac, red and gold. The towns of Reggio and Messina, facing each other across the straits, look clean and grey against mountain backgrounds. Land at 6:50 a.m. and march through the wrecked streets of Reggio, enjoying marvelous view of the harbour, ships plying the straits, and Sicily. Breakfast at 2:00 p.m. and move off again at 4:30, going northeast over hills and ravines that would make the Cheddar Gorge look like a ditch. I am soon drenched from head to toe in sweat. Evening comes, then night, and we march on through villages reeking of squalor and poverty. I am feeing weaker; no food, and one foot dragging behind the other. Bridge blown, but engineers already doing wonderful work. At midnight still marching, though men beginning to fall out (young fellows too).

5 September Stop briefly at 1:00 a.m. and sleep where we drop. No sleep last night and evidently very little tonight. One meal only yesterday. At 2:00 a.m. men line the road, fallen by the wayside dead-beat. I can't go much farther. I am nearly done. It is pitch black here in the avenues of woods. I am sweating with weakness. At 2:30 a.m. we overtake men of

---

[21]The Saskatoon Light Infantry (M.G.) were support group to the brigades of the 1st Canadian Division.

the Patricias and kip down. Too dazed to remember much. John Gowan gives me two biscuits, a lump of bully beef (like chicken) and a bar of chocolate. Sleep on rocks with just my gas-cape over me. Get up at 7:00 a.m. stiff with cold and wet, stale sweat. Blessed tea, and two pieces of hardtack and cheese. One mile from our objective, they say. (I wonder?) The sun rises at 8:15 and warms us as we march off. Soon we near the summit of Mount Basilica. Forests of pine, beech, poplar and elder wood. Settle at 1:30 p.m. at big convalescent hospital for children and sleep for six hours in a real bed. Had almost forgotten it was the Sabbath. Have a feeling God will understand. . . .

6 September   Pitch dark and very cold when we move off. My legs are stiff from yesterday's march, but we warm up as we go. By 10:00 a.m. fog lifting from nearby hills and sun trying to break through low-lying clouds . After brief rest in the afternoon move off at 3:30 for long haul of 22 miles, much of it, they say, across country. As night falls we overtake men of the Edmontons and wait, then push on. Tired by now. My knee shows signs of giving out and cramp follows. Damp and cold as we start a seemingly endless rise into the mountains.

7 September   Arrive very early at Santa Christina, a fair size town, where we are met by civilian police in ornate uniforms. Rain pours down in sheets and with great vehemence. An Italian opens his house for the drenched troops; he speaks a little English, having lived in the U.S.A. for nine years. His shop has nothing to sell now, he says, with despair and defeat in his voice. . . . On we go beneath leaden sky and glowering, inky black clouds, and pray to God for a rainless night. Eventually pass through the Edmontons' lines and catch up with the Colonel, who has been recceing a campsite. We carry on endlessly up and up in spiral fashion, following the mountain sides, sometimes going in opposite directions and seeing rear troops below on the same road. We reach the top eventually and proceed across country in the gloaming. The whole battalion seems to lose its way in the dark; we travel in circles.

8 September   At 1:30 a.m. we stop and I slump in the ferns, sharing a blanket with Orr,[22] who has a fever. Up and on the go again at 6:30 a.m., cold and hungry. March for two hours, then breakfast on half-rations in a valley by a stream. Resume march, feet dragging, past hovels of

---

[22]K53110 Pte. G.B. Orr: batman, more properly, general assistant to the Padre.

surprised peasants. At 3:00 p.m. arrive at long last at our destination. What destination? Establish ourselves, and I find a quiet spot on the hillside overlooking the sea, which is distant and far below me. Fix up my gas-cape as a tent, eat and turn in. Exhausted.

———————

Extracts from an Interview with Lieut. J.O. Moxon, dated at Vancouver, B.C., 22 July, 1960.[23]

McDougall: Do you remember anything except tiredness about the long advance up Italy?

Moxon: The thing I remember is we became expert at rolling up our blankets and moving the battalion. We had blankets, so this must have been after some of our vehicles had caught up. We could move that battalion in about 15 minutes. I remember we would just get bedded down, and the next thing we would hear would be a motorcycle and someone shouting "Prepare to move!" Then everybody would start to swear.

McDougall: And cold at nights? You're up high?

Moxon: Yes, very cold at nights. We seemed to move more by night than by day, though, and I heard later that the idea was to impress on the Germans that there were a lot of battalions there. Was that right?

McDougall: Partly. There was also the problem of relieving some of the pressure on Salerno.

Moxon: It seemed to me at one time we got orders to make as much noise as we wanted to. .... Incidentally, the maps were very poor in this whole business.

McDougall: It was perhaps difficult to issue them quickly enough to keep up with the move.

Moxon: Maybe so. But I think even the ones we did get were poor, because it seemed to me we were getting lost all the time. I remember climbing up to a plateau we were supposed to get on to; we were in single file, and of course the Germans had blown all the bridges, and there were

---

[23]Lieut. Moxon was, during the period discussed, with "D" Company, under the command of Capt. J.H.T. McMullen.

plenty of them, so that we couldn't get any of our heavy vehicles across. We were on our own, and we had had nothing to eat for what seemed like days, except what we carried with us, which was hardtack. It was surprising how hardtack and margarine were just the most delicious things we ever ate. At last we got up on to the plateau, and as far as I was concerned I thought we were halfway up Italy. When I eventually got a look at a map I couldn't believe that we'd just gone across the toe of the boot. Well, up on the plateau we were stretched out in line, and you know how it is, you concertina. Then every time you stop, the line closes up. With "D" Company at the end, as it seemed to be most of the time, away the rest of them would go, and then we'd be running. The boys were getting pretty unhappy, and after this stumbling and starting and stopping had been going on for hours we swore we had passed the same place about three times. So the fourth time we passed this same spot, some joker sang out, "Put another nickel in and we'll go round again!"

McDougall: A crack like that could help when tempers were thin.

Moxon: It certainly could. What got me was that we seemed to be climbing day after day, and we'd end each march with as few as eight fellows out of our platoon. I know that I cried, my knees hurt so much. Going down especially. We'd see the road across the way, and we'd take short-cuts and go down thump, thump, thump. My knees were just agony. But I was proud of myself keeping up, which I had to. I admired Hoffie tremendously; not only did he do this march, but he was up and down the line, exhorting us on. He must have marched four times the distance we did. We got to hoping we would run into some Italians or Germans so that we could stop.

McDougall: Do you recall being seaborne at one stage of the advance? Some elements of the battalion were lifted up the coast by L.S.Is. on the 19th.

Moxon: No, I don't, though I do remember a whole series of quick lifts by transport which took us pretty quickly right up to Potenza. At first we moved on our own "F" and "A" Echelon vehicles, then it was big trucks handled by Italian drivers. There were stops for a day or so here and there, of course, and I remember one, I don't know exactly where, when word came down from above that we were to eat off the fat of the land. It can't have been very official, because we weren't supposed to take food needed by the starving populace. But I guess we were a starving enough populace ourselves by then. Anyway, we were fortunate enough to have a fellow in my platoon who had been a butcher, and we found a little calf pretty smartly and made ourselves a wonderful feed. I think the chap's name was Deschene. Eventually we made him a corporal. . . .

Patrol Report Submitted by Lieut. A.L. Robinson of "C" Company and dated 23 September, 1943.[24]

On the 22nd of September I received instructions from Capt. Thomson to take 20 men on patrol to obtain the following information:

1. Whether the town of Baragiano was occupied by the enemy.[25]
2. Condition of bridges on road Ruiti-Baragiano.

Patrol left battalion at 0930 hrs. Reached Baragiano at 1530 hrs. No enemy in town. Received following information from civilians. 1. Mines and booby-traps on road Ruiti-Baragiano. 2. Small bridge blown on same road but large bridge O.K. 3. Bridge on road leading into Baragiano was mined. 4. Enemy had tank and four machine-guns at Stazione di Baragiano, and guard of 30 men. These troops wore death's-head badge. 5. Large force of enemy estimated at several hundred at Stazione Bella Muro and on hills beyond.[26] 6. 12 to 20 machine-guns and two anti-tank guns of heavy calibre on road Stazione Bella Muro to Bella. 7. Heavy concentrations of enemy at both Muro and Bella. 8. No enemy on road or on hills between Stazione di Baragiano and Ruiti.

Having received above information, it was decided to send patrol back on a course parallel to road Baragiano-Ruiti under command of the Sergeant, with the intention of confirming information re bridges on this road, while the platoon commander and his runner remained in Baragiano to observe Stazione di Baragiano, and the road and ground to Muro and Bella, and to obtain any further information possible. Main patrol left

---

[24]W.D., Seaf. of C., September, 1943, Appendix 10.

[25]Baragiano was about 15 miles northeast of Potenza. Seaforth of C. were to patrol this sector while the Patricias patrolled north in strength to Melfi.

[26]Muro was about 8 miles beyond Baragiano on the axis of the patrol's advance. "Stazione" signifies the town's railway station, often some distance removed from the town itself.

Baragiano approximately 1700 hrs. En route confirmed information re bridges and met personnel of 5 Div.[27]

After patrol has left, contacted Carabiniere H.Q. and arranged for accommodation for the night and concealment if enemy patrol should return to investigate. Obtained services of interpreter and arranged to have civilians and farmers in vicinity brought in for questioning.

Gave all information to runner with orders to return to BHQ immediately if I did not return by 1900 hrs. It now being 1800 hrs., I proceeded to high ground overlooking Stazione di Baragiano and, not being able to see any enemy movement, borrowed Italian shirt and proceeded down cliff toward station. On reaching vineyard 400 yards from station, observed enemy soldier approaching. Returned to town and found several civilians waiting to be questioned. Elicited much of the information given above.

Realizing that information about the enemy at Stazione di Baragiano was not reliable and might cause unnecessary delay unless confirmed, it was decided to dress in civilian clothes, take guide and go to the station on the morning of the 23rd. Written report was then given to runner and he was sent with guide to return by quickest route to BHQ. It subsequently transpired that he met a 5 Div. Recce Unit beyond Pacherno,[28] who were much interested in report. Runner reached our BHQ at 0900 hrs. 23 Sep.

Obtained complete set of civilian clothes, discarded all marks of identification including watch, money and arms, retaining only binoculars, and left Baragiano with guide at 0630 hrs. Proceeded down cliff, crossed river and road, and approached Stazione di Baragiano from N.E. Wandered along talking to civilians and finally reached station. No sign of enemy except tank tracks on road. Civilian reported machine-gun at white house directly across from station. Walked around house but could not see gun. Believe it was in woodshed or inside house. Decided closer investigation would be indiscreet and proceeded to find tank. Guide took covered route through orchard to edge of road, about 150 yards behind station. He pointed out location of tank, but I was unable to see it. Went to edge of road, when burst of machine-gun fire disclosed it immediately across the way. Heard two enemy talking. Tank was against grey stone building, under large lone tree, and was heavily covered with freshly cut branches. From 10 yards it was very nearly invisible. Guide suggested it would be unwise to return immediately, so proceeded toward Bella road to confirm, if possible,

---

[27]The 5th (British) Division, working on the left of the 1st Canadian Division.
[28]Picerno?

reports of machine-guns and anti-tank guns on high ground overlooking road. Got within 400 yards of road and met two Italian soldiers who advised Germans were shooting at anyone approaching road. Guide led way to large two-storey house owned by friends of his. Observed country from top-storey window, but could not locate enemy positions. This due to road running through defile between two long, low hills. Located Anti-Aircraft gun on reverse slope of small feature about one mile from station.

Returned then to Stazione di Baragiano and decided to try again to locate machine-gun posts. Met by boy at corner of white house who warned us away. Proceeded across ploughed field heading towards Baragiano. When about 200 yards from house a shot was fired into ground immediately beside us. Taking this as a warning to change course, we did so and approached farm house. Immediately there was another shot and a civilian, walking 100 yards in front of us, fell. We again swung toward Baragiano and a third shot was fired into ground between us. Proceeded to farm house and found above-mentioned civilian badly wounded. There being nothing we could do, proceeded north into hills and made uneventful return by circuitous route to Baragiano. No enemy sighted and all civilians reported none east of Bella road. Arrived Baragiano approximately 1100 hrs.

Had meal, changed into uniform and rested for an hour. Left Baragiano at 1300 hrs and proceeded into hills N.E. of town. Cut back to river bed and headed north to Ruiti. About two miles from Baragiano, sighted troops on road across riverbed, which turned out to be 5 Div. Recce Unit. Gave officer in charge all information. Then made way back to BHQ, arriving 1700 hrs.

A.L. Robinson, Lieut.

II

Decorata Crossroads and Baranello

Between the 1st and the 20th of October the Seaforths were to fight two engagements ten days apart in the course of a crab-like movement more west than north which took them from the vicinity of Troia, just south of Lucera on the edge of the Foggia plain, to a point deep in the heart of the Apennines where Highway No. 17, running west by north, intersected the important Naples-Termoli lateral at Vinchiaturo. In making this movement they would, as part of the left-flank brigade of the 1st Canadian Division, squeeze out the neighbouring 5th (British) Division against a high mass of mountains (the Matese) to the southwest which neither the Germans nor the Allies would care to dispute. The shift of axis to the west would also have the curious effect of sending the Seaforth Highlanders of Canada and other units of the 1st Division at an angle across the line of withdrawal of Herr's 76th Corps, whose main task had been to back up the 14th Corps in attacks upon the Salerno bridgehead and who were now moving northeast, under pressure, towards what the Germans hoped would become the winter line of the Sangro River some 50 miles up the east coast.[1] The 26th and 29th Panzer Grenadier Divisions on Herr's right, together with the 1st Parachute Division on the left, were under orders to deny the intervening ground to the Allies for at least a month, from the 2nd of October to the 1st of November.[2] The Seaforths would therefore find the Panzer Grenadiers, with whom they would be immediately concerned on the Canadians' left, an enemy somewhat confused by the complexities of their plan of withdrawal but nevertheless stubborn in their resistance. They would also find the Germans, as usual, much aided by the rugged nature of the terrain and themselves much hindered by the coming of the autumn rains.

Since the illness of General Simmonds on the 29th of September had placed Brigadier Vokes in command of the 1st Division and, in turn, Lt.-Col. Hoffmeister in command of the 2nd Brigade, it was Major J.D. Forin who led the Seaforths north from their positions near Potenza on the

---

[1]The withdrawal to a "winter line" on the Sangro River was covered in Hitler's orders to the German Tenth Army on 30 September. See Nicholson, *The Canadians*, p. 238.
    [2]*Ibid.*

1st of October. That evening, between Canosa and the coast, the battalion convoy had to yield roadspace for the night to transport of the 78th (British) Division streaming up Highway No. 16 towards Foggia and Termoli; but the next day it made good time over the long straight stretches that crossed the plain, and had soon turned sharp left (marking the westerly shift of its axis) to take the Benevento road to a cluster of buildings called Stazione di Bovino about 20 miles due south of Lucera. The Patricias, who were to advance for a time on the right of the Seaforths, were that evening in Troia, ten miles to the north, and farther north still, on what was to be initially the main divisional axis, the 1st Brigade had already begun to attack west of Motta along Highway No. 17 in the direction of Vinchiaturo and Campobasso. The Scout Platoon, which had preceded the battalion, reported the new area clear of enemy.

The bearing which the Seaforths were now to follow in their advance to Vinchiaturo split evenly the angle between Highways No. 87 and No. 17 as these converged on Vinchiaturo crossroads, respectively from the south and from the east. The route would be for the most part across-country (tracks would serve as roads) over ground that was reasonably open, but extremely hilly, and sometimes stony, and everywhere laced with streambeds beginning to fill with water at this time of year. Only one major road traversed the sector, running from Highway No. 87 on the left at Benevento to Highway No. 17 on the right at Volturara and forming with the two converging highways the crossbar of the letter A. At the point at which the Seaforths' axis cut this road was the town of Foiano and, just west of it, the hill called 1007.

After some delays on the 3rd, pending clarification of the situation in San' Bartolomeo and Alberona on the right flank, the Seaforths were lifted forward on the morning of the 4th in T.C.Vs. over a tortuous country road to its junction with the main lateral five miles east of Foiano. "C" Company, in the role of advance guard to the battalion, had by the time the remainder of the companies debussed already advanced along the lateral and through Foiano to another road junction five miles west of the town, where they reported coming under shell and mortar fire from their right flank. Beside a blown bridge on the near side of the town, "A" Company, BHQ, "D" and "B" Company crossed a small stream (which was in fact a tributary of the Fortore River towards which the 3rd Brigade were at that moment attacking along Highway No. 17, a dozen or so miles to the north) and proceeded through Foiano to positions a few hundred yards behind "C"

Company. Of the battalion's forward transport, two jeeps alone were able to cross the stream. Major Forin had in the meantime gone forward with the I.O. to establish a command post with "C" Company, beyond which again the Scout Platoon was searching the area assigned as the battalion objective for that night.[3] This was Mount Faggi (or Hill 910) half a mile west of "C" Company's position at the road junction, and the secondary road which led off from the junction skirted the base of this hill on the right to wind north between other hills for six miles to a country crossroads and cluster of houses named Decorata. The entire district was very hilly, but while there were trees near farmhouses and in the many draws, the hills themselves were for the most part bare. Leaving "B" Company in reserve, Major Forin moved his other three companies onto Mount Faggi after dark.

If Mount Faggi was clear, however, the hills to the north were not, and especially the hill called 1007 (or Mount San Marco) which on the morning of the 6th showed up plainly to observation from a forward knoll of Mount Faggi across the dip of the intervening valley. At eight o'clock the 2nd Brigade was under orders to take and hold Decorata crossroads, but when a report came in almost simultaneously that four armoured cars and a carrier of the 4th P.L.D.Gs.[4] had been knocked out and eight men killed by a concentration of fire from Hill 1007, it became clear that any plan to take Decorata crossroads must take account of Hill 1007 as an intermediate objective. Accordingly, under an inclusive plan which called for "B", "C" and "D" Company to advance and consolidate around Decorata crossroads, Major Forin ordered "C" and "D" Company to attend first to Hill 1007. In this preliminary task they would have the support of a regiment of medium guns, a platoon of heavy mortars and a platoon of medium machine-guns. Neither tanks nor the 17-pounder anti-tank guns of the artillery were available to help them against armour.[5]

---

[3]Postings at the moment included "A" Company, Capt. T.C.B. Vance; "B" Company, Capt. W.G. Harris; "D" Company, Capt. J.E.T. McMullen; 2 i/c Battalion, Major H.P. Bell-Irving; Adjutant, Capt. E.A. Anderson; I.O., Capt. K.S. Murdoch; Scout Platoon, Lieut. A.W. Gray; Support Company, Capt. F.H. Bonnell.

[4]The Princess Louise Dragoon Guards, which had served since the landing in Sicily as Divisional Reconnaissance Regiment.

[5]Approaches from the south and west appear to have been blocked at this time to heavy vehicles. Tank resources, moreover, were still meagre for a variety of reasons associated with the long advance up Italy. "A" Squadron of the Calgary Regiment arrived in Foiano late on the 6th from Volturara. See Nicholson, *The Canadians*, p. 246.

The attack on Hill 1007 went in, as planned, at three o'clock that afternoon. "D" Company, given the special job of securing a knoll immediately forward and to the left of Mount Faggi and from there providing covering fire for "C" Company's assault, had no difficulty in reaching its objective. But "C" Company, entering the intervening valley from the right soon after, came under merciless fire (some said as heavy as anything the Seaforths had experienced since operations began) and the assault was in danger of losing momentum completely until Major Thomson, with the cheery confidence which had already become his mark in battle, renewed in his men the will to get up and go. He called for "B" Company and all supporting arms to strengthen their fire against the top of Hill 1007, then took his men over the remaining 600 yards of ground to drive the enemy from the feature.[6] Nine men were killed and 23 wounded in the afternoon's action. The defending Panzer Grenadiers, well dug in and effectively supported by armour, were probably less badly damaged than the Seaforths. "C" Company consolidated on the crest of the hill, where large boulders and the German emplacements offered protection from enemy countering fire, and there they were shortly joined by "D" and "B" Company.

Darkness was now setting in on this chill October evening, but there was to be no respite. Assuming command of the three companies on Hill 1007, as he had earlier been instructed to do by the C.O., Major Thomson set the scene with his company commanders for the necessary phase to follow, which was the advance to Decorata crossroads. Well before midnight the trek began, the companies strung out in single file, the route across-country but held to the axis of the road on the right, with which members of the Scout Platoon with marvellous ingenuity kept contact throughout the night. The moon helped the Seaforths keep direction and contact within their ranks for the first half mile, but soon its light was blotted out by fog, and men a few feet from one another disappeared as if by magic into the black shroud. The head of the column pushed on as best it could.

Then trouble began. For the ground beyond Hill 1007 was firmly held, and held by armour, and the advance to Decorata crossroads, laid on with the idea of a deep thrust forward on a narrow front, soon became a series of savage and inconclusive skirmishes in the dark as Major Thomson's force stumbled upon enemy positions scarcely knowing they had done so

---

[6] A/Major (Capt.) S.W. Thomson, was awarded the M.C. for his part in this action. K42641 Pte. (A/Cpl.) D.R. MacDonald and K52839 Cpl. R.E.M. Thomas were awarded the M.M.

until they were on top of them. Surprise became a mixed blessing and a curse. "D" Company, which was in the lead, dealt effectively with several machine-gun posts, but before long they were in contact with tanks. A burst of fire from these at point-blank range killed four, including the company commander and a sergeant, wounded a number of others, and scattered the forward platoons.[7] Control of the attenuated column, never easy that night, was by this time all but impossible to maintain. Major Thomson concluded that the position of his companies, perhaps a mile short of the protection of the houses at Decorata crossroads and unsupported by anti-tank weapons, would become quite untenable in daylight. He therefore asked for and received permission to withdraw, and by dawn his companies had made their way back, bringing with them under great difficulties their wounded, to Hill 1007. Here "B" Company remained to hold the boulder-strewn crest, while "C" and "D" Company moved back to Mount Faggi to reorganize.

Thus the record of the 6th of October, a day memorable in so many ways for the Seaforths, was marred by anti-climax. It had begun with a remarkable success against Hill 1007, and it had ended in uncertainty. Yet the nightmare march of the three companies towards Decorata crossroads had done all that could be expected of it in the circumstances, and indeed may well have pushed the Germans to a more hasty departure than they had intended. Depart they did, for when on the 8th the Patricias were on the point of launching a second attack against Decorata crossroads, this one supported by tanks, a patrol of two men of the Seaforth Scout Platoon penetrated the position and reported it clear. The 2nd Brigade resumed its advance, swinging west again towards San Croce and Cercemaggiore as it closed on Vinchiaturo.

It was not at Vinchiaturo, however, that the Seaforths fought their second engagement in October, but rather at Baranello, a town set in the hills three or four miles beyond Vinchiaturo and halfway between the Vinchiaturo-Campobasso road on the east and the Biferno River on the west. A week separated the two actions at Decorata crossroads and Baranello, and a week is a long interval for an advance of scarcely thirty miles without serious opposition. In part the difficulty was the one commonly encountered in Sicily and Italy of moving relatively large and heavily

---

[7]The company commander killed was Capt. J.E.T. McMullen; the sergeant, George Fairweather. Both were men of the highest calibre, and their loss was deeply felt within the battalion.

equipped forces in a confined area. But there was also the mud of recent rains to contend with, the uncertainty, as always, about the extent of the German withdrawal, and the inevitable caution in the face of uncertainty which recent casualties imposed.[8] On the 9th the Edmontons were in Castelpagano, four miles west of Decorata crossroads, unopposed; and on the 12th, after a carefully prepared attack had proved unnecessary, the Seaforths took San Croce, five miles west again of Castelpagano. That night the Patricias were in Cercemaggiore, six miles up a twisting country road which ran north from San Croce to join Highway No. 17 just east of Vinchiaturo crossroads. Then, taking this road briefly as their axis, the battalion moved forward on the 14th through Cercemaggiore to Highway No. 17, where they stood by to attack Vinchiaturo (ceded to the 2nd Brigade as an objective by the 1st and 3rd Brigades, which had turned northwest from Highway No. 17 against Campobasso) as soon as the Edmontons and the Patricias had secured the intermediate ground in the vicinity of a crossroads two miles east of the town.[9] But once again attack was unnecessary. Early on the 15th, Seaforth scouts reported Vinchiaturo clear, and the brigade commander ordered Major Forin to proceed immediately through four successive areas of concentration (reporting "Gin", "Whisky", "Rum" and "Rye" as each was passed) towards Baranello, which patrols had already approached and found defended.[10] A platoon from "C" Company occupied Vinchiaturo.

Safely on "Rye", the Seaforths were beyond the Vinchiaturo-Campobasso highway and astride a secondary road which led away from the highway at right angles to make its way through low hills and eventually over rising ground to Baranello. Three landmarks divided the distance between the highway and the town: a railway station and a brick factory, almost directly opposite one another, a mile or so off the highway; a

---

[8]On the 9th, 14 mules with Arab muleteers under a British N.C.O. arrived at BHQ to be attached for all purposes. They set to work immediately to carry rations and kitbags to "A" and "B" Company, which could not be reached by transport because of the soft and muddy approaches to Hill 1007.

[9]Called, logically enough, Vinchiaturo crossroads (though not so named on the maps) and formed by the intersection with Highway No. 17 of a secondary road passing from one end to the other of the arc described by Highway No. 87 between San Giuliano to the southeast and the Baranello cut-off to the northeast of Vinchiaturo.

[10]Between Agira and Baranello, and especially in the later stages of the advance, the Scout Platoon provided invaluable service. Conditions were ideal for them, and they had excellent leadership under Lieut. A.W. Gray and Sgt. G.K. McKee.

commanding piece of ground (Hill 702) at a bend in the road a mile beyond the station; and a cemetery, surrounded by high walls as usual, a mile and a half beyond the hill and only a few hundred yards short of the town. "A" Company advanced quickly through the deserted brick factory and railway station to occupy Hill 702 on the night of the 16th, and on the following day Lt.-Col. Forin (whose promotion to command had just come through) issued his orders for the capture of Baranello. "D" Company under Captain D. Newson would make the attack, supported by the regular complement of heavy mortars, machine-guns and artillery. The guns of the field regiment would lay down a concentration on the town for 20 minutes, then lift to the high ground to the south. Two anti-tank guns (17-pounder) were established near "A" Company on Hill 702, with orders to fire on targets of opportunity. The attack was to go in at 5 o'clock the next morning. The night was quiet except for spasmodic shelling by the Germans and an occasional salvo from Allied guns.

The attack went in early on the 17th, and it was a good attack against very light opposition, although nearly five hours were to pass before Lt.-Col. Forin learned definitely of "D" Company's success since wireless communications were poor to non-existent throughout the early stages of the action.[11] Encouraged by the news he eventually received, the C.O. sent scouts into Baranello to gather all the information they could of the situation there and proceeded to bring up the tail of the battalion (Rear BHQ and "F" Echelon) to the railway station where he had maintained his command headquarters for the past 24 hours. Then, late in the afternoon, came a disturbing message form "D" Company: counterattack was imminent from a strong enemy force observed moving up from the Biferno River to the west of Baranello.[12] Battalion communications at this crucial moment failed. "D" Company withdrew and were back on Hill 702 by dusk. That night a "B" Company patrol sent against Baranello suffered five casualties on the outskirts of the town; the new German garrison was vigilant and plainly determined not to repeat the morning's easy surrender of the position.

---

[11]There was at this time a critical shortage of battery replacements for the No. 18 sets. The shortage compounded the difficulty of maintaining wireless communication in country where intervening hills constantly created "dead" spots in reception.

[12]This was No. 7 Company, 9 Panzer Grenadier Regiment, which had been in divisional reserve.

There were therefore two attacks on Baranello, and the second attack had to do the hard way what the first had so readily accomplished. As a precaution in the face of what was now obviously a difficult situation, Lt.-Col. Forin at 7 o'clock the next morning sent "A" Company under Capt. T.C.B Vance to secure the Seaforths' left flank by occupying high ground (Hill 763) more than a mile to the southwest, from which there had been enemy interference the day before. This force had a quick success against light opposition.[13] Behind Hill 702, now held by "D" Company, "B" Company under Captain W.G. Harris had been readied for the attack on Baranello itself, and at 9 o'clock, after a preliminary bombardment of the town by Allied guns, they set off in extended formation for the cemetery. To forestall the communications failure of the previous day, Lieut. F.R. Perrett, the Signals Officers, laid lines for the field telephones behind the advancing company. The cemetery, surprisingly, was not held, and the leading platoon reached it without difficulty. But here, and along the line of some adjacent buildings, the company stopped. The open ground in front of them, between the cemetery and the town, was swept by fire, and repeated attempts to cross it were broken up. For several hours Capt. Harris kept his platoons concentrated under cover while German defensive fire rained down on them and a counterattack on their left flank materialized, was dealt with, and disappeared. He then called for a new concentration of artillery and mortar fire to be brought down on the near edge of the town, and under the protection of this barrage he took his men quickly across the intervening ground and, after stiff fighting on the fringes, on into the town itself. By 4:30 in the afternoon Baranello was clear. "B" Company had taken 18 prisoners and counted 20 German dead in the streets and houses of the town. Seaforth casualties were 4 killed and 11 wounded.[14]

On the 17th of October Lt.-Col. Forin had told his company commanders that the 1st Canadian Division was going into army reserve and that the Seaforths would be consolidating as soon as their present commitments were fulfilled for a prolonged stay in the area. With the fall of Campobasso,

---

[13]Capt. Vance had a squadron of tanks to help him (W.D., Seaf. of C., 18 October, 1943). Tanks do not seem to have been used in the main attacks on Baranello; the approaches were perhaps too exposed. Lieut. D.R. Barrett-Lennard was killed by machine-gun fire during the action against Hill 763.

[14]These figures are for the 17th and 18th combined; separate figures for the second attack are not available.

unopposed, to the Royal Canadian Regiment on the 14th, plans for some time in the making had been promptly put into effect to establish this quite handsome town (a provincial capital, population 17,000) as a Canadian leave centre. Baranello, as it turned out, would be specifically the home of the Seaforths. The Seaforth picture was of course only a small piece of a much larger panorama of operations, and there were still some important tasks to be performed locally following the battalion actions of the 17th and 18th. The responsibilities of the Canadians went beyond the Biferno, and on the 23rd the Edmontons and the Patricias attacked the villages of Colle d'Anchise and Spinete, respectively, immediately across the gorge of the Biferno from Baranello. To the south the Carleton and York Regiment on the same day took Campochiaro on the steep shoulder of the Matese Mountains, while to the north the 1st Brigade, after a hard contest for Oratino and San Stefano on the near side of the Biferno on the 20th, crossed the stream successfully on the 24th in the direction of Molise and Torella on the heights beyond. All these advances were pushed with some urgency since they were the necessary preliminary to the recommitment of the 5th (British) Division to the left flank of the Eighth Army in a drive north and west of Isernia. But for the Seaforths the taking of Baranello was the beginning of the end of a long spell of involvement which had begun 48 days before and over 400 miles away when the battalion convoy had pulled out of "Happy Valley". Now, to the east on the Adriatic coast, General Montgomery had established a new corps, the 5th, to bring the major weight of his army operations to bear on the winter line (so-called) to which the Germans were retreating after their defeat at Termoli and in the country to the west. The new commitments of the Seaforths, five weeks distant and a wealth of happy living between, would be in this coastal sector north of the Sangro River.

Extracts from the Diary of Capt. B.G. Parker, 2 i/c "C" Company, dated 5–8 October, 1943.

5 October   Cold and wet last night. Scrounging meals, which the lads do very handily. Have plenty of eggs, despite 100-odd being smashed in the jeep while we crossed diversion over the river bed near Foiano yesterday. We move up in the afternoon on foot six miles into the hills to our respective companies. Scrap going on to our front; medium machine-guns and 4.2" Mortars giving support to Baldwin's platoon on the hillside.[15] Pte. "Curly" MacLeod killed, and Bob Bonner wounded by dud shell bouncing off edge of slit trench.[16] Reach company at dusk. Syd Thomson away with "D" Company directing artillery fire onto German tanks and infantry most successfully.

6 October Up at dawn after a good night on straw bed shared with Syd. Six others also in tiny peasants' cottage. Go forward to observation post, then guide company across-country to new area. Mortared and shelled on the way, but no casualties. Syd with three companies under command, "C" Company leading, takes in attack on 1007 at 1500 hrs. Come under heavy shelling and mortar fire, all too damn close. Fortunately earth is rain-soaked, greatly reducing casualties. Company attacks into the sun, which makes fire from enemy tanks, guns and machine-guns hard to spot. Word comes back that Ptes. Leith, Williams, Toomer, Olynyk, Robertson, Diggens and Moore killed. All good men. Major Forin, Don Colquhoun[17] and I have narrow escape when shell lands 25 feet away. Companies consolidate on Hill 1007 and push on in darkness.

7 October Very dark night, and we lose contact often. Enemy flares go up. Continually fired upon by M.Gs., armoured cars and tanks. Have more casualties, and a number missing, including Jim McMullen. Look for Jim and others for two hours without success, then return to original feature at 0430 hrs. Fog a blessing, though so heavy at 1000 hrs. that we have to ask BHQ to fire shots to guide us back to new company positions. Had great difficulty evacuating wounded over rough country, but with never a complaint from them. The medical section as usual does a tremendous

---

[15]Lieut. J.W. Baldwin. The "hillside" would be Mount Faggi.

[16]K52166 Pte. Alexander MacLeod, as his army number indicates, was one of the "originals" of the battalion, having enlisted on 27 September, 1939. Padre Durnford, in his diary entry for 6 October, writes: "I hear that 'Curly' MacLeod has been killed and move forward to search him out. I bury him, removing his boots since Italians are now known to be pillaging graves in their desperate need for footwear. 'Curly' was 45 years old, probably older, a solid chap and a restraining and inspiring influence upon the younger lads. We shall miss him." The "Bonner" referred to was Lieut. Robert W. Bonner of "A" Company, recently come to the battalion (13 August) and within a few hours of entering his first action carried out still clutching, unfired, a .45 revolver of prodigious weight given to him by his father for use as his personal weapon.

[17]Lieut. F.D. Colquhoun was at this time commander of the Anti-Tank Platoon of Support Company.

job, especially Cpl. Thomas, who worked tirelessly throughout the night to bring casualties in to the R.A.P. Some of us volunteer to go back to look for Jim McMullen, but we are refused permission by brigade. . . .

Extracts from the Diary of H/Capt. Roy Durnford, Regimental Chaplain to the Seaforth Highlanders of Canada, dated in Italy, 7–9 October, 1943.

7 October I get up at 4 a.m. to a slight rain over a misty landscape and prepare to move forward to "Tac" BHQ, leaving John Orr behind to keep an eye on our effects. Out on the road, which is rapidly becoming a supply route for others besides ourselves, I get a lift with an English medical truck (Eighth Army) and arrive safely in the front lines, where I lose no time digging a slit trench. Everything is MUD. We have had 53 casualties in two days. At least five are dead, we think, of the group who went towards Decorata last night, and Capt. McMullen is missing. I cannot do any burying because the position is still in enemy hands. I slush about during the day, then rain comes on again at night, and after supper I retire to a dirt bed, wet and cold and wrapped in my gas-cape. An hour later the enemy opens up all over and around us. The Adjutant and one other are wounded.[18] I see them off down the line and return to bed. There is more shelling, but no damage is done. I sleep, after a fashion, until 4 a.m.

8 October I make tea at 5 a.m. and rejoice the hearts of a few frozen soldiers. Then off to bury Reimer of "D" Company, who was killed yesterday, and return at 11:30 to find that a welcome rum issue has arrived for distribution to the companies. The allowance is a "tot" (about 2 ozs.) per man, issued on the C.O.'s orders when circumstances require and permit. It is dark stuff, and very strong. I can remember on civvy street thinking of it as "old demon rum", but here it is a blessing to cold, tired and harassed troops. On my rounds later I find a peasant sleeping, as I think, but actually dead, having been hit by a sniper's bullet through the head. After dark I go forward to the observation post to watch directed fire of our artillery and machine-guns. I sleep again in a slit trench.

---

[18] The Adjutant (replacing Capt. J.H. Gowan, who had been posted to 2nd Brigade headquarters on 12th September) was Capt. E.F. Anderson. Capt. F.H. Bonnell replaced Capt. Anderson.

9 October   Get at last to our killed near Decorata. German tanks had caught them at close quarters in the dark, and the bodies are terribly shattered, though God knows the Italian peasant I thought was sleeping was no better off than these. We bury four in the morning and seven in the afternoon. At both services the men are in tears. These are harrowing experiences. ... Kit-bags come up, and we very gladly get out of our tropical clothes (some tropics now!) into battle-dress.

Extracts from an Interview with Lieut. J.O. Moxon, dated at Vancouver, B.C., 22 July, 1960.

McDougall: You were on the night-march to Decorata crossroads, were you not?

Moxon: Yes, I was. And just before that was Hill 1007. This was the first contact we had had with the Germans since I joined the battalion in "Happy Valley", and one of the things I remember vividly was that this was the first time I had had to go through all the routine we had learned at Gordon Head[19] about "O" groups, and so on. It wasn't like Gordon Head. When Jim McMullen came back from the "O" group at BHQ, he called the platoon commanders up on to this ridge to go over the plan with them, and the first thing that developed was that there was a great deal of confusion as to which was Hill 1007.

McDougall: Were there intervening features?

Moxon: Oh yes, there were two or three ridges which it could be — knolls, I suppose you would call them. Well, eventually we decided which one was 1007, and we got our orders. "D" Company was to move up onto the first ridge to our front and from there give covering fire to "C" Company, who would take Hill 1007 from the right. My batman, Wally Reimer, a little dark chap, was killed just 10 feet from me on that ridge. That was my first experience of someone being killed.

McDougall: Shelling?

---

[19]Gordon Head Camp, located at Victoria, B.C., was the basic training centre through which most officer reinforcements to the Seaforth Highlanders of Canada passed during the earlier years of the war.

Moxon: Yes, he was killed by shelling. And being green myself, I didn't know what the blazes was coming off with all those shells coming down. I remember one of the reinforcements who had just come up to the battalion was a great big chap who had somehow managed to bypass most of the replacement depots down the line; and I asked him how he had managed this, and he said well, when I was in England I was the best with the Bren gun and so they selected me to come straight out. But when it came time for us to get up onto the ridge, I remember this chap was in tears. So I went back to him and said, well, come on lad, this is it, what's the matter? Well, he said, I don't think I know how to fire this gun. So the corporal took the Bren from him right there, and we moved on. We made the ridge without much trouble, and by and by when we looked down we could see "C" Company moving up on the right.

McDougall: They would be in extended order.

Moxon: They were spread out, the old routine. They were pretty well in the open, of course, and they were supposed to get some cover from smoke. Ken McBride went in as one of Syd's platoon commanders, you know, and I remember joking with Ken afterwards about the smoke because there was so little of it. Well, I said, how did that go? And Ken said that Syd had turned to him and said, well, K.G., there's your smoke, get going! And here's these two miserable smoke bombs, that's about all, and a wisp of smoke drifting across the front to give cover. Anyways, we had no trouble seeing "C" Company go up the hill, and I remember, even as it was, being worried about shooting up our own fellows, because they eventually got very near the rocks on the top of the feature and charged. I said to Ken after, I said well, it must have taken a lot of guts to go running in there where all those guns were, and hell, he said, that was the only safe place, amongst those rocks.

McDougall: There were a number of big boulders?

Moxon: A lot of big boulders, and a sort of cone on top. And I remember that night, after it was all over, we went down into the country beyond, towards Decorata, and we kept running into these mobile guns or tanks, whatever they were, which would pull back, and then we would run into them again. It was black as pitch. We were in single file, and we tried to establish some sort of system of signals so that we would keep together. But it was pretty hopeless. I know I was lost myself for a while, from everybody, with a few fellows. I think I lost a whole section that night. Yes, I did. I lost Cpl. Smirle, and he showed up the next day. Where he got to I don't remember. He was a first-class man. Eventually I think Syd decided it was just senseless to go on, because we'd go only a little distance, perhaps a hundred yards, and these damned things would open up. There couldn't have been any moon; it was absolutely dark.

McDougall: It started off moonlight, according to reports, but very soon it clouded over, then fog came too.

Moxon: That's right. So it seems to me we ended back on 1007; and I remember this, that I slept right on top of my Tommy-gun that night. It rained, and we had our gas-capes, and we put our gas-capes around us, and I slept right on top of my Tommy-gun. I was so tired I just slept. In the morning the Germans had gone. . . .

Letter from Major J.D. Forin to Mrs. Forin, dated near Vinchiaturo Cross-roads, 14 October, 1943.

My dearest Vivian:

I have been up since 5:30. This, if I get to bed at all, is now my normal reveille. The last ten days have been filled with rain, mud, German rearguards, shell-fire (theirs and ours), moving up, and fighting with little cease and little rest. Our unit seems still to be destined to pick the hottest spots, and we have had a couple of good shows — successful, but with some losses. What wouldn't I give for a bath! Our battle-dress is here, and we are changed into it, which gives us comfort in the wet and cold. Our food is good and we have not missed many meals. It is simply astonishing the number of eggs which come in when we pause, even for a few hours. The Italian farmers bring them, and they do a good business.

There have been many rumours in circulation about our returning to England for training and ultimately some other effort; but one never obtains confirmation until the eve of such a move. It would be wonderful to get back, though what a bed would feel like, the Lord knows.

Yesterday evening the battalion was moved up to this spot for the night in anticipation of today's show. At the last stop my BHQ was situated in a pleasant farm-grove area, with stretches of grass under tree-cover. Frank Bonnell went to one of the farm-houses to arrange for our use of a room so that we could work with lights — impossible otherwise in the open. He simply told the farm people, through one of our interpreters, that four officers would be there "tonight", and when he next came back, there was the room with a huge bed prepared and four straw ticks laid out. Needless to say, it had to be made plain that all we wanted was a table, a chair or two, and a fire in the fireplace.

We are about to leave now. In the distance we can hear the sound of demolitions being set off by the Germans, generally their last act when they are pulling out, and also our gun-fire as the two other battalions of the brigade go up. We go up later. Am feeling fit, though a bit battle-tired. I am still unscathed, by God's grace. Loads of love to you and the babes.

Ever,

Douglas

Extracts from the War Diary of the 26th Panzer Grenadier Division, dated 16–17 October, 1943.[20]

16 October In the Baranello sector sudden artillery attacks on our own batteries indicate that the enemy has completed his artillery preparations. The careful manner of his reconnaissance would seem to indicate that he believes himself to be in the area of a strong defence line. Contrary to previously held beliefs, the Canadian Division seems to be no less systematic than our recent American opponents. ...

17 October 1035 hrs. 67 Panzer Grenadier Regiment reports that after 45 minutes of heavy artillery preparation the enemy is attacking its outposts in the Baranello area.[21] In view of the enemy pressure and the hostile attitude of the civilian population, the outposts were forced to withdraw. ... 1050 hrs. 7 Company, 9 Panzer Grenadier Regiment (in Divisional Reserve at Cantalupo) is placed under command of 67 Panzer Grenadier Regiment for the purpose of rectifying the situation at Baranello. 1700 hrs. The counter attack of 7 Company on Baranello makes good progress. Baranello is taken at 2130 hrs. ...

---

[20]Quoted in Report No. 18, Historical Section (G.S.), Canadian Army Headquarters, p. 32 (mimeographed).

[21]This would be "D" Company's attack.

A Narrative of War

Extract from an Interview with K38637 Pte. G.A. Reid, dated 23 July, 1960, at North Vancouver, B.C.

McDougall: Scouts were sent out on the afternoon of the 17th of October to get all possible information about the situation in and around Baranello. I believe this is where you and Sgt. McKee came into the picture. Did you know that "D" Company was successfully into the town?

Reid: Oh, yes. They went in and we went through them. We took off down the point, Baranello is on a sort of projection, and we went to two or three houses down on the flat. This would be to the right of Baranello as you face it.

McDougall: Just you and Sgt. McKee?

Reid: Yes. We went into Baranello with three, but the other chap was sent back with information. I don't remember who he was.

McDougall: You were to get all possible information?

Reid: Yes; we were to try and find out who was on our front, and bring back a prisoner if we could. So we headed across these flats at the bottom and checked the houses. As a matter of fact we had a plate of spaghetti in one of them, and that was the last meal I had for two days. Well, we crossed a river, quite deep, which ran through the flats, then came back to our side and went up to a little house on quite a high hill. We stopped there; I'd torn my pants, and so a fellow mended them for me. He had no sooner mended them when this little Italian came running up and yelled "Tedesci, Tedesci". And so we asked him where, and he said they were coming from the west, heading east into Baranello.

McDougall: You are in the northeast part of the town now?

Reid: We're out of town, on the northeast edge. So, we thought well, we'd better get back and warn the fellows at least. We asked the Italian how many Jerries there were, and he said, oh, a couple of hundred. So we went up a mule trail not far from where we left town, and when we got into the town we couldn't find "D" Company, couldn't find anybody. Apparently the Jerries had taken the town again, and they watched us come right in. So we walked into this police station, and the people in the station thought it was kind of funny us being there, but they figured maybe the Canadians had come back into the town. Just then, there's a knock on the door, and

102

this fellow said in very good English, better English than mine, would you tell the Canadians to come out, we're withdrawing. Or something like that. So I opened the door, and the minute I opened the door this fellow grabbed me by the binoculars.

McDougall: Let me get this phrase again: tell the Canadians to come out, we're withdrawing. . . .

Reid: I guess he wanted us to think just what I thought, that it was the Canadians outside, and, well, it worked, because I opened the door and he grabbed me. Then Sgt. McKee emptied his pistol through the door, but we were off to one side by then. Anyways, this Jerry, he was a major, started slapping me around right there, and he said, what are you doing up here? I said, I'm just up to get some wine. I didn't want him to know I was a scout. So he said, where's the other man? I said, there's no other man. Yes, he said, there is, we saw him go in. I said, Oh? No, I just sneaked into town myself to get some wine.

McDougall: You were in uniform or course? You hadn't put on civvy clothing?

Reid: Oh no, though we'd done that once in Sicily. Well, just then the Carabiniere and the Sergeant must have made their way upstairs, and they dropped a whole box of these Italian hand-grenades and showered the whole bunch of us. One Jerry had his knee cut, I know, and in this schamozzle I decided to make a break. So I ran down the main street, and the Jerries' machine-gunners saw me and started shooting. But they were shooting at my feet. They must have wanted to get a prisoner too. I made it round the corner, and I laid down in behind a plant. You remember how they had them growing in buckets. I lay down because this street was a dead end and I couldn't get over the wall, so I thought, well, I'll just play possum and they might think they've got me and buzz off. They started marching, and I counted 19 of them walking by the end of the alley, but one of them came up and looked at me and said, Kaputt? And I just laid there, but I guess he heard my heart beating, because he kicked me in the side, and, well, he knew I wasn't dead then, so he said, Ah, nie Kaputt! So I got up, and they made me tie my shoes around my neck and they loaded me down with ammunition.[22]

---

[22]It is not clear why the Germans should have been taking ammunition out of Baranello at this time, when it was their plain intention to hold the town against a second attack. The

McDougall: It was getting dark by now?

Reid: Yes, it was getting dark. Then they took me to a building right on the outskirts of the town, and they started shooting questions at me, like the usual, who are you with, why are you fighting over here and not minding your own business. Then they said, why were you in Baranello? And I said, I just wanted some wine. They said, oh, don't give us that. I said, well, I was after a girl if I could get one, you know. I tried to make it sound as good as I could. I don't know if they believed me or not, but anyway they quit slapping me around. They didn't hit hard, you know, they just slapped me. At that point I heard machine-guns up the other end of town, and I thought, well, at last they're coming to get me. But we shoved off, about seven of us, a bit before dawn, and I packed the ammunition, those big metal boxes of theirs, packed two cases of that, and we'd got darned near to the river when our 25-pounders opened up and gave us the worst shellacking I've ever been in.

McDougall: What was the machine-gun fire you heard?

Reid: I don't know. I think it might have been the Sergeant, because he apparently made a break for it. As a matter of fact I heard he had made several breaks, and they shot him.

McDougall: Yes, that's the story. When "B" Company finally took the town, the Italians told them that McKee had made several attempts to escape, and on the last one they shot him. But you never saw McKee after you were taken?

Reid: When I went out of the police station I yelled up to him the outfit, the number the Jerries had on their shoulders. That's what we were sent out for, and I figured, well, if McKee gets back our job is partly done. But he never did get back.

McDougall: What happened after you got clear of the shelling from the 25-pounders?

Reid: Well, I thought now we've got to cross that river we crossed earlier on patrol, and it had been quite deep, so I'll just grab one of these ammunition boxes, empty it, and swim underwater, like in the movies. But

---

ammunition may have been for weapons or guns not in the possession of the garrison. Pte. Reid was apparently evacuated by a small carrying party which would perhaps return the same night to Baranello.

the river we crossed wasn't any deeper than our knees, so that was that. From there I was taken to the next little town and sent back. ...

From a Telephone Conversation Between the Chiefs of Staff of the German 76th Corps and the Tenth Army, Colonels Henning Werner Runkel and Fritz Wentzell, dated 19 October, 1943.[23]

Wentzell: How is your situation? Increasing pressure?

Runkel: Yes. A small mishap occurred unfortunately at Baranello where the enemy squeezed into the place from the rear.[24]

Wentzell: One cannot deny that 26 Panzer Division has been fighting well these last few days. ...

Letter from Major J.D. Forin to Mrs. Forin, dated at the Brickyards, Baranello, 21 October, 1943.

My dearest Vivian:

It is like an Indian Summer's day, with soft sunshine, bracing mountain air, blue sky, and clumps of fleecy clouds. There is a slight breeze in the trees, and above all, peace. That is, comparative peace, for still in the distance one can hear the guns, and at times shells from German heavy guns land not far off. I am seated at the open window of an Italian house, of which we have the ground floor; it is of stone, with tile floors and long, narrow windows with shutters. It is close by the road, and vehicles pass, for now that the forward battle areas have moved up, shelling of the roads has almost ceased. In the railway yard close by stand a locomotive, a Third-Class railway car, and a tank car, demolished by the Germans before they left.

I have been in command of the battalion for over two weeks, and three days ago I was made a Lt.-Col. So there, now you have a colonel for an

---

[23]Quoted in Report No. 18, Historical Section (G.S.), Canadian Army Headquarters, p. 34 (mimeographed).

[24]Runkel describes, not quite accurately, "B" Company's attack on the 18th. The German line faced generally south; entrance into Baranello from the east might well be considered entrance from the "rear".

old man. .... We have seen our hardest fighting so far and have succeeded very well in three attacks made in the above time. Our work has brought new credit to the Regiment. As for me, I confess it is a great satisfaction to see one's views and plans proved sound, and with relatively few casualties. You may read about the fights and you may see my picture. You may even hear my voice, for yesterday, the fighting over, the Press and the C.B.C. came down on us and took up our time, and I obliged by recording an incident about one of our sergeants who was killed on patrol. I had just come back from the village and had seen his body. I can't tell you what a brave, fine lot of men I have. I am more proud of command and their performance than of anything else in a material way at present within my grasp. ....

Budge Bell-Irving has just today been made a Lt.-Col. and is being flown back to England tomorrow to command an officers' training school. He has done a wonderful job out here. Syd Thomson now becomes my second-in-command. I remain the only original officer. To celebrate Budge's going we are in our kilts, which have been brought up, and we will have a drink or two tonight. Saw John Gowan today; he is out of hospital, on a diet. Jaundice, I think. Now I must go. All the love in the world. Am certain I'll be seeing you soon.

Ever,

Douglas

CENTRAL ITALY

24 November 1943 – 8 June 1944

I

The Taking of San Leonardo

By the middle of November, 1943, the main German defences in Italy were established along a line which ran from the mouth of the Garigliano River on the west coast across central Italy to the mouth of the Sangro River on the Adriatic. Both ends were well dug in behind water courses which in the present season of heavy rains were formidable barriers to tanks and vehicles. Between the ends lay a range of mountains, the Abruzzi region of the Apennines rising to nearly 10,000 feet in the peaks of Il Gran Sasso and Maiella, where a handful of men would serve to contain a division. If the ground had until now been unfavourable to the invaders from the south, it would be even less favourable in the country north of the Garigliano-Sangro line.[1] Blocked by the mountains in the centre, the Allies would be compelled to direct their efforts against two corridors on the flanks, which together offered scarcely 25 miles of front for the deployment of their forces: on the western side, and pointing straight to Rome, the valley of the Liri River, and on the eastern side a narrow coastal plain which was indeed much less a plain than a kind of washboard of escarpments and gullies closely spaced and running at right angles to the Adriatic. The Germans might fear Allied mobility by sea, but not by land. They were reasonably confident that their positions could be held as a winter line. And in this, as events were to prove, they were not entirely mistaken. The extent to which they were out in their calculations was to be determined in part by the operations in which the Seaforths were involved throughout the month of December.

Information about impending action filtered down to the Seaforth companies at Baranello in the third week of November and took its place in a context of signs, by now quite familiar, of an early move. The Allies, it would seem, had decided to maintain pressure on the Germans despite the

[1]Writing later of the phase of Allied operations about to open up, Field marshal Viscount Alanbrooke regretted that General Alexander had not done more to break up and destroy Kesselring's forces in the more favourable country south of the Garigliano-Sangro line. Hindsight of war provides many such regrets. One can only say that the Seaforths in Italy throughout September and October worked hard and fought with skill and courage within the limits of the plan set for them.

onset of winter. With an eye doubtless turned to Rome as the attractive prize offered by a successful passage of the Liri valley, they had chosen the western sector for their main effort. But the left hand would need the help of the right, and General Montgomery had been ordered to mount a good battle in the Adriatic sector in order to contain German troops and if possible threaten Rome itself by securing the eastern end of the Rome-Pescara lateral. The Eighth Army, so the story went, was now being readied to attack the Sangro line.

On the 25th of November the 1st Canadian Division was notified that it was to relieve the 78th (British) Division in a bridgehead which was to be established as soon as weather permitted on the high ground beyond the Sangro. Within a few days the Seaforths were packed up and away, and by the 30th the battalion convoy had taken its place in an almost solid chain of vehicles moving sluggishly north from Termoli.[2] The main assault, delayed several days by torrential rains, had by this time gone in: British and Indian troops were now secure in Mozzagrogna and Fossacesia on the far side of the Sangro Delta, and exploitation towards Lanciano on the inland road and San Vito on the coast road had begun. Earlier, in a special message to all troops under his command, General Montgomery had said that the forthcoming operations in the Adriatic sector were designed to hit the enemy "a colossal crack". The Germans were by no means in full retreat; but they had suffered heavy losses and the first line of their defence was broken. The Canadians were to be committed to maintain the momentum of the attack towards Ortona and beyond.

Huddled in T.C.Vs. and jeeps and carriers which were poor protection against a cold northeast wind and heavy rain, the Seaforths had a miserable time of it for the six hours it took them to cover the last few miles to the front. But when finally the companies were unloaded just before midnight on the 1st of December along the ridge overlooking the Sangro, the skies were clear and the stars shining. The way was down now, following the switchback of the narrow road, over a footbridge which spanned the swollen river, then across the wide flats of the valley to an assembly area below Fossacesia. Men and vehicles were everywhere. To the left of the Seaforths, on the Li Colli feature, the Shermans of the 1st Canadian

---

[2]Such density of movement by day was of course possible only under conditions of complete air supremacy. The Seaforths came to take this kind of protection for granted. With a few minor exceptions they had no experience throughout the entire Mediterranean campaign of what it was like to be vulnerable to attack by air.

Armoured Brigade which were to support the attack across the Moro clattered and rumbled into harbour. Allied guns flashed and roared in the dark pit of the Sangro throughout the night.

The three days which followed were days of mounting tempo as the Seaforths scrambled to come abreast of the forward elements of the 38th (British) Brigade, now under command of the 1st Canadian Division for purposes of relief and closing on the Moro River 12 miles to the north. By noon on the 4th the companies were sited in a large olive grove on a ridge west of San Vito, from which, the day being clear, the men had their first view of Ortona. But that afternoon they moved again, and by midnight, having relieved the Inniskillin Regiment as required, they were strung out along the south escarpment of the Moro River on either side of a cluster of farm houses called Sant' Appollinare. To their left, 2000 yards upstream opposite the village of Villa Rogatti, were the Patricias. To their right, between Sant' Appollinare and the sea, the 1st Brigade stood ready to relieve the remaining elements of the 38th. Shelling and mortaring had again become part of the daily life of the battalion.

When, on the morning of the 5th, Lt.-Col. Forin had his first good look at the Moro River, and San Leonardo beyond, he was well aware of the difficulty of the situation which the Seaforths faced. The divisional commander had chosen the road through San Leonardo as the main axis for the Canadians,[3] and the Seaforths were to lead the advance along this route while the Patricias attacked simultaneously farther inland at Villa Rogatti. Forin knew that he would have to commit the battalion quickly since the division had been ordered by 13th Corps on the 4th of December to "get over the River Moro as soon as possible".[4] Little information was available about the enemy. What was left of the 65th (German) Infantry Division, badly cut up at the Sangro, was reported relieved by the 90th Panzer Grenadier Division on a front extending six miles inland from the sea,

---

[3]The road through San Leonardo was no longer, strictly speaking, the "coast road". A new highway, not shown on available maps, ran north from San Vito along the waterfront to Ortona.

[4]From 1 Canadian Infantry Division Operations Message Log, 4 December 1943, quoted in Report No. 165, Historical Section, C.M.H.Q., p. 20 (mimeographed). Writing later of this stage of operations, Lt.-Col. Forin expressed the uneasiness he felt at the time: "No definite information as to German strengths or dispositions, no time allowed for patrolling, no supporting fire. It looked like a rush job, and always rush jobs have spelt to us unfavourable settings and advantage to the Germans" (W.D., Seaf. of C., December, 1943, Appendix 7).

and all indications were that the Germans, in their determination to deny Pescara to the Allies for the remainder of the winter at least, would make a strong stand south of the Arielli River and the useful Ortona-Orsogna lateral.[5] Between the Moro and the Arielli lay a plateau of unusual depth for this part of the country, where tanks, German or Canadian, could be used to good advantage. The key to a successful passage of the Moro would therefore be the ability of Canadian armour to cross in close support of the infantry. Canadian armour was ready, though support generally was threatened by the fact that all bridges across the Sangro had been washed out the night before. The real problem was the ground to the immediate front, plainly visible to the C.O. on the morning of the 5th: the blown bridge, the flooded stream, the mud and the many small cliffs of the Moro valley.

By ten o'clock Forin had given his orders. The Moro had been reported not more than ten feet wide and two feet deep in front of the Patricias' position upstream, and easily negotiable by infantry. Both engineers and tank crews, moreover, seemed satisfied that tank crossings could be established where the main-axis road met the river below San Leonardo, and again, upstream, below Villa Rogatti. Assigning San Leonardo as the battalion's first objective, Forin ordered "B" Company to cross the river directly in front of its present position just east of Sant' Appolinare, climb to the small plateau beyond and seal off the hamlet of La Torre on the left flank. "C" Company was to cross the river farther downstream and approach San Leonardo by way of the main-axis road leading up out of the valley. Zero hour at the river line for both companies was to be twelve o'clock that night. Half an hour later, "A" Company, crossing still farther downstream, was to follow the route of what appeared to be a covered draw in a right-flanking attack on the town. "D" Company would reinforce either "A" or "C" Company, depending on which had the greater success. All crossings were to be without preliminary bombardment, though divisional artillery would be on call throughout. Engineers would complete a diversion for tanks below San Leonardo as soon as a bridgehead was secure.

The attack went in as planned that night, a silent beginning to what was to be perhaps the noisiest and most lethal three weeks of action in the history of the Seaforths. The silence was soon broken on the right. "C" Company, having crossed the bed of the Moro without incident, had

---

[5] 90th Panzer Grenadier Division was fresh, having come from the Venice area, and before that from Sardinia, where it had been formed early in the summer of 1943.

advanced less than 200 yards towards the hairpin bend in the road leading up to San Leonardo when it came under machine-gun fire from the high ground to the west.[6] It was not badly hurt, but its sections were scattered and pinned down. "A" Company fared no better. Crossing downstream to the right, it was no sooner over the river than it ran into the same type of fire that had stopped "C" Company. The company commander was blinded temporarily by an explosive bullet, the C.S.M. killed, and several were wounded.[7] As word of these setbacks reached Lt.-Col. Forin at his command post in the early hours of the morning, a group of men from "A" Company, little more than a platoon in strength, had withdrawn under the direction of Lieut. J.W. Baldwin to the south bank of the river and were about to attempt another crossing on "C" Company's route. "B" Company, on the left, was an unknown quantity. It had been swallowed up into the night as effectively as if it had been dropped into a bottomless pit. The story of its battle, except for confused sounds and two brief messages which got through to BHQ much later, was to remain untold and unreadable for nearly 24 hours.

As far as Forin could judge, the first phase of the Moro engagement was over. At dawn on the morning of the 6th he reported to Brigade that the Seaforths had gained a bridgehead across the Moro against strong enemy resistance. But San Leonardo had not been taken, and the bridgehead was so weakly held and so shallow that it could not be considered sufficient protection for the main-axis crossing on which the engineers must work before the tanks could add their weight to the battle.[8] Was any exploitation possible? Some tanks had already been lost in the mud of the river bed or shot up attempting to cross without benefit of a proper diversion; and, as the morning wore on and the valley came under massive defensive fire from the enemy, other tanks were to try repeatedly but without success to get over to the infantry on the far side. In the end, the best they could offer

---

[6]Here, as elsewhere in this section, true compass directions are likely to be confusing. Below San Leonardo the course of the Moro River is north and south rather than east and west. I have formalized orientation in earlier parts of the narrative and do so again now. I have assumed that the Seaforths were heading north, with the Apennines on their left or west flank and the Adriatic on their right or east flank.

[7]"A" Company commander at this time was Capt. T.C.B. Vance; the C.S.M. was M.A. Blaker.

[8]Supporting tanks were those of the 4th (British) Armoured Brigade until the evening of 7 December, when they were relieved by tanks of the 1st Canadian Armoured Brigade. See Nicholson, *The Canadians*, p. 298.

was hull-down support from the Sant' Appolinare feature. It was a grim yet familiar impasse: the infantry unable to escape from its containment without the help of armour, the armour unable to help the infantry without penetration deep enough to cover the necessary crossings. "The prospect," Forin wrote later, "left me uneasy and uncheerful."[9]

Still uncertain of the fate of "B" Company, and still without much hope of getting armour across the river in support of his companies, Forin nevertheless decided to commit his reserves now (consisting of "D" Company and some remnants of "A") at a point slightly to the left of the main axis in an attempt to regain the momentum of the attack. But at two o'clock in the afternoon, just as the leading platoons were ready to set off, word came from the commander of the tanks that the fire-support promised for the new plan had had to be cancelled in favour of prime targets which now had appeared in the form of enemy armour manoeuvring near San Leonardo. The Seaforths stood down, on thirty minutes' notice to move. Shortly after, as a result of a meeting between Brig. Hoffmeister and the divisional and corps commanders at the tank command post on the ridge, Forin was notified of a change in the brigade plan. The main axis was to be shifted upstream. The Edmontons would be passed through the Patricias, who had taken Villa Rogatti that morning and held it throughout the day with the help of five tanks which had successfully crossed the river in their sector.

Plans to reorganize the Seaforths again south of the Moro were soon in motion. First the part of "A" Company that had come under the command of "C" Company, then "C" Company itself, were withdrawn. "B" Company remained a problem. At a quarter past seven that morning its commander, Capt. W.H. Buchanan,[10] had sent back word by runner (the No. 18 set was out) that he was consolidating somewhere on the plateau in front of La Torre, where he was "meeting opposition from enemy M.G. fire". At ten o'clock he had reported that he was still meeting opposition but was "in the process of cleaning up same".[11] All after this, however, was silence until late in the afternoon when Capt. Buchanan, in a third brief message,

---

[9]W.D., Seaf. of C., December, 1943, Appendix 7.

[10]Capt. Buchanan, together with Lieut. J.C. Allan, had joined the battalion on the 14th of November, at Baranello. Originally officers of the Calgary Highlanders, these were the first of a number of postings under the "Canadian Loan" scheme which brought Canadian officers from the U.K. to units in the Mediterranean theatre, theoretically for a tour of duty, but often in practice to stay. They became Seaforths and almost without exception made outstanding contributions to the record of the battalion.

[11]W.D., Seaf. of C., December, 1943.

asked for permission to withdraw his company. Within a few hours the regrouping of the Seaforths south of the river was complete.

The postscript to the record of this disappointing day is the story of "B" Company, which, ironically, was the one bright piece in the picture missing from the situation report at BHQ. Unlike the companies on the right, "B" Company had been able to exploit the element of surprise made possible by the absence of artillery preparation the night before. It had also been fortunate, as it turned out later, in hitting the enemy at a soft spot in his defences, which was the boundary between the 361 and 200 Grenadier Regiments. At a time, therefore, when the bulk of the battalion lay badly scattered and immobilized below San Leonardo, the left-flank company had been busily engaged in what already promised to be a successful fight. By first light it had got well up onto the long spur of ground leading to La Torre and had taken 12 German prisoners. By noon it had advanced 500 yards along the edge of the gully that ran at an angle across its front between La Torre and San Leonardo. By nightfall it had over-run 16 enemy posts, and had taken 60 prisoners at a cost to itself of only two killed and six missing. "B" Company, of course, like all the intruders north of the Moro that day, had needed the support of tanks, and in the end, threatened by a counter-attack by a strong force of Germans reinforced by armour, it had had to withdraw. But it had withdrawn in good order and virtually intact.[12] Its success was reason for satisfaction, but frustrating beyond measure for Lt.-Col. Forin, who had been unable to make use of what it had achieved.

For the next 48 hours the Seaforths passed into brigade reserve. From the time of the arrival of the 1st Division at the Moro, messages and orders coming down from above had given the impression that passage of the river would be short and sharp, followed by a number of rearguard skirmishes such as the battalion had been engaged in between Foiano and Baranello in October. The reality had proved different. The 90th Panzer Grenadier Division, after 24 hours of bitter fighting which had cost them 76 prisoners and the equivalent of two companies killed,[13] had not only

---

[12]Symbol of "B" Company's success was the award of the M.M. to Pte. (A/Cpl.) John Herbert Teece for a day of courageous fighting highlighted by the evacuation under great difficulties of Capt. Carter, the artillery representative with the Company. (N.B. I have not been able to find Teece's name in the Master Nominal Roll of the battalion. This omission should be checked.)

[13]Report No. 165, Historical Section, C.M.H.Q., p. 33 (mimeographed).

kept the Seaforths out of San Leonardo but had denied the Canadians all the ground north of the Moro with the exception of Villa Rogatti on the left and a small piece of river bed and bank won by the Hastings and Prince Edward Regiment in a diversionary attack up the coast road to the right of the Seaforths on the night of the 6th. An intelligence summary put out by the 1st Canadian Division on the 7th of December faced the sobering facts:

> We have assumed that the enemy will fight his forces with determination until it is clear that we have succeeded in seizing a bridgehead which allows the full deployment of all our arms, and have supply routes which wipe out the river as a tactical feature. When he judges that point has been reached he will begin withdrawal to a new line. It appears that the enemy does not think that point has as yet been reached.[14]

The same summary noted that the Germans were thought to be able to bring to bear on the Canadian sector a full divisional artillery regiment of 48 guns, and had at their disposal in addition up to 10 infantry and two or three heavy guns of 17 centimetre calibre.[15] The Seaforths in their reserve positions south of the Moro were shelled heavily on the night of the 7th.

A new plan designed to break the deadlock, however, was in the making. General Vokes' intention of switching the main axis to exploit the success of the Patricias at Villa Rogatti had had to be abandoned almost as soon as it was formulated. On the afternoon of the 6th the engineer officer given the task of reconnoitring the site for the vehicle diversion below Villa Rogatti which would be indispensable to large-scale operations had returned to report "no diversion possible". The first phase of the new plan, which originated with Corps Headquarters and which was to be completed by the evening of the 7th, called for the 8th (Indian) Division to take over the Rogatti area.[16] Vokes was then to regroup his forces on the shortened front and commit two brigades (rather than one as before) to the job of restoring the main axis at San Leonardo. At the divisional level, in the next phase, Vokes' orders called for an initial two-pronged assault on San Leonardo by units of the 1st Brigade. From the coast-road bridgehead, still held by the Hastings and Prince Edward Regiment, the Royal Canadian Regiment were to attack westward along the line of a track

---

[14]*Ibid.*, p. 37.

[15]*Ibid.*, p. 36.

[16]This meant, in effect, simply an extension towards the sea of the front of the 8th (Indian) Division, which had been advancing on the left of the Canadians.

which followed the edge of the escarpment into San Leonardo, while at the same time the 48th Highlanders were to make their way directly across the river from Sant' Appolinare, and, as "B" Company of the Seaforths had done on the first crossing of the Moro, secure the spur between San Leonardo and La Torre. The 2nd Brigade was then to exploit towards the original divisional objective, which was the junction of the San Leonardo road with the Ortona-Orsogna lateral. This junction was hereafter to bear the code-name "Cider".[17] The fire plan for the operation was to include bombardment from four field and two medium regiments of artillery and strikes by 13 squadrons of Kittyhawk bombers.

The morning of the 8th was clear and sunny, and sorties of Allied planes engaging targets towards Ortona and beyond soon reduced the shelling which had pounded the battalion the night before. Orders received by Lt.-Col. Forin at eight-thirty made plain the battalion's role in the brigade plan. The Seaforths would attack again across the Moro and would capture an intermediate objective some 600 to 700 yards beyond San Leonardo; this done, they would provide one company, under command of a squadron of tanks, to make a thrust in the direction of a stretch of rising ground to the left which led to the Ortona-Orsogna lateral.[18] The Edmontons would attack through the main battalion positions and capture "Cider" crossroads, and the Patricias and the Seaforths, wheeling right, would then exploit towards Ortona. Back at BHQ, Forin informed "D" Company, now under the command of Capt. A.W. Mercer, that it was to cross the river the next morning on the backs of tanks at the site of the proposed diversion below San Leonardo. The company was to pass from his command that night and marry up with the Calgary "A" Squadron in harbour.[19] The remaining companies would follow "D" Company as the situation permitted.

The situation on the morning of the 9th was from the outset unfavourable to the Seaforths' attack, which had been based on the premise that San Leonardo would become untenable by the Germans under pressure from the two regiments of the 1st Brigade converging on it from the flanks. The R.C.R., severely mauled, had come to a halt 1000 yards east of the town, and the 48th Highlanders, though secure on the La Torre spur

---

[17] As things turned out, ten days were to elapse before "Cider" crossroads was finally taken.

[18] The route on the left was to be called later "Lager Track".

[19] Tanks of the 1st Canadian Armoured Brigade replaced those of the 4th (British) Armoured Brigade in support of the Seaforths on the 7th of December.

to the west, were in no position to force the deep gully which lay between them and the division's first objective. Higher command, however, was not disposed to wait. Throughout the night sappers of the 3rd Field Company R.C.E. had worked under constant shelling on the diversion below San Leonardo, and by six o'clock in the morning the crossing was ready for tanks. Within an hour, the base across the Moro having been judged sufficiently secure,[20] "D" Company of the Seaforths was mounted on its tanks and on its way down the steep and exposed descent to the river.

How little this was to be a mission of exploitation for the Seaforths was soon apparent. Two tanks were casualties almost immediately when they failed to negotiate the switchback road leading down into the valley and toppled over a thirty-foot cliff. The appearance of Canadian armour, moreover, was the signal for intense concentrations of shelling and mortaring, and the river bed soon began to fill with casualties.[21] The engineer work party, and its bulldozers, not yet free of the area after the difficult assignment of the night before, suffered badly. The Seaforths, on the other hand, having by this time learned useful lessons about cooperation with armour, were quickly off their tanks and across the river on foot 100 yards upstream. Ten minutes later, in the lee of a steep embankment which marked the two traverses of the road up to San Leonardo, "D" Company joined forces with six tanks of the Calgarys, under Major E.A.C. Amy, which had managed to negotiate the diversion. The situation looked bleak. "D" Company was already much depleted in strength, and the way forward was blocked by the lead tank, which had no sooner arrived on the scene than it had been blown up on a mine at the hairpin bend in the road. The entire force was under heavy fire from their front and from their right flank.

But there was to be no second denial at San Leonardo. Capt. Mercer dispatched one platoon of "D" Company, commanded by Lieut. D.M. Owen, to contain the fire on the right flank. The remainder of the company, with a platoon commanded by Lieut. J.F. McLean in the lead, then charged up the bluffs in front of them, and the tanks turned off the road and followed. It was a stiff test for the Shermans and their drivers, but with skill and

---

[20]Lt.-Col. Forin was under the impression at this time that the bridgehead had been reported secure, and that the R.C.R. were therefore in San Leonardo. See his personal narrative, W.D., Seaf. of C., December, 1943, Appendix 7.

[21]"Moaning Minnie", the Germans' six-barrelled *Nebelwerfer*, was making its first showing on this front. It made a great deal of noise on firing and at the point of impact, but it was not a particularly lethal weapon.

determination they gained the heights, and from there on infantry and armour drove relentlessly over the relatively flat stretches of vineyard and olive grove which led up to San Leonardo. Fire support from the tanks was close and devastating, and Seaforths came on Grenadiers in slit trenches firing straight up into the air in their efforts to keep their heads down. By nine-thirty McLean's platoon had over-run one anti-tank gun and ten machine-gun posts, killing eight Germans and capturing eighteen, and had begun, with whatever help it could muster, to clear the town itself against continuing stiff resistance.[22]

"D" Company's strength was now reduced to 39 all ranks, and only three Shermans remained of the six which had crossed the river that morning. It was a small force to cope with a counter-attack, but it proved itself quite up to the task when the Germans at this point threw into the battle for San Leonardo, along the eastern approaches to the town, 12 Mark IV tanks and supporting infantry. Major Amy's troop promptly engaged the enemy armour, and when the German lead tank was blown up the others did not press the attack. German infantry was for the most part cut up or dispersed, though some managed to infiltrate into buildings on the edge of the town. The situation was in fact to remain unstable for several hours. Eventually, however, the arrival of Lieut. Owen's platoon from its protective role on the right flank, then of a much reduced "B" Company of the R.C.R., and finally of the remaining Seaforth companies with another troop of tanks in support made possible a thorough clearing of the objective. San Leonardo was reported firmly held by 5:45 p.m.

Consolidation in this kind of close and stubborn battle is likely to be about as costly as initial assault. From the time of "D" Company's

---

[22]For their share in this conspicuous achievement, Lieut. McLean was awarded the D.S.O. (a decoration seldom given to subalterns) and K53341 Cpl. (A/Sgt.) G.F. Horan the M.M. In heavy fighting such as took place at San Leonardo it is of course difficult to attribute action categorically to one platoon or section rather than another. The components of a company become thoroughly shaken up, and while some elements disappear altogether, others coalesce in unexpected ways around centres of leadership. Lieut. McLean was undoubtedly one such catalyst and agent on this occasion, and it seems certain that the group around him represented at one time or another most elements of the company, including company headquarters and even, it is reported, a Calgary troop commander, Capt. Charbonneau, who, having lost his tanks to enemy fire, was still eager for a fight and joined the Seaforths to finish the battle on foot. If the company commander's role seems less than glorious at times like these, it must be remembered that his first responsibility is to control the parts of his force and preserve what he can of their flexibility in the battle. Capt. Mercer filled this role admirably at San Leonardo.

crossing that morning the ground between the diversion and San Leonardo had been a clamorous, blistering interdiction of shell and mortar fire, and to this inferno the reserve companies of the Seaforths and BHQ were confined throughout most of the day. There were important jobs to be done, doubly difficult under heavy fire. "B" and "C" Company had to be joined up with tanks and sent forward to support "D" Company in clearing operations and in extending the battalion positions beyond San Leonardo. Rations and greatcoats had to be taken across the river later in the day, ammunition hauls made by mule train, and the R.A.P. set up in the town. And, as always, the C.O.'s command post had to be pushed forward as close as possible to the perimeter of battle. It was on one of those moves, on the morning of the 10th, after a confusing and exhausting night shuffling a force under his command which now included parts of the Edmontons and the R.C.Rs., that Lt.-Col. Forin was wounded by shrapnel. The same shell killed Forin's batman-driver and a BHQ signaller, and wounded the I.O., Lieut. D.S. McLauchlin. A few hours later, on the south side of San Leonardo, a shell bursting outside the door of a house which was the temporary location of Rear BHQ riddled the room with shrapnel and wounded Capt. B.G. Parker, 2 i/c of "C" Company, and the Adjutant, Capt. F.H. Bonnell. Major Thomson took over command of the Seaforths late in the afternoon of the 10th, with Major J.H. Gowan as his second-in-command. The second and this time successful battle of the Moro River had cost the battalion over 50 casualties, killed, wounded and missing.

Extracts from an Interview with Lieut. W.F.J. Gildersleeve, dated July 20, 1960, at Vancouver, B.C.

McDougall: You joined the battalion after the fighting was over at Baranello?

Gildersleeve: Yes, I took over the Signals Platoon from Frank Perrett. The Signals Officer up to that time had been a regimental officer; I was Royal Canadian Corps of Signals. . . .

McDougall: Until you became a Seaforth.

Gildersleeve: Yes, until I became a Seaforth.   But that was much later.[23]   There were three other R.C.C.S. personnel in the platoon: the rear-link wireless operator, a spare operator, and a driver.[24] The rest were Seaforths, usually trained with the unit, but sometimes sent away for a course. W.J. Hicks was my sergeant, and Cpl. Duxbury and Cpl. Meade were there then too. You were saying that the action was over when I came to Baranello. Yes, it was, though the heavy artillery was still firing from the brickyards when I settled in there in a room over the Signals Office. I shared the room with Freddie Middleton and Dusty Rhodes, and I remember that Freddie and I were suffering from the runs.[25]

McDougall: What was the relation of the brickyards to the railway station?

Gildersleeve: The brickyard building was the first building you came to going west along the road into Baranello. Then you went on another 100 yards or so, and there was the railway station. The Pioneer Platoon had put the bridge over the railway tracks back into shape when I got there. The Padre slept for a time in one of the kilns at the brickyards. It was at the brickyards that I first met Tony Fiorillo, who was in hiding there with his sister. He was a professor from Milan University, and later, when the unit moved into the town of Baranello proper, he was asked to come over and give us some lessons in Italian. Fiorillo became a good friend, and I've been in touch with him several times by letter since the war. . . .

Letter from Antony M. Fiorillo to Mr. W.F.J. Gildersleeve, dated November, 1948, in Italy.[26]

. . . If I close my eyes to retire for a little while within myself, I suddenly find myself in a small simple village, Baranello, whose name is well known to the Seaforths. It was an isolated village, in spite of the great traffic of

---

[23]Lieut. Gildersleeve, after outstanding service with the battalion as Signals Officer, received permission to transfer from R.C.C.S. to Seaforth of C. in September, 1944. He became a platoon commander with "D" Company.

[24]The rear-link was by No. 22-set to brigade.

[25]Capt. F.S. Middleton still commanded "B" Company; Lieut. D.C. Rhodes commanded the Pioneer Platoon. The "runs" was of course dysentery.

[26]What follows is not a translation; the letter was written in English.

121

troops that came to it, and the consequent activity unusual in a place where nature and man are accustomed to slumber in the warm sun of summer, as well as in winter. . . .

Just before the Seaforths arrived, and for a time afterwards, it was a problem to reach Baranello, and only when the war was getting far from those snowy mountains did we finally have an opportunity to re-enter the town and thus meet the new inhabitants who in time became friends to us all.

There were Major Thomson, Colonel Forin, Dr. Sutherland,[27] Chaplain Durnford, yourself, Sgt. Smith of the Pipe Band,[28] and many others I could name because they are still alive in my memory. Yes, a gesture, an expression, an episode, a personal characteristic is sufficient to bring all of them back to my mind, as well as the Italians who enjoyed their company. It is no strain on the imagination to picture them again: here I see Major Thomson, so kind and a true gentleman, always sparing of gesture, attractive even in his being left-handed; here comes Lieut. Gildersleeve, with his honest, spontaneous and smiling expression; and here also is Capt. Sutherland, who cured his patients in the Church of Saint Mary, and who concluded his conversations with an habitual "Who knows?" And what is one to say about the chaplain, who chose an oven as his home? It was a kind of rural oven, having all the appearance of a dwarf house where one would like to withdraw with one's thoughts and experiences.

Recently I have been in Baranello. I arrived there by means of a comfortable and rapid train. It was natural to make a comparison with the 1943 travel, although now I had reversed my direction, coming this time from the direction of Rome. In 1943 I had hitch-hiked all the way, by trucks, jeeps and lorries driven by soldiers from different countries, through torn up roads and over temporary bridges which substituted for those destroyed by the retreating Germans.

Five years have passed since that unforgettable 1943, and many things have changed, though Baranello is always the same small village which welcomes the traveller with its stretching valleys and the blue expanse of its sky. At the entrance still stands the old gloomy barone's building where the Seaforths once had their headquarters; and just up the hill the charming bells of the church call the people from the farms to go and

[27]Capt. W.H. Sutherland joined the Seaforths on 26 August, 1943. He was posted to the 5th Canadian Field Ambulance at the end of the stay in Baranello.

[28]K52111 L/Sgt. J. McL. Smith, bass drummer with the Pipe Band.

adore God. It is the same Church which five years ago was sounding with soldiers' footsteps, and which received like a mother the wounded and the sick. Leaving the village behind, just near the station you can see the same oven where Padre Durnford retired with his load of memories and experiences. The bridge over the railway has been re-built, and little by little the real signs of a past war are fading away, just as any indications of military barracks or field hospitals have disappeared. But these memories are always green in our hearts, and we can wander within valleys still echoing the passage of the Canadian armies.

People are back again at their work, no longer curious about the novelty, absorbed in their misery or in their quest for riches; but passing amongst them, even in after years, one can still hear them talk of a certain October evening when the first Canadian patrols arrived to bring us back the peace we seemed to have lost forever. . . .

Extracts from a Letter Written by K534897 Pte. George Ableson to Mrs. Agatha Summers of Vancouver, B.C., dated "North of the Sangro", 3 December, 1943.[29]

. . . The cigarettes are most welcome, and thank you very, very much. They travel well, and the white package with the familiar "Sweet Caporal" on them look beautifully crisp and new when we break them out of the cartons. Didn't they have "Sweet Caporals" in the first war? I remember Uncle Frank talking about "woodbines", which I believe was the name of a cigarette, and I seem to remember the name "caporal" too. Perhaps it was just a common name for issue tobacco.

I think sometimes about these connections with the 1914–18 war because the links turn up frequently in the Seaforths, who pay a good deal of attention to traditions even in the midst of this theatre of a new war. Uncle Frank will be interested to know that on the 25th of October, when we were in rest at Baranello far south of here, the battalion commemorated the battle of Passchendaele in a round of ceremonies that began in the afternoon and went on for some at least until the small hours of the morning. The commander of the 51st Highland Division was there, and a Lt.-Col. Ainslie of the 6th Battalion Imperial Seaforths, as were also, of

---

[29]Fiction: see note p. 11.

course, Brig. Hoffmeister and a number of other officers who have been posted to staff elsewhere but who lose no chance of coming home to the battalion for a visit. And there was an officers' dinner, which they say was a great success despite the fact that the cook was pronounced drunk half an hour before the dinner began. But what, one asks, is Passchendaele to us? I stood beside Leo Greig, our Sanitary Corporal, when the Pipe Band played in the streets of Baranello on the 25th, and Leo remembers Passchendaele, having joined the Seaforths in 1939 (God knows how) at the ripe age of 52. "Postie" Sinclair may remember it too, because I have seen first-war ribbons on his tunic. But for most of us it is nothing but a name for what history books have told us was a spectacularly senseless waste of human life. Yet it is something else too. It is not a recollection of people, obviously, or of a place, but rather a kind of celebration of a thing done honourably within the family. The Seaforths did well at Passchendaele, and the crazy determination to carry out an assignment that brought them distinction then somehow reinforces the present, just as what we do well now may somehow reinforce the future. Sgt. Elaschuk and I figured this out one day (though not in so many words) while cleaning a Bren gun. We were feeling philosophical. The links are not chains, however, and that's a blessing. There seems to be enough new blood running in this battalion to keep it fresh.

Perhaps the present needed reinforcing at Baranello, because Baranello was a slack time for the Seaforths in a beautiful but slightly ominous way. The leaves were turning when we were there, and the whole countryside was a picture of autumnal loveliness with its changing colours, its green valleys, its pleasant well-tilled slopes, and the snow-capped mountains in the background, not far away. We lived well, and there was leave for most of us to Bari and Naples, and shorter visits to Campobasso nearby, where everything one could reasonably expect was laid on for the comfort of the troops. Of course we trained and marched hither and yon in the usual rest-area fashion, and so kept fit in body. But it's a sad thing, Aunt Agatha, that when the pressure's off the spirit sags. Some remember their loneliness, and a great many unhappily remember more of the self than they do when the going is tough. There was a great deal of grumpiness and backbiting at Baranello, often without much cause. To be fair, jaundice may have had something to do with it. It has grown to be a regular epidemic over the past two months, and it is undoubtedly the most depressing disease imaginable. The C.O. has been trying to fight it for weeks. I saw him today as he left for a recce of our new positions to the north of here, and he looked thoroughly miserable. . . .

Extracts from an Account of the Crossings of the Moro River, by Cpl. John Doe, formerly of the Scout Platoon, the Seaforth Highlanders of Canada, dated at Vancouver, 8 July, 1960.*

It is the 4th of December, and we are just forward of San Vito, on the coast road to Ortona. To our right the Adriatic sparkles in the sun. To the north the buildings of Ortona gleam whitely. Immediately ahead of us is a stream bed which forms a gully. Farther up the gully, but covering the road, is a sniper. Any traffic across the gully receives his immediate attention.

We are in no hurry anyway. We have until evening to make contact with the Irish Brigade of the 78th Division up ahead. From the sounds of mortar and machine-gun fire, they appear to be busy, and we feel it would be impolite to interrupt them at their work. On the left of the road a lane runs through a lawn up to a large house. Mr. Gray and most of the two sections of scouts occupy this house. Denis Coen, Chuck Townsley and I have moved into a little shack on the right of the road to warn passersby about the sniper. Our orders are to observe, not to get involved in fighting. This suits us. We have been warned about mines, and soon a demonstration takes place. A turbaned Indian and two mules appear, walking on the grass beside the road. An Italian box mine disintegrates the mules. They vanish, leaving only a smear. The Indian must be of tougher stuff, or else the mules block the blast. His uniform is ripped to shreds and he is wounded in several places. He shrugs away our door, which we offer as a stretcher, and walks out. He still has the halter rope in his hand, and the turban on his head. . . .

It is now the evening of the 4th, and we have taken up positions on the ridge above the Moro, near Sant' Appollinare. Shelling is heavy, but we are snug in our caves by the cemetery. In front and below us is a valley, with the shallow river on the far side. The bushes in the valley have lost their leaves and provide little cover. A road spirals down our side, crossing to the blown bridge, and twists its way up the far bank. Winter and the

---

*The footnotes are those of the author of the account, who appears here anonymously as "John Doe". "John Doe" is, however, a real person, unlike the fictional "George Ableson" introduced earlier in this text (see p. 9).

smell of fire and explosives mix with the odour from the cemetery. A truck blows up nearby from a direct hit. This is serious business. The "egg campaign" is over.

It is noon, the 5th of December, and we have been given our orders. The Seaforths will cross the Moro tonight, without armour or artillery support, in a surprise attack on San Leonardo. "B" Company will be on the left, "C" Company in the centre, "A" on the right. Our concern is with "A" Company, so Mr. Gray, Davis and I visit the rear-guard of the British troops still in the area. They point out a path that disappears down the bank out of sight into the brush. No time for a recce. Besides, every movement on the bank draws mortar and artillery fire. We return to BHQ for a supper of bully and tea.

I am to take "A" Company across the river. Once across, I'm told, my job will be done. It is dark, with clouds overhead and no moon. We leave "A" Company area and wind our way along the bank. To the left, on the other side of the valley, bright flashes show where a battle is in progress. The Engineers are probably trying to begin work on the diversion. Shells burst ahead of us on the ridge, and we detour into dead ground. A message is passed up from Major Vance for more speed. I locate the path leading down into the valley and am joined by Major Vance, Lieut. Baldwin of the leading platoon, and Angus Blaker, C.S.M. I accept, under protest, a bodyguard of one section, and start downward. The noise of the men with me seems more dangerous than their protection is worth. I drop them off as guides at each turn in the trail.

The brush is head high. Every few minutes a flare blossoms in the sky to sparkle brilliantly for a minute or so. I freeze, and look at the bleached landscape. The trail is good and no German patrols seem to be using it. I reach the river, hardly more than a stream, and cross. There is a steep bank. Lieut. Baldwin and his platoon join me on the higher ground 100 yards ahead. I tell him that my job is officially over. However, since BHQ is to cross later tonight if all goes well, there seems no sense in going back and then over again. Besides, Jerry knows something is up. He is shelling our back trail. The flashes decide me, and I stay with "A" Company. We move off. Clinking equipment, boots squelching in the mud and the muttered curses of the men sound more clearly to me than the distant noise of battle. My rope-soled shoes and lack of all metallic gear, except helmet and pistol, allow me to move silently. Word comes up that the rear platoon is missing.

126

I am crossing a gully, ten feet in front of the lead platoon, when a stream of fireflies arches lazily through the blackness.[†] Then the night is shattered by the rip of Spandaus. There are shouted commands behind me, and then the pop-pop-pop of the Brens.[‡] I am officially a guest at this battle and lie low. Other Spandaus join in laying down a cross fire. "A" Company is pinned down. There is much shouting, but after a time this stops, and I conclude the company has withdrawn. I crawl over to a shock of grain and worm inside. I can now stand without exposing an outline, but there is nothing to be seen. The German fire slackens, except for occasional bursts. I decide to go home. I work my way back across the river and climb the south bank just as it is getting light. . . .

December the 8th. Another attack is in the wind. We have been living in a house half a mile south of the Moro, in an orchard, after returning from a 24-hour rest, a mile or so back from the front. We have washed and shaved, and, except for some shelling, had some peace. Colonel Forin had a close one here when a dud shell landed a few feet from him. Yesterday my friend Coen was hit. The wound was painful but not serious. He left, happily full of morphine, amid the congratulations of the rest of us. I remark to Mr. Gray on his luck. Christmas in bed. He tells me to make sure not to get lucky myself.[§] Some genius has found a number of bottles of wine. We sit on the floor with our backs against the wall, discussing everything except the coming battle. I rarely drink before or during a show,

---

[†]Tracers always seemed to move as slowly as the arching spray from a garden hose, and resembled fireflies in the dark. Their other main characteristic was that they always seemed to be coming directly at you.

[‡]According to my observations, we always seemed to fight a much noisier night battle than the Germans. On this occasion, as on others, there seemed to be much shouting back and forth, from our side, In the short periods of silence it was possible to hear the quiet, disciplined voices of the German machine-gunners through the darkness. One got the unfair impression that they were the better soldiers. However, had the situation been reversed, and the Germans the victims of a night ambush, caught without cover, I'm sure they would have made just as much noise as we did. . . .

[§]Denis Coen was a remarkable youngster. He joined us in 1940 in England. He was the absolute minimum age, and looked it. Because he was good tempered, eager to learn, and young, he took a constant ribbing from the old-timers, some good natured, some not. He and I became fast friends from the start. I watched him grow from a naive if intelligent boy to a hard, intelligent soldier, and about as unboyish as General McNaughton. He came back after this wound, and after doing good work as a Scout was N.C.O. in charge of one of the "Wasp" flame throwers that did such an excellent job at the crossing of the Yssel River in Holland towards the end of the war.

but somehow tonight it seems called for. Outside, shells are bursting in the orchard, and the Mortar Platoon house right behind it is hit, though there are no casualties. There is a kind of whispering silence, then a faint whine grows into the banshee scream of a salvo coming our way. Drinks pause on the way to our mouths. Then, after the crumps, conversation resumes and another round of drinks. The diversion below San Leonardo is about ready, and we are to take the town in the morning. "D" Company is to cross on tanks. . . .

Word comes to move. "D" Company is across, and the Scouts follow a draw to the left of "D" Company's route. Shell, mortar and machine-gun fire come from all points of the compass, but overlook us. The body of an R.A.P. man lies beside the trail; I think I recognize him, but can't be sure. A few yards farther along, four Seaforths form the spokes of a wheel. The hub is a shell hole, with the smoke still drifting from it. We go in single file. Word comes from behind to speed up.

An Indian mule driver and mule, carrying ammunition, are with us. We start up a gentle slope and are mortared, inaccurately. The mule proves his common sense by lying down and refusing to continue. We leave him and the Indian, circle the slope crossing the San Leonardo road and get into dead ground. Here we halt. It is late afternoon now, and a light rain is falling.

There is Spandau fire on our right, and the battle in the town doesn't slacken. German planes swoop out of the clouds, dumping bombs and cannon fire on the transport and reserve tanks across the river. They swing towards us, and I dive into a shell hole half full of water. Through my mind goes the thought, "This is December 9th, and we're going to be living in muddy ice-water until next Spring." The prospect is not attractive. The planes disappear.

Orders come to move on. We climb the hill to San Leonardo. Most of the houses on the south side are blackened hulks, with some still burning. They smell as usual of shell-bursts and the dead. It is getting dark. We are to spend the night here, and so our section takes over a house.

It is not a bad house. It is dry and has an upstairs full of rubble to absorb shells from above, with a room or two on the north side for protection. These are the principal qualifications of a first-class residence in battle. An unexploded 25-pounder shell is embedded in one of the walls. We make ourselves comfortable and put out sentries. Mr. Gray sends orders for a subsection (three men) to act as guides for the tanks in the morning.

Pat Hill, Roy Tennant and myself are elected, and we are not too happy. However, the orders are cancelled. In the morning L/Cpl. Wharton, John Wilson and "The Cowboy" are to leave on a patrol through enemy lines.

December the 10th. BHQ is to move forward, and we are to lead them, moving half a mile or so to the north to a gully running east and west, where we will set up shop. Immediately outside the town there is a grove of trees. On the other side of this there is a large open meadow which extends to the gully. On the left is the road, sheltered by trees, and on the right again are more trees and bush. To the north of the gully the ground rises gradually towards a still larger gully just short of "Cider" crossroads.

Intelligence says that the enemy has no observation on the meadow. My section is therefore to advance across it in open order, BHQ following. But we come under fire from "Moaning Minnies" halfway to the gully, and I conclude that Intelligence has been misinformed. So far we appear only as a rifle section. We can get up and dash the rest of the way easily enough. But what of BHQ, with its No. 18 sets and other heavy equipment? The moment they appear they'll be spotted as a headquarters of some sort, and they can't travel quickly. The trees on the left, on the other hand, offer good cover. There is some shelling on the road, but under cover BHQ will look like just another body of riflemen and not worth special attention. I wave my section back to the trees, and they follow in file to the left, with BHQ behind. We make our way to the gully without incident.¶

On the far side of the gully is a house. The door facing us is barred. I turn to get help in lifting it off its hinges. Colonel Forin arrives. Also a German shell.

It is like being hit in the back of the leg, hard, with a club. I roll to the bottom of the gully, yelling something. I look at the leg. It looks as good as ever, except for a tear in the trousers over the calf. A piece of shell fragment is somewhere in there. "Good," I think, "Christmas in bed!" No more water-logged shell holes for a while.

¶When I signalled my section to retire to the start line, I was not prepared for the speed and efficiency with which they carried out the order. I have a shocked memory of seeing nothing but the soles of their shoes. I wondered if they would stop short of the Moro. Robbie (J.R.G. Robertson) was on my flank, nearest the road, and he looked flabbergasted at my changing the order, as well he might. However, at my signal to follow by way of the covered road they all wheeled into line like the excellent soldiers they were, and, as already mentioned, we proceeded to the gully without incident. It has occurred to me often since that time that, had Colonel Forin and I both remained unwounded, I should probably have been in serious trouble for changing what, to me, seemed orders based on faulty intelligence. However, the point was never raised officially later.

There is a lot of shouting. Groans come from nearby. I crawl over and find Lieut. McLaughlin, the I.O. His legs are full of shell fragments and he is in considerable pain. However, his colour is good and he has the strength to curse. Not so King, the Colonel's runner. He is hit in the stomach and going fast. A few feet away is the body of Beaton, one of the BHQ signallers. Someone says the Colonel is hit too, though no one knows how badly. The German gunner who fired that one made it pay. It had hit a tree behind us at chest level.

An R.A.P. man arrives some time later. He does what he can. Sgt. Portwood and three others pack out McLaughlin and King, using a ladder as a stretcher. I find I can hobble without too much trouble.

Advance R.A.P. is a house 50 yards behind the gully. It is full of wounded and shell-shocked men. King is beside me, still breathing. A tank takes shelter behind the R.A.P., and Mr. Gray goes out to protest. We expect to be fired on at any moment, but Jerry either doesn't spot the tank or refrains because he knows it's an R.A.P. He is still shelling the area heavily. An R.A.P. jeep arrives, and Lieut. McLaughlin, King and I are loaded on it. King is unconscious, but breathing. He has said little and doesn't appear to be suffering much. I've wet his lips a few times when he's complained of thirst. He can't drink because of the stomach wound. The jeep crawls cautiously down the shell-pocked road to San Leonardo. I think that if I were driving I'd go all out. Shells blossom on the road and on both sides. But the driver has critically wounded aboard; to hit a shell hole at high speed might kill them. He risks his life and takes his time. We arrive safely at San Leonardo.

The R.A.P. is a dark room in a battered house. Lights from car batteries hang over blood-stained stretchers. Shells are still falling outside. Their crump is varied occasionally by the peculiar whirr of slate shingles blown from nearby roofs. There are many wounded.

The M.O. takes a quick look at King and he is carried through to the back room. He glances briefly at the field dressing on my leg. I suddenly realize I am also hit in the head and hand, scratches only. He seems satisfied. My friend, Harry Doan, who is in the room, comes over and chats.|| Later I overhear him saying to "Moose" Molson that casualties in the battalion are very heavy. He goes through a list of familiar names, many

---

|| Harry and I were old friends. He was killed a few days later while driving supplies up to the rifle companies in a Bren Carrier. He was taking the place of another driver whose nerves had collapsed.

dead, more wounded. He is waiting for orders to take supplies forward, or evacuate wounded.

The door opens to a weird noise. Two men come in. One is over six feet and heavy. He is only a boy. His eyes are glazed, and from his open mouth comes a scream that rises and falls with the noise of shelling outside. Behind him is an R.A.P. man. He has his hands over the youngster's ears, and is talking to him in a soothing voice. The boy is an advanced case of shell-shock. The M.O. sends him into the back room to make way for the wounded. . . .

Fresh casualties keep arriving. Capt. Anderson is desperately tired, but he never stops working or loses patience with the shock cases. He is talking to another of these, not as bad as the boy. This one is a friend of mine. He has had this trouble before and has been evacuated for it. But he is always sent back up. He is a bundle of nerves, but he never asks for a favour and gives everything he's got until he snaps. The M.O. is talking to him. "Are you hit anywhere?" "No." "Is there anything physically wrong with you?" "No." He probes his man but quickly comes to the conclusion that this one is genuine and has to be taken out. There is deep humiliation in my friend's face as he goes back to join the dead, and the screaming case, in the back room. He thinks he has let his friends down. He will be back again and again, shaking like a leaf every time we see action, going on to the breaking point. He will finish the war unwounded, and carry a sense of shame for the rest of his life. He is a very brave man.

Later, two R.A.P. men, Lieut. McLaughlin, the young shell-shock case and myself are in a jeep heading south over the Moro. The boy is sprawled across my legs, still moaning steadily. We cross the repaired bridge and start up the other side. There is a hairpin bend ahead that comes under fire regularly. The R.A.P. men go this way often. There is tension in their voices. I hold my breath and wonder how I'll control the boy if we get a close one. We pass the turn safely. The R.A.P. men and I suddenly feel talkative as the strain eases. We are over the bank on the south side. Ahead is Rear R.A.P. It is night, and for me the battle is over.

II

The Gully and Ortona

For many Seaforths the type of warfare which developed north of San Leonardo between 10 and 18 December brought to mind an image which they had inherited from an older generation of the fighting in World War I. Until now, despite the mountains and defiles of Sicily and southern Italy and the narrow fronts which these had imposed, they had retained a sense of freedom of movement in the performance of their tasks. Now they were to be confined and crowded. Boxed within not much more than a square mile of relatively flat and open ground, they were required, before the week was out, to share this small space with all the fighting troops and a great many of the supporting arms of the 1st Canadian Division. They were to live in surroundings made absolutely derelict by prolonged and intense bombardment: trees bare arms against the sky, the few farmhouses mere heaps of rubble, vineyards a tangled chaos of wire and vine, earth scorched and barren. They were to know with a new acuteness the miseries of living and fighting in mud, the pervasive stench of cordite and death, the terror of imminent counter attack. They were to share in the new and disturbing experience of seeing one battalion after another of every brigade in the division committed to unsuccessful and sometimes disastrous frontal assaults against a prepared line of defence manned by a stubborn enemy. They were to suffer 110 casualties and count themselves lucky in the number since other battalions were to fare much worse; and they were to see companies reduced in size to one quarter their proper fighting strength, with no immediate prospects of reinforcement.[1] It would be as close as they had come or would come to paralleling the conditions of attrition and bloody stalemate familiar to veterans of the war of 1914–18.

---

[1]Killed were 2 officers and 38 other ranks; wounded, 7 officers and 63 other ranks. The week which followed, the week of Ortona, produced as many casualties again. No comparable period in the war (casualties at the Hitler Line, which were higher, were incurred in a single day) created as severe a drain on Seaforth resources. The problem of reinforcements, moreover, became acute for the first time during these last weeks in December. Seaforth field returns for the week ending 18 December were asking for postings of 8 officers and 129 other ranks. On or about 14 December the division was reported down 104 officers and 1569 other ranks. These deficiencies were not properly filled until the close of the battle for Ortona.

Yet the stalemate was, after all, only a matter of days, not of weeks or months as it had been on the western front in World War I. Towards the end of this extraordinary week the lid of the box was pried open. Major Paul Triquet of the Royal 22me Régiment won at Casa Berardi, near the by this time notorious "Cider" crossroads, the first Victoria Cross awarded to the Canadians in the Italian campaign, and the sequel was the street battle for the town of Ortona itself, which was fighting of a different order again. The Seaforths fought a decisive action at the crossing of the Moro, and a second decisive action in the streets of Ortona. In between, with the exception of a single action on the afternoon of 13 December which for a moment threatened to loosen the entire front, the story of the battalion loses its identity within the confused unfolding of a corporate slugging match.

When Major Thomson took over command of the Seaforths on the afternoon of the 10th, the battalion was still committed but had surrendered the initiative of the attack to others. Late on the 9th, Colonel Jefferson had moved the Loyal Edmonton Regiment up to San Leonardo, where he had joined Colonel Forin in strengthening the still weak hold the Canadians had on the escarpment north of the Moro; and on the morning of the 10th, the Germans having in the course of the night spent most of the reserves of 90 Panzer Grenadier Division in fruitless attacks against the ridge line, the way had appeared open for the Edmontons to exploit the Seaforths' success. Accordingly, a little before nine o'clock Jefferson's companies had begun an attack 500 yards north of San Leonardo which was intended to take them in two bounds to "Cider" crossroads. The Patricias were to pass through the Edmontons and turn towards Ortona. In the meantime, "A" Company of the Seaforths had been required to protect the Edmontons' left flank by occupying rising ground to the northwest, in the direction of what was later to be called "Lager" track, while "B" Company had been sent half a mile east of San Leonardo to a position astride "Royal Canadian Avenue", now vacated by that regiment, which had withdrawn to the south bank of the Moro to reorganize.[2] These battalion tasks, carried out under heavy fire, had just been completed when a German shell brought about a change of command for the Seaforths.[3]

---

[2] R.C.R. casualties had been the heaviest sustained by any unit involved in the Moro action: 21 killed and 53 wounded or missing. See Nicholson, *The Canadians*, p. 303.

[3] As in the case of royalty, there is no break in battalion command: Capt. W.D. Blackburn of "C" Company took charge while Major Thomson was being brought forward. Amongst the fatal casualties sustained on the movement out from the San Leonardo-La Torre area on

The time of that shell was 11:30 a.m. "A" Company was well forward, having better than halved the distance between San Leonardo and the neck of raised ground which carried "Lager" track around the end of a long gully to the Ortona-Orsogna lateral. Shelling was intense and German snipers were active. On the battalion's right the attack put in by the Edmontons up the main-axis road had at first appeared to be going well. At ten o'clock Jefferson's companies had sent back word that they were "now proceeding on the final objective"—that is, "Cider" crossroads—and on the strength of this report Brigadier Hoffmeister had ordered the Patricias "to be prepared for exploitation towards Ortona."[4] But although a later report from the same companies described them as actually consolidating on the final objective,[5] the truth was that at noon on the 10th, the Edmontons were no farther forward than "A" Company of the Seaforths and still short even of their intermediate objective, which was a low ridge more than a mile south of the crossroads. They were being hit hard — sufficient excuse, the difficulty of the ground also considered, for mistaken messages. Early in the afternoon, the situation confused and success still of necessity assumed on the main axis, the Patricias began moving out from San Leonardo. Unable to get through to the Edmontons' positions, they were themselves caught and badly cut up in the rain of defensive fire which now covered the entire area. At nightfall on the 10th the Seaforths dug in on the left, the Edmontons to the right on Route 16, and the Patricias slightly behind the Edmontons and between Route 16 and the coast road. Here, by the sea, the Hastings and Prince Edward Regiment had also dug in, having been able to do no more on the 10th than consolidate their gains of the past three days. No unit of the division had as yet closed with the feature of the ground in front of them which was the source of their trouble.

This feature was The Gully: within a few days it needed no other designation. The Gully was a kind of modest valley into which the gently rising ground beyond San Leonardo dipped before lifting again, this time more sharply, to the high ridge which provided passage for the main road from the west into Ortona. Flanked by formidable bluffs at its seaward end, just south of Ortona, it ran inland between more moderate contours, crossed the main-axis road a few hundred yards short of 'Cider" crossroads,

---

the 10th was Lieut. R.A. Wilson, a young officer who had served the battalion well since the landings in Sicily.

[4]W.D., H.Q. 2 C.I.B., 10 December, 1943.

[5]W.D., H.Q. 2 C.I.B., December, 1943; Appendix 1, Intelligence Log . . . Ser 10.

then continued westward for another 1000 yards before losing itself in the rise of land which "Lager" track followed northward to the lateral. It was a water-course in season, but although the rains, after a week's respite, were to begin again seriously on the 11th, it was not as a water obstacle that The Gully proved capable of holding the Canadians up for eight costly days. With great ingenuity, and drawing upon lessons learned at the Sangro, the Germans had made The Gully into a defensive locality of a peculiarly effective kind. Instead of relying chiefly upon domination of the feature by firepower from above (they had made provision for this too) they had placed their main network of weapon-pits in The Gully itself, and especially on the enemy side of The Gully where the reverse slope marked the first fall of the land after its rise from San Leonardo. It was these latter positions that played havoc with the Canadian attackers. Canadian guns, of which there was certainly no shortage, could not get enough crest clearance to search the positions out, and the defenders were too well dug in to suffer much from mortar fire. Allied fighter-bombers, of which there was also a good supply, could not accept a bomb-line as close as this one would be to Canadian troops. Covered by ample registrations of German guns over the length and breadth of the slope down to San Leonardo,[6] the crest of the ridge on the Canadian side mined and booby-trapped, tanks in support for enfilade fire, the German line of The Gully was all but impregnable.

It took the Canadians some time to recognize this fact. The official history of the Canadians in Italy remarks with monumental simplicity that there were only two alternatives open to Canadian troops at this time: either they could try to cross The Gully from the front, or they could try to go around it on the left and roll up its defences from behind.[7] As it turned out, the first alternative was given priority: the assault would be from the front, with one or at most two battalions up at any given time. Late on the morning of the 11th, therefore, the sequence began with orders to "A" Company of the Seaforths to attack the ridge on the near side of The Gully immediately to its front. Tanks would be in support, and one platoon from "B" Company and one from "C" Company would protect the right flank as the company drew beyond the Edmontons' positions. After nearly two hours of difficult struggle up the muddy slope, "A" Company reached its objective. Depleted in strength before it began the attack, it now had

---

[6]Between 7 and 9 December the registration of hostile batteries on 5 Corps front (a front of about 4 miles) rose from 26 to 76. C.M.H.Q. Report No. 165, p. 54 (mimeographed).

[7]Nicholson, *The Canadians*, p. 305.

a strength of 45 men. Its tanks had fallen behind. At one o'clock the company commander, Capt. E.W. Thomas, reported a heavy concentration of enemy preparing to attack the position, and on the advice of Major Thomson the company withdrew to its starting point in order to allow the artillery to bring down defensive fire. Meanwhile, far to the right, on the Edmontons' other flank, the Patricias had begun another attempt to close with the ridgeline south of The Gully. This attack was to meet with no better success than the Seaforths', and it was to cost the Patricias much higher casualties. On the 12th and 13th the story was to be repeated: first an attempt to push the West Nova Scotia Regiment to The Gully through the Seaforths' positions, then the Carleton York Regiment through the Edmontons' positions. Casualties mounted; no appreciable amount of ground was gained. After three days of fighting the division was almost totally committed between the Moro on the south and The Gully on the north, "Lager" track on the west and the sea on the east. It is difficult to say how long this situation might have continued if two developments on the 13th had not undermined the Canadians' acceptance of the alternative of frontal assault.

The two developments were really one, though their exact connection is not clear. On the night of 12/13 December a patrol of West Novas, drawn from a company left behind in San Leonardo to form the basis of a mobile reserve for the brigade, discovered near the "Lager" track end of The Gully a harbour of German tanks. At seven o'clock on the morning of the 13th a West Nova platoon, carried on three Ontario Shermans, burst into this harbour and destroyed four tanks and an anti-tank gun before the Germans were awake to their danger. By ten-thirty this success had been reinforced by the arrival of the remainder of the West Nova company and a second squadron of tanks, and the entire force now wheeled right, around the head of The Gully, and set course for Casa Berardi and "Cider" crossroads. They did not reach the crossroads; but before they were stopped by a deep ravine which lay across their path, and by a stiffening German resistance, they had made a deep penetration, perhaps 1000 to 2000 yards, behind The Gully's defences.

That same morning, the 13th, a second scheme had taken shape, independent of the first though very like it in conception and execution.[8]

---

[8]Nicholson (*The Canadians*, p. 309) says that the Seaforth infantry-tank team "was organized by Brigadier Wyman (Comd. 1st Armoured Brigade) with the authority of the G.O.C." Since the divisional Operations Message Log for the 13th makes clear that Brig.

Acting on instructions received from brigade headquarters at ten o'clock, Major Thomson relinquished his "A" Company to the command of "C" Squadron of the Ontarios, and in the afternoon the infantry and tanks set out on what was apparently designed as a raid in force to test the strength of the enemy around the head of The Gully, then east along the lateral road as far as opportunity would permit.[9] As it turned out, opportunity was almost unbelievably favourable. The Seaforths, not more than 40 strong and under the joint infantry command of Capt. E.W. Thomas and Capt. D.S. Harley, proceeded, with their tanks, directly to their front, crested the rise, and firing all weapons at their disposal swooped down a shallow incline towards a culvert which offered passage to the higher ground and the lateral beyond. Before they had reached the culvert they had taken, almost without protest, 78 German prisoners, including one battalion commander, his adjutant, and four platoon officers. Having passed the prisoners back, they moved on by way of the culvert, losing one tank but reaching the lateral road without further difficulty. Here they turned east and with their left flank anchored on the Ortona road continued their penetration. They were deeper into enemy territory than the West Novas had been, but they encountered little resistance. When they stopped, it was because their third tank (their second had been lost at the road junction) became bogged down in the mud, and the tank commander had orders to withdraw when his tanks were gone. The force returned by the way it had come to "A" Company's original position. The Seaforths suffered no casualties in this remarkable action.[10]

It is idle to speculate what might have happened if the Seaforths and the West Novas, singly or together, had been able to hold their points of farthest penetration or exploit them, or what might have been the outcome if communications had been such, and reserves so available, as to make possible immediate reinforcement of their success. By the evening of the

---

Wyman was fully informed about the West Nova's successes that day, a close connection can be inferred, through him, between the two raids. Information about the Seaforths' exploit was of course slow in getting back. C.Q.M.S. Jones of "A" Company seems to have provided in person the first firm news at seven o'clock that night (W.D., Seaf. of C., 13 Dec., 1943).

[9]The Seaforth War Diary records that the raid was "to help the Carleton and York reach their objective" (*ibid*). The Carleton and York attack through the Edmontons' positions went in at 6 a.m. on the 13th.

[10]The suggestion that this action "almost loosened the whole front" is to be found in W.D., H.Q. 3rd Infantry Brigade, 13 Dec., 1943.

13th the essential clue was in General Vokes' hands, and early on the morning of the 14th the Royal 22me, the only regiment of the division not yet committed against The Gully, attacked along the same route taken by the Seaforth raiding party the day before. But where the way had been easy for the Seaforths, it was now tough. The Germans resisted stubbornly the new threat to their flank, and resisted with a new strength given them by the arrival in the Berardi area on the night of the 13th of elements of 1 Parachute Division sent to relieve the decimated and battle-weary Grenadiers.[11] And even with Casa Berardi taken, at considerable cost and with great credit to the French Canadians, there was still "Cider" crossroads to be made good 1000 yards beyond. On the morning of the 15th, while the build-up of Canadian armour continued in the Berardi area, the Carleton and York Regiment was committed once again to a frontal assault against The Gully on the main axis. The attack failed, and this was the last of the many costly attempts made by single units to force the line of defence from the south. The final stages of the approach to Ortona saw a reversion to the use of the ground on the left over which the Seaforths and the West Novas had already made passage. On the morning of the 18th the 48th Highlanders and the Royal Canadian Regiment, under the most massive artillery preparation yet undertaken in the Mediterranean theatre of war, launched an attack designed to take first the 48th at an angle from "Lager" track across The Gully and over the lateral road to cut the road to Villa Grande a mile to the west of "Cider" crossroads, then, in a second phase, the R.C.R. along the north side of the lateral to the crossroads itself. The operation was called "Morning Glory", and despite severe setbacks in its second phase it was eventually successful. The R.C.R. occupied "Cider" on the evening of the 19th.

In all these events, since the 13th at least, the Seaforths had played a relatively passive role. There were minor adjustments to be made to company positions, and one major shift on the 14th which moved the weight of the battalion back towards La Torre and farther to the west. But throughout they maintained their place on the left flank of the division, sending out patrols towards Villa Jubatti to test for enemy infiltration and to keep contact with elements of the neighbouring 8th (Indian) Division.

---

[11]The commitment to the Ortona sector of troops of 1 Parachute Division, a first-line formation, and Kesselring's decision on the 14th to commit to the same sector his Army Group Reserve (Regiment Liebach) are measures of the importance the Germans attached to holding the Canadians back at this point.

With the completion, however, by the 1st Brigade of its initial tasks in "Morning Glory", it was time once again for the 2nd Brigade to take a hand. It would be their job to secure Ortona. Early on the 19th Major Thomson received orders to take over the positions on the coast road occupied by the Hastings and Prince Edward Regiment.

Since the first Canadian Division now controlled two miles of the Ortona-Orsogna lateral north of The Gully and the 8th (Indian) Division and the 2nd New Zealand Division were both across the same road in their respective sectors, Ortona might have been expected to fall into the hands of the Allies like a ripe plum. Canadian commanders seem to have thought that it would, and Brigadier Hoffmeister's early decision to make Ortona a one-battalion attack reflected this view. The next natural line of defence for the Germans appeared to be the Arielli River three miles to the north, and Ortona itself, with its narrow streets and crowded houses perched on the top of a cliff overlooking a meagre artificial harbour, had few of the marks of an important piece of military real estate. The Germans themselves may at one point have made a similar appraisal, for when Casa Berardi fell on the 14th the diarist of 76 Panzer Corps Headquarters had remarked phlegmatically enough that the enemy would now "bring up further forces and tanks, and in the exploitation of today's success will presumably take Ortona".[12] But somewhere along the way the situation changed. Ortona was to be contested. And it followed that the more it was contested the more bitterly it was attacked, so that the struggle which eventually developed took on the character of a "prestige battle" to which both sides became stubbornly committed without either being fully convinced of the net tactical value of the objective for which they fought.[13]

---

[12]Quoted in Nicholson, *The Canadians*, p. 313.

[13]Nicholson is my source for the phrase "prestige battle", as applied to Ortona (*The Canadians*, p. 329). Correspondents of the Associated Press, who found Ortona eminently newsworthy, may, oddly enough, have had something to do with the deepening of commitments on both sides. Nicholson quotes Kesselring in a telephone conversation with the Commander of the German Tenth Army on Christmas Day: "It is clear that we do not want to defend Ortona decisively, but the English have made it appear as important as Rome." "It costs so much blood," Kesselring went on, "that it cannot be justified; [but] you can do nothing when things develop in this manner; it is only too bad that . . . the world press makes so much of it" (*ibid.*, p. 328). Contemporary clippings from Vancouver newspapers in my possession refer to Ortona as "a key Adriatic port", and "a vital communications centre".

It was by such curious means that the Seaforths acquired another battle honour for their colours.

Arrived at the seaward end of The Gully on the evening of the 19th, the Seaforths set up headquarters in a house whose second-storey windows commanded an excellent view across what was here a wide and deep valley to the approaches to Ortona and to the town's white cluster of houses beyond. The next morning BHQ became also the 2nd Brigade Command Post, and at nine-thirty Brigadier Hoffmeister came forward to put the Seaforths in the picture and to establish control over the new phase of the battle due to begin within the hour. The main effort of the attack would fall to the Loyal Edmonton Regiment, who were to make a long leap of almost 3000 yards from "Cider" crossroads up Route 16 to the outskirts of Ortona.[14] The Seaforths, in a role of which they had been advised the previous night, were to protect the Edmontons' right flank by attacking with a company directly across the valley towards a church easily distinguishable 300 yards beyond the sharp edge of the escarpment at the end of a ribbon of houses reaching south from Ortona. The Patricias would provide a firm base inland, on the near edge of The Gully between the Seaforths and the Edmontons. The barrage supporting the Edmontons' advance would begin at ten o'clock, and the Seaforths were to be down into the valley by noon.[15]

The task fell to "C" Company, now commanded by Capt. D.S. Harley.[16] "C" Company was to be supported by "D" Company, under Capt. A.W. Mercer, which was to clear the ground first to the peak of a long spur overlooking the mouth of The Gully, then from the forward slope give covering fire to the attacking company, which was to pass through its position. "D" Company, as was to be expected, was hit heavily for its pains by defensive fire; but it was so far successful in attracting the attention of the Germans that "C" Company got down into the valley, past a brick factory which lay to the right of the road at the bottom, through a minefield, then to the right up the steep face of the cliff without suffering any casualties. But the Germans were now alert to their danger, and as the Seaforths neared

---

[14] At "Cider" crossroads Route 16 out of San Leonardo turned right to become identified with the lateral road into Ortona.

[15] The Edmontons' attack seems to have been almost two hours late in starting, a fact of some consequence to the Seaforths' attacking company.

[16] Capt. Harley had taken over command of "C" Company from Major W.D. Blackburn, who was evacuated on 19 December.

the top of the cliff they were showered from above with grenades. Men began to fall. Most, however, gained the crest of the plateau, bayonets fixed, where they quickly cleaned out a score of weapon-pits which the enemy were busy evacuating.[17] Recognizing the danger of being pinned to the edge of the cliff and perhaps knocked back over it by the counter-attack fire beginning to come in on them, Capt. Harley decided to make for the church, now plainly visible through the thin trellis-work of vines to his front and as plainly a rallying point for the Germans. He asked for another force of Seaforths to be sent up the beach to his right to forestall German infiltration up The Gully behind him, and he called for counter-fire from Canadian artillery. It was now more than three hours since the attack had been launched, and the original force of 86 men, small enough to begin with, had been cut to almost half that number by casualties — two of these, platoon officers.[18] But the attempt on the church had to be made. While one platoon under Sgt. J. Elaschuk steadied the left-flank approach to the church, a second platoon under Sgt. J. Mottl worked round to the right and charged the position from the seaward side. This charge, bravely made, weakened and failed when Sgt. Mottl was killed and half of his small group fell before withering fire. As it happened, however, this pressure coincided with a new pressure of which the Germans became aware as the Edmontons at their backs took the first houses on the fringes of Ortona, where Route 16 entered the town. By six o'clock Capt. Harley had established contact with elements of the Edmontons on his left and had been placed temporarily under Colonel Jefferson's command. Early the next morning "C" Company occupied the church — identified as the Church of Santa Maria di Constantinopoli — unopposed.

The task now to be undertaken by the Edmontons, and, as it turned out, by the Seaforths as well, was that of a town-clearing operation against strong resistance, an operation sufficiently rehearsed in battle-schools in England, but one in which both battalions in the week to come were to develop a number of practical refinements. The simplicity of the task from a tactical point of view was out of all proportion to the bitterness of the struggle itself, and indeed stood in marked contrast to the complexity of the practical responses which the fighting required of Seaforths and Edmontons of all ranks. Ortona, as already noted, is a narrow town,

---

[17]Here as elsewhere the Germans showed their dislike for perimeter defence to the last man; they seemed to prefer to preserve strength for counter attack in force.

[18]Killed was Lieut. A.L. Robinson; wounded, Lieut. D.C. Hanbury.

confined to a width of about 500 yards by a deep valley on the left and sea-cliffs on the right. It is divided slightly to the right of centre by the Corso Vittorio Emanuele (a continuation of Route 16 entering from the southwest), and at the Piazza Municipale, which is the town square, the Corso bears left to become the Via Tripoli, which then descends into the valley beyond to cross a small stream, rise again, and become the main highway north to Francavilla and Pescara. On either side of the Corso the Canadians were confronted by a network of extremely narrow streets in which three-storey and four-storey houses stood wall to wall and back to back. These houses, together with a hotel, a school, a church and a factory, were occupied at one time or another by the Germans that Christmas week and had to be cleared. Buildings at street-corners had been blown outward to block the intersections. The streets themselves, covered by small-arms and anti-tank fire, were no-man's-land in the attack. It was a setting which promised little room for manoeuvre, though ample opportunity for ingenious solutions to the problem of clearing houses.

When it became evident by mid-morning on the 21st that the Germans did not intend to give up Ortona easily, Brigadier Hoffmeister ordered Major Thomson to relinquish a second company in support of the Edmontons' attack. But at one o'clock the orders were changed: the experience of the Edmontons in securing a score of buildings on the outskirts of the town had already made clear the extraordinary demands on manpower to be expected in a type of operation in which an entire platoon could be swallowed up in the clearing of a single house. "C" Company was returned to Major Thomson's command and the battalion as a whole committed to the battle. At four o'clock "D" Company began the relief of a company of the Edmontons on the inland side of the Corso Vittorio Emanuele, and by eight o'clock the following morning they were ready to begin their work. The remaining companies were now disposed in a semi-circle just south of the town, with BHQ established at the Church of Santa Maria. Mortaring was heavy over all the approaches to Ortona on the 22nd.[19]

What "D" Company experienced in the next twenty-four hours set the pattern for the days to come. In the first stages of clearing at least, they were not to be greatly troubled by shelling or mortaring, for friend and foe were too closely engaged for that kind of support, and, where a building

---

[19]BHQ came near to losing its vehicles on the morning of the 22nd when a bomb set fire to an ammunition truck parked behind the church. With quick thinking and considerable courage the C.O. and a number of headquarters personnel got their vehicles out of danger.

might change hands more than once in a single day, their positions were too uncertain. Yet the bursting of bombs sporadically in great thunder-claps of noise which hammered at the ear-drums through the echoing streets began the war on men's nerves to which so much was soon to be added. The fighting edge of the company, it was clear, would have to be small groups of men, a section or a platoon at most. Streets of houses were to be taken, both sides, and to this extent the orders were simple and systematic. But execution of the orders varied according to the temperament of individuals and the quick readings of the situation they had to make. A section would perhaps storm its way into a house at the head of a block, clear it to the top, then blow a way through at roof-level into the adjoining house, where it would clear to the bottom.[20] Then back it would go to the top, through the wall and down again; and so on, the Germans withdrawing on the other side of the street as the houses opposite were taken. Others under different circumstances developed a preference for criss-crossing the street, entering buildings always from the ground level. First, smoke grenades would be thrown up the street and the door opposite smashed with bullets;[21] then, one group giving covering fire, a second group would race across, burst into the house and clear it from the ground up. Sometimes there would be help from supporting arms for these operations — perhaps from the Seaforth anti-tank guns, which saw good service in Ortona against particularly stubborn enemy emplacements, perhaps from the Seaforth mortars or the medium machine-guns of the Saskatoon Light Infantry, occasionally from tanks, though these had to be used sparingly in the rubble-filled streets where they were extremely vulnerable to enemy fire. And always, of course, there was the resourcefulness and determination of the paratroopers to be reckoned with: houses taken by the Seaforths during the day re-occupied by the Germans at night; snipers infiltrating positions, especially from the exposed left flank; doors booby-trapped, buildings mined with delayed charges. There was a basic pattern, "D" Company discovered, but the detail was and had to be infinitely varied.

So the days passed, though the Seaforths really knew neither day nor night as they pressed forward. Up the muddy, rutted road out of The

---

[20]The "beehive", a conical demolition charge developed for use principally against pillboxes, proved useful in these "mouseholing" techniques.

[21]I have it on good authority that the Boyes Anti-Tank Rifle, then obsolescent but still carried in battalion stores, came into its own in Ortona for the first and only time during the war as an extremely effective weapon for smashing door-locks.

143

Gully the company carriers began, on the evening of the 22nd, which was a Wednesday, to haul ammunition and rations forward from "F" Echelon. At eight o'clock that night "D" Company moved into the southwest sector of the town preparatory to employment the next day on streets to the left of the Corso, between "D" Company and the Edmontons.[22] On Thursday morning the C.O. (now promoted to the rank of Lieutenant-Colonel) set up his command post on the second floor of a green-shuttered hotel which stood on a corner of the *piazza* at the entrance to Ortona, and late that afternoon he ordered "A" Company forward to link up with "B" in house-to-house fighting. Objectives for the three companies on Friday included a large church, partially demolished, the town school, and command of a main intersection named "Dead Horse Square". These positions were gained by the end of the day and held tenuously throughout the night — in one case under conditions of double occupancy which saw the Seaforths bowling grenades down a long corridor towards the end of the building still occupied by the Germans. "A" Company lost a section of men when a building they had taken during the day was blown up under them at night by prepared charges.

Saturday, Christmas Day, was cloudy and cold, and the companies were heavily committed. It might have been like any other day of that week if the Quartermaster, Capt. D.B. Cameron, and his staff had not decided that nothing was impossible, not even a Christmas dinner, with all the trimmings, in the midst of battle. On the Friday afternoon they had brought cooking equipment and supplies up to the Church of Santa Maria, and at eleven o'clock on Christmas morning "C" Company, which was the reserve company, sat down to a sumptuous meal, beautifully set, to be replaced two hours later by "A" Company, whom they relieved in their forward positions, "A" Company then relieving "B" Company, and "B" relieving "D", until by seven o'clock that night the last man of the battalion had had his fill of food and wine and fellowship.[23] But even as the tables were cleared the situation worsened in the town on the left flank, and "D" Company, slated for reserve, were hurriedly committed again to the fight.

---

[22]On 23 December the boundary between the Seaforths and the Edmontons was established as "the second street N.W. of the main road through the city" — that is, two streets left of the Corso Vittorio Emanuele. See W.D., Loyal Edmonton Regiment, 23 December 1943.

[23]When Capt. Cameron was later awarded a periodic M.B.E. for long and distinguished service as Quartermaster to the battalion, his remarkable achievement on Christmas Day at Ortona was used as the basis for his citation.

Sunday dawned wet and cold again. Having stabilized the positions weakened by infiltration the previous night, the companies resumed their advance.[24] Reinforcements of 6 officers and 85 other ranks, many of them novices and all of them brought in under most difficult conditions, nevertheless stiffened the fibre of the battalion. The line was well forward now, with three-quarters of the town cleared and the Edmontons reporting penetration on the right almost to the entrance of the square dominated by the Church of San Tommaso. Back farther on the left, which was the hinge of the German withdrawal, elements of "C" Company of the Seaforths on Monday morning occupied the basement of a factory, but found it strongly fortified and were unable to drive the Germans from the main floor of the building. New plans were laid that afternoon: "A" Company would attack the factory early the next day, taking with them enough explosives to demolish it; then, to tip finally the scales of the fighting, the Patricias would be brought in to drive through the Seaforths and the Edmontons towards the cemetery on the far edge of the town. These plans, however, did not mature in quite the form they were made. Sometime before first light on Tuesday, 28 December, the remnants of the two regiments of 1 Parachute Division to whom the defence of Ortona had been entrusted withdrew across the valley to the north. The battle was over.

It had been a costly battle. For the period 20–28 December, 1 Parachute Division reported to Tenth Army Headquarters total casualties of 455 men; in the same week the Canadians lost 650 all ranks, killed, wounded and missing.[25] The Seaforths had had one company commander, Major T.C.B. Vance, killed in the streets of Ortona, and a second, Capt. (now Major) D.S. Harley, severely wounded. Some 30 N.C.Os. and privates had lost their lives. The figure for those wounded, again within the town itself and not including the preliminary attack on the Church of Santa Maria, was 64, of whom 5 were platoon officers. It had been a hard fight because the enemy had been skilful and fanatical in his resistance and had had ideal cover for defence. It had been made doubly difficult by the fact that

---

[24]The infiltration (which, it should be noted, had nothing to do with the arrangements for Christmas dinner) resulted in the capture of two sections of a platoon from "C" Company. When "C" Company moved to restore the situation at noon on the 26th, the Germans released the prisoners. In the ensuing action 16 paratroopers were taken prisoner and a number killed.

[25]Nicholson, *The Canadians*, p. 333. The second figure is of course for the Canadians as a whole, not just the attacking battalions at Ortona.

the left hook intended to take the 1st and then the 3rd Brigade, beginning on 22 December, from "Cider" crossroads through San Nicola and San Tommaso, behind Ortona to Torre Mucchia at the mouth of the Riccio River, had encountered so many setbacks that it was not completed until well after Ortona had fallen. But if it was a costly battle, it was also a battle which displayed richly the courage and skill of a very considerable number of Seaforths whose stories remain unknown or known only to a few. The emblem of this excellent conduct was the D.S.O. awarded to Colonel Thomson for his and his battalion's role in the taking of Ortona.[26]

Extracts from an Interview with Major D.S. Harley, dated 7 June, 1961, at Toronto, Ontario.

McDougall: I've read you the piece from the War Diary which connects you with the "Lager" track affair. Now what I'm asking you to do is to recall if you can the setting for this operation, how it went, what you felt about it. . . .

Harley: You'll have to let me just ramble here. I remember I was told about noon or a little after that I was to join June Thomas up at "A" Company in order to make this attack with a troop of tanks. Soon after I arrived, we decided that we'd go right up the steep incline in front of us to get to the top of the slope which went down into The Gully. We were to advance more or less in a straight line, with the tanks in between us — so many men, a tank, so many men, and so on. . . .

McDougall: This was to be in broad daylight?

Harley: In broad daylight. We launched the attack about three in the afternoon. Well, at first there was a deathly silence, but we had agreed that everybody should let off everything when the tanks let off everything. And the tanks had their fast pup-pup-pup-pup guns, and everything went

---

[26]The battalion's performance at Ortona was first-rate; I have no doubt about that. Yet curiously enough, of the five D.S.Os., three M.Cs., and seven M.Ms. won by Canadians participating in the battle (including tank crew and artillery-men) only one D.S.O. and one M.C. were won by Seaforths. I conclude that we did not press our claims as hard as we should have. It took the battalion a long time to learn to do this in the face of the generally high level of performance expected of and received from its members.

off suddenly, and with that we were in a thin red line, and we all advanced up the axis of this track.

McDougall: Did you meet opposing fire?

Harley: No, we didn't meet much. We put up the fire. We had fixed bayonets, and we were all to shoot as we went over the hill, and go as fast as we could. We breasted the ridge, and as we came over the top making a helluva noise — to me it sounded as if the whole Canadian army was in action — there was a certain amount of fire from the Germans.

McDougall: Small arms?

Harley: Small arms; that was all.

McDougall: No shelling?

Harley: No shelling at that period. It seemed to us that we took them completely by surprise. Whether it was the time of day, or what it was I don't know; but there was very little opposition, and we were all yelling and letting off our rifles happily. The tanks were pouring out ammunition.

McDougall: Just let me stop you a minute here. You speak of going over a rise. In front of you is ...

Harley: The Gully.

McDougall: Rising then on the other side to the lateral road.

Harley: To the lateral road, right on the other side. And we met absolutely nothing until we got to the top of that ridge. And one of the first things I remember at the top of that ridge was one of the tanks set a haystack on fire on the lateral road, and that blazed up and lent atmosphere to the whole thing because there was a terrific lot of smoke and fire going on. In The Gully was a road, going across The Gully, over a sort of culvert; and one of the tanks let loose at a German vehicle or tank, and that caught fire. Then we all went running down towards the culvert.

McDougall: Did the tanks get ahead of you?

Harley: No, they were never ahead of us, never. And it was then that the Germans literally poured out and surrendered.

McDougall: As soon as that? Before you reached the road?

147

Harley: Oh, long before. As we came over the rise, it seems that they thought that instead of one company coming over, it was the whole brigade. That was the impression I got. There was so much clutter, you see, we were all laterally formed up, there was no depth to our attack at all; with all the noise, everybody letting off everything he had, it must have seemed as if we were just the first instalment of a big attack. . . .

McDougall: But you did go farther. You went beyond this?

Harley: Oh, yes. There were the Germans coming towards us with their hands up, and it seemed to me there were hundreds of them. It created havoc; the troops all stopped, and our problem was to keep them going and let the prisoners go through us. It was at that time that the C.O. of the Germans and his adjutant were asking who our commanding officer was. He was brought to me to surrender, and he clicked his heels and said, to you I surrender, or something like that. Very formal. Well, we got runners to take the prisoners back, and we got going again, down through the culvert area. There was a lot of equipment around, and I remember a burning German tank, with its gun. It was obvious we had hit their headquarters, with a very thin screen in front of it.

McDougall: Do you remember seeing slit trenches?

Harley: Yes, there were slit trenches just on the reverse slope, and the headquarters seemed to be below that, where there was a little group of buildings. But the slit trenches were very lightly manned, and they obviously felt that the strength coming over was too much for them to resist, so they surrendered.

McDougall: Now let's go on . . .

Harley: Well, we re-formed quickly on the other side of the culvert — June on the left in the middle of perhaps 20 men, and me on the right in the middle of another 20. And at that moment I think our first tank was knocked out. What hit it, I don't know, but it stopped and blazed. So we went on with two tanks, and we swung onto the lateral road. But we didn't go along the road; we were south of the road, though we used it as our axis, with our left man on the edge of it. We were going along through fairly open, undulating country; and soon after we'd swung to the right we lost the second tank. There again I don't remember just what happened, because we were ahead of the tanks at the time. Then, very shortly after, we ran into a German position based on the road — rather like a road-block type of position, with slit trenches, but pointing towards The Gully. We took them laterally. And I remember we ran into what seemed to us heavy fire, and all the troops immediately took to the ground and opened fire, because I remember myself lying down and aiming, and it was the only German I shot in the whole war, that I knew I'd shot. I had a rifle at the time; I got him moving, shot him, he must have been a hundred yards away. But they were surprised because we were coming in laterally to them, perhaps a little behind them, and they were a little bit nearer to The Gully than we were. They were trying to form round into a line to meet us. Now how far we went through that area, it's hard to say. Perhaps a mile?

McDougall: Do you remember what led to your decision to stop?

Harley: Ah, yes. We went on and on doing this, and the final tank that we had with us broke a track, got into boggy ground, got bogged, I remember, and we stopped, because the tank was behind us. It was shooting over us. And the tank commander of that tank, if I remember rightly, hopped out and ran up to us, and there was a huddle, and he said that he was bogged down and couldn't get forward, and his orders were that if his tank bogged down he had to destroy it. The decision then was that as we had no support, and it seemed to me it was getting twilight, we had to withdraw. So they set the tank on fire. By that time there was no opposition — we weren't being fired on at all. We re-formed and came back quickly the way we had come. No trouble, over The Gully, onto the high ground the other side, just over the high ground, and we dug slit trenches there for the night. We were heavily shelled there with those whizz-bang mortars.

McDougall: Let me go back, then, to what your orders were when you set out. The tank commander was officially in charge, I gather.

Harley: Yes.

McDougall: But I presume you received some orders too. What was the intention? A raid in strength?

Harley: As I recall, the intention was to get up to the lateral road, turn right towards the coast and go as far along the lateral road as we could, until we got to the crossroads.

McDougall: "Cider" crossroads.

Harley: And we were told to take "Cider" crossroads. But it was a raid with a view to feeling out enemy strength. If we were successful we would consolidate around the crossroads. But on no account were we to let the Germans take our tanks. If our tanks were knocked out, we were told to come back.

McDougall: Now what was your communication back? Was it effective throughout?

Harley: There was no communication.

McDougall: No communication?

Harley: We lost communication. The set went wrong.

McDougall: Why?

Harley: Oh, don't ask me. I mean, you say to the signallers get through, and they say they can't . . .

McDougall: They weren't wounded or killed?

Harley: No, no. It was on the guy's back, and they were fiddling with it as the Sigs always fiddle with things, and they could get no signal back. They were giving out their reports but they could get nothing back.

McDougall: Did you feel at the time that you had achieved success?

Harley: Terrific . . .

McDougall: And would have reported success.

Harley: Terrific disappointment on the part of the troops that we were held and made to come back, because we felt that we could go through without the tanks. We gave up when we had defeated all resistance, and the huddle we had, and the decision to burn the tank and come back was greeted with something like disgust.

McDougall: At the moment you turned back there was actually no further opposition?

Harley: Nothing, absolutely nothing. There was nothing in front of us then; there was nothing behind us. It was just a question of going back to billets. The scheme was over. . . .

McDougall: The scheme was over. That's very well put. Now let's go forward to Ortona, the move into Ortona. It's the 19th of December. The brigade has sent the Edmontons in on the left, up the main road, and the orders are that the Seaforths will support and join with the Edmontons by moving up on the right flank, across the seaward end of The Gully, up the cliff, close to the Church of Santa Maria. The main sequence is clear, but I want to pick up a few points. How did you come to be commanding "C" Company?

Harley: Davie Blackburn was in charge of "C" Company when we moved over to the coast. Then Syd Thomson got us together to give out the orders, and having listened to the whole thing, and feeling very content that I was with "A" Company in reserve, Syd suddenly turned to me and said, Oh, by the way, Don, you're in command of "C" Company; Davie is not well and he's going back. That was about ten o'clock in the morning, and if I remember rightly we were to be into the valley by noon. I immediately got the jitters. However, I had the orders, and I went to "C" Company and took command. There wasn't much time, but I did manage to get forward with the three platoon commanders to a position from which we could look over the brick factory, across the valley to the church and Ortona . . .

McDougall: When you got down into the bottom of The Gully, I believe you ran into a minefield, is that right?

Harley: We did indeed. We were in arrowhead formation — one platoon up, with two back on the flanks, and company headquarters in the middle. Sgt. Elaschuk led us down with his platoon. There was no fire at all, except for the supporting fire from "D" Company, and the 25 pounders. Then Elaschuk got into a minefield; there was quite a solid one at the bottom of the valley which hadn't been obvious to us as we went down the hill. Elaschuk yelled back that he was in the mines. However, we had to go on, we were in open country, and so I said to go on, we'd have to hurry. We started doubling, and soon we could see the mines all around us. I remember so well there were mutilated bodies of Germans in that valley and in the minefield. But the miraculous part was that we got right through the minefield without casualties; we could see them, they were humped, and it was a question of stepping over them as we ran. We really ran very fast.

McDougall: How did you get up the cliff? It was very steep.

Harley: On all fours. I had a rifle, and I remember slinging it over my back and getting down on my hands and knees.

McDougall: Can you give us some glimpses of what happened in the position you secured at the top?

Harley: Well, we had this perimeter with the cliff absolutely behind us, and the vineyards and a sort of open space in front of us ...

McDougall: There was a real trench system up there?

Harley: Yes, there was a trench system. Not like the First World War systems, but a slit-trench system — very definitely a system, because there must have been 20 or 30 slit trenches which we were able to get into. There was not much foliage in the vineyard, so that you could see through it, and on the other side was a hedge, and the churchyard beyond the hedge. The open Gully behind bothered me. I was in contact then with Syd Thomson by radio, and I remember looking down and seeing this tremendous opening, and I said to Syd, what if we get a counter-attack down that flank and up The Gully, and he said, all right I'll keep that watched, don't you worry about that.[27]

McDougall: Communications were good this time?

Harley: Excellent. Then I asked Syd for support, and he said, well, I can give you the 25 pounders. We had an artillery officer with us, and he called down the 25 pounders, but unfortunately some of the shells fell short and did some damage amongst the wounded we had gathered on a little bank or shelf about 10 or 15 feet below the top of the cliff. I think it was because of that experience that some of those who could walk started back on their own at nightfall across the valley. I don't think many made it through the minefield; I know there was explosion after explosion behind us, and I remember going down to them and saying, for God's sake don't move, everything's all right if you stay there. But the minute one's back was turned they began fading off into the darkness.

McDougall: Did you take any prisoners at the top of the cliff?

Harley: Yes, perhaps a dozen. And that reminds me of an interesting sidelight to this attack. After I'd got my orders, when I went forward with the platoon commanders to make a recce, with me was a little guy in a trenchcoat and an ordinary army peaked cap and brown shoes, no

---

[27] A platoon of "A" Company was subsequently sent up the shoreline on the right as flank protection to "C" Company.

battle-dress, an ordinary uniform. He was the *Manchester Guardian* correspondent, and he said, do you mind if I come forward with you while you make your assessment of the position. Well, he came, and when we went into the attack he asked if I'd mind if he came along with me across the valley; and I said, not a bit. He was with me, this little guy, unarmed, nothing, trench-coat, peaked cap, and his ordinary serge trousers, all the way across. And when we were up in the vineyard he was still there with me, and we were cut off. We had collected perhaps a dozen prisoners there, and I said to him, I can't spare any men to take these prisoners back, will you? He said, well, I'm unarmed, I can't take them. And I said, we'll give you a Tommy-gun to take them back. He said, I've never fired a T.S.M.G. in all my life, and I said, well, just wave it about and take them back. And he said, I can't, I'm a non-combatant. Which of course he was. I suppose I sent back the prisoners with the walking-wounded. I don't know. Anyway, we were on top, and I had this little guy with me the whole night.

McDougall: It must have been a grim night.

Harley: It was. Syd and I talked regularly on the set, and I remember so well his making some crack, and I said, well, I'd rather be at the Savoy, Syd, than sitting up here; and he said, you wouldn't see the fireworks at the Savoy that you're seeing here. And I said, well, I sure could do with a drink, chum, would you send one over? And he said, right, I'll arrange that. He was a wonderful C.O.

Letter from K534897 Pte. George Ableson to Mr. John Ableson of 2876 West 5th Ave., Vancouver, B.C., dated 27 December, 1943.[28]

Dear John:

I have only a few minutes. A truck will be here at ten, it's after nine-thirty now, and then I'm off down the line to "A" Echelon, which is five miles back. With any luck (should I be ashamed to say this?) I'll be out of the frontline fighting for a while, perhaps for good. Not wounded either, so you don't need to worry about *that*. I'm an escaped prisoner of war, believe it or not! Was held by the Germans in a house in Ortona for part of one night, that's all. It was a nightmare end to a nightmare week. We had had

---

[28]Fiction: see note p. 11.

a bloody time of it for several days, clobbering and being clobbered in the streets of the town, then came Christmas day and a wonderful Christmas dinner in a little church we took on our way into Ortona, then back into the streets again to relieve "A" Company. We took another house that afternoon, Sgt. Elaschuk and I and half-a-dozen others, and settled down to keep it for the night, but something went wrong, I don't know what, and the next thing we knew the place was full of German paratroopers, Schmeisers in our faces, and that was that. But it wasn't to be the end in the way we expected. For some reason they kept us in the house. It was like going backstage, seeing them like that, young fellows, lean-faced, going about their business. Came dawn, Capt. Harley I guess came to check our position, got fired on, put in an attack with the rest of the company, and we became surplus to the Germans, who needed every man to fight back. So they did a deal with Sgt. Elaschuk, there's hardly a section in the company doesn't have at least one man can speak German — said they would let us go if we promised not to fight again. Johnny promised, and we went. I don't know whether that kind of promise is covered in the rules of war, but while they're figuring it out we're going back. Suits me. I reckon Johnny and I and some of the others are about saturated anyways. You get so very, very, tired, and the tension in you just builds up and there's nothing you can do about it. But I'm all right, and I've done my best. There's the truck, must go. Love to Martha and the boys.

Yours,

George

———————————

Extracts from the Diary of H/Capt. Roy Durnford, Regimental Chaplain to the Seaforth Highlanders of Canada, Christmas Day, 1943.

. . . Went forward as soon as I could to Main BHQ at the church, travelling by Red Cross jeep with Tom Mercer and Paddy (Leo) Hawkins, the Bailey bridges jammed with traffic. Preparations for Christmas dinner were well advanced when I arrived, chiefly the result of Borden Cameron's tireless work for the past twenty-four hours. The companies came in in rotation — "C" Company first at eleven o'clock, "A" Company at one, and so on until seven o'clock at night. The men looked tired and drawn, as well they might, and most of those who came directly from the town were dirty and unshaven. "Well", I said, "at last I've got you all in church." The floor had been cleared and tables set up, and it was a heartwarming sight to see the white table cloths and the chinaware which some of the boys had scrounged from houses we had occupied, and the beer, cigarettes, chocolate bars, nuts, oranges and apples laid out as extras. For the dinner itself, there was soup to start, then roast pork with apple sauce, cauliflower and mixed vegetables, mashed potatoes and gravy, Christmas pudding and mince pies for dessert, all of it excellent and a great credit to the cooks. Plates were heaped high, as much as any man could eat ...

So the tables filled and emptied and were filled again all day, and I saw many a tense face relax in the friendly warmth that grew up within the walls of the battle-scarred church. What a concert of noise it was! As the sense of relief took hold, the talk became louder, and shouted greetings and jokes were exchanged from one table to another. Up behind the altar, in a ruin of church furnishings, the company cookers hissed and sizzled, and the plates clattered as they were cleared from the tables and piled high on the altar itself. I might once have thought it a desecration of the Lord's Table, but it did not strike me this way today. In one corner, the battle still being in progress in Ortona, the signals bell would ring urgently and there would be shouted snatches of conversations on the radio sets. Above the din one could hear sometimes the distant chatter of machine-gun fire and the whistle and crump of shells landing not far from the church. And through it all visitors came and went. Colonel Thomson was there for a while, and Brigadier Hoffmeister, who misses no chance for a visit with the Seaforths. Both spoke briefly and got a rousing cheer from the men. Reporters from the newspapers were there too — a man from the *Daily Express*, and one from the *Manchester Guardian*, also some foreign Public Relations Officer who was led around by "Postie" Sinclair and introduced to all and sundry as "a Highland Gentleman from Siberia and Hong Kong." It was wonderful to hear so much laughter so close to so much death and suffering. "Postie" brought with him a sack of mail which was greeted with shouts of pleasure.

I don't know how many remembered Christ today, but I felt that most of these men, whether they knew it or not, remembered the things that Christ stood for — compassion, faithfulness to a cause, self-sacrifice. At each sitting I began a little service in the cloisters at one side of the church, being careful to make it voluntary, and I was pleased to see how many gathered around. We had just a few short prayers, and then some carol signing — Wilf Gildersleeve playing the harmonium we found in the church, while "Postie" and Major Gowan manned the bellows. I have done what I could. I have talked with many men in the course of the day, most of them, I'm sure, fearful of what lies ahead, but they are fine men and I know they will give the best that is in them. My heart grieved to see them, after their brief two-hour respite, turn their faces again to the battle . . .

———————

Extracts from an Interview with Brigadier S.W. Thomson, dated 15 July, 1960, at Victoria, B.C.

McDougall: For the write-up on Ortona, then, you would build the Seaforth role a little, over and above what the official record gives?

Thomson: Yes, because of the weakness of the diary. It probably wasn't properly written up. We were tired and depleted. There's no mention of that left-flank threat we had all the time.

McDougall: What was the ground like out to the left?

Thomson: Just like any compact Italian village, the houses thinned out and it dropped away down into a valley. That's where at night the enemy would come in, a few of them. It wasn't so much patrols; they sent in snipers and then raised hell with us during the day. It would take all day to find them. It was such a big blank we couldn't possibly control it. They would get into the houses we had already cleared.

McDougall: Do you remember how you worked your companies?

Thomson: It was very simple. Actually, it's probably the simplest of any kind of operation, town-fighting, as far as the battalion is concerned, because the features were sitting right there on the map in front of you, or the photos,[29] and we could say we own this house and not that one. Next day we'd decide to take this one or that street, and so on.

McDougall: Did you each night plan the work for the next day?

Thomson: It was a continuous thing; there was no night and day, as far as the fighting was concerned.

———

[29]Good aerial photographs of Ortona were available to commanders. See Nicholson, *The Canadians*, plate facing p. 305.

McDougall: They didn't shut down at night at all?

Thomson: In some cases they did for a while, but you could never depend on it.

McDougall: How did you handle your orders?

Thomson: The orders were given either by runner or by me directly — somebody going from company to company all the time, a continuous round. We never had an "O" Group where the company commanders came in; we were always committed. Oh, there may have been odd nights when we could get them all in, but generally it was a piece-meal development. One company would get one house, or one street, ahead of another company, then you'd have to bring them up into line.

McDougall: Did you have them all committed, you might say?

Thomson: At times we did, because those that were out of the line were trying to protect that left flank. It was the strength of the company and its ability to fight at the moment that determined who was in the front line. Company strengths, of course, were very poor, very poor. Not much more than half what they should have been.

McDougall: There was an Army pamphlet on street-fighting brought out, wasn't there, which made use of the experience gained in Ortona?

Thomson: Yes, there was; but all these things, mouseholing and so on, had already been taught in battle-school before we left England. It's true there were innovations that the boys thought up while they were there; but it was all done by the front-line soldier, not by the colonel or even in most cases the company commanders. They just ran into a problem, and they found some way of solving it. One of the things I got the biggest laugh from in England when I went back was when I said they used the Boyes anti-tank rifle to blow locks off doors, so they could get into them when they were attacking a house. Somebody thought, it's a very accurate thing with a high muzzle-velocity, clearly the thing for the job, and it worked. I don't know how often it was used, perhaps only once or twice. But that was the way problems were solved. . . .

McDougall: Do you remember a tunnel under Ortona?

Thomson: Yes, I do. There was a single-line railway that went right under the town. We discovered not long after we'd been in the town that

157

that's where the majority of the civilians were. It was quite safe there. And we also suspected that the Germans were using it from their end to conceal themselves at night, and this was verified after the town was taken when we found that the Germans, some of them, had spent their Christmas there, because there were several Christmas trees. The place was completely filthy by the time we found it.

McDougall: What happened to the civilians when you went into the town. Were they all gone?

Thomson: No, they weren't gone by any means. There were civilians in town all through, in the cellars, quite a few. For the older people and the children it was pretty terrible.

McDougall: Give me a picture or two that stays in your mind.

Thomson: Well, one is of an old woman in a square in front of one of the company positions, and she had gone off her head, I suppose, and was wandering about with her hair down, yelling and screaming. Then she was shot, and we couldn't get to her, and when the tanks came up later they ran back and forth right over her. It was terrible, though she certainly didnt' care by then. I'll tell you another thing I can still see very clearly. The Germans used a horse-drawn vehicle for evacuating casualties. I don't know whether they were short of transport then, or what, but there's no question that we used to be able to see them coming up to the bridge at the far side of the town in a wagon with a big cross on it, drawn by two white horses; and we would watch them coming into the town and going out again. It was lovely to see.

McDougall: In your experience, the Germans honoured the Red Cross?

Thomson: There was no occasion in the war when I could say they didn't . . .

———————

Extracts from Letters from Lieut. R.L. McDougall to Mrs. R.I. McDougall, 512–15th Street East, North Vancouver, B.C., dated 20 December, 1943 to 6 February, 1944.

20 December, 1943 (Convalescent Camp, near Phillipville, North Africa) . . . Since I am temporarily in charge of 200 men in the depot, I now live

in great magnificence with a tent all to myself. At the moment I'm sharing
it with a couple of field-mice, but they don't take up much room. A few
minutes ago one of them made a sally from beneath my raincape, which is
draped over a box against the tent wall. He looked at me for a few seconds,
very intent, eyes brightly reflecting the lamplight, as if expecting me to say
something, then withdrew. I do have lamps now, you see, and can therefore
draw up my box to the little writing-table in the evenings. The Canadian
soldier has a genius for improvisation. The writing-table I speak of is
just a putting together of odds and ends of lumber and broken-up boxes
but is quite presentable. On its few square feet of surface are set out my
three lamps, which doesn't leave much room for writing. But the output
per lamp is low, and concentration is necessary. They run on coal-oil and
range in size from small to large, from simple to fairly complex. The first
is merely a round cigarette tin (Players) with a wick drawn through a hole
in the lid. The second is a half-pound tobacco tin with a broad wick raised
above the lid by an inch or two of tin wrapping. The third is or was a
hurricane lamp, and for want of a proper globe it wears crazily over its
flame a beer bottle from which the top and bottom have been chipped.
So the three of them throw their soft yellow light over this page, leaving
the rest of the tent in shadow. ... I remain ridiculously healthy in this
unhealthy land. My leg continues to improve. An hour ago I heard faintly
some snatches of Christmas carols — one of the padre's sing-songs in the
Canteen hut, I suppose. ... Five days to Christmas ...

26 December, 1943 Sunday night. Again my little table, my three lamps
lit and ranged before me. There is a sharp nip in the air this evening, which
is probably as close as this country comes to frost. My feet are incredibly
cold. There is coconut matting on the floor of the tent, but it is no proof
against the chill of the earth. ... Still, things might be much worse, will
be much worse I expect in Italy. Down below in the lines the men have
kindled their little fires, cheating the cold and dark of their tents with the
simple bounty of a fire, light and warmth and a friendly atmosphere. I was
out a moment ago to get a drink from the washstand at the end of the lines
and stood for a few minutes looking at the little city of lights below; and
then beyond to right and left where the lights from other camps broke the
darkness. You will gather that the blackout is not taken seriously here. ...
In the officers' lines there are fires sometimes too at night. If you walked
with me in the soft sandy soil up and down the rows of tents, you would see
a remarkable assortment of stoves made of tiles or petrol cans or biscuit

tins. On these the batmen heat water for shaving, or boil clothes, or brew tea. Around nine or ten at night the flames of one or two fires flicker against the brown canvas of the tents, and a circle of half-lighted figures stands grouped, talking, perhaps cooking snacks from parcels. . . . Unfortunately it was not possible for me to get to church on Christmas morning, but I sent you special thoughts. In the afternoon the officers served the men their Christmas dinner in the huge N.A.A.F.I. hut which is the recreation hall for the camp. There was a bottle of beer apiece, doubtless muscatel on the side, and turkey and pork with dressing, green peas, potatoes, mince pies and pudding. In the evening six of us went to a nearby hospital on an invitation to a nurses' dinner and dance. A very pleasant evening. . . . On Christmas Eve, Freddy McLean (Johnny's brother) and I borrowed the Colonel's jeep and went down to another hospital to visit some Seaforths, taking with us beer and cigarettes. That too was enjoyable. I came across two of my old platoon, and we had a good talk. The wards, large Nissen huts, were very cosy and Christmassy with their Christmas trees and decorations. . . . I expect to leave here soon and begin the long trek back to the unit . . .

5 January, 1944 (Avellino) We crossed Italy by cattle car yesterday, and I am now at a base reinforcement depot. Conditions get more primitive as I go up the line; no lamps here of any kind and only a meagre supply of candles, so that when daylight is gone we pack off to bed. . . . I am beginning to run into old friends from the regiment. Davie Fulton is just down the road, and I have also seen Frank Bonnell. Best reunion has been with Don Colquhoun, whom I have been with, off and on, since Currie Barracks days. He is having a rest near this camp, recovering from jaundice, which seems to be taking a great toll of the troops. . . . I am, by the way, still cold; I think I was cold when I last wrote you. Now we are really chilled by the wind coming off the snowy hills. Bare trees again, and a general wintry look, quite like January at home. . . .

16 January, 1944 (Lucera) Here in this little town there will be a check in my movement forward. From the last camp, as a matter of fact, I went right forward one day, but only as conducting officer for a draft going up the line and so had to return. But I did manage half an hour at the battalion, which is resting now at Ortona after a strenuous battle there, and it was wonderful to renew contacts with the few who remain from my time with the battalion in Sicily. There have been many changes, and promotions of course for those who have survived and done well, but it's amazing how the character of a unit, the feel of it, endures in the face of an almost constant turnover in personnel. Roy Durnford is still around, and Pipe-Major Esson, "Pay" Williamson and Borden Cameron, and I guess others that I didn't see. Colonel Thomson is on his way to England, and Colonel Creighton now has the command. Johnny McLean, who had No. 14 Platoon alongside of me, now has "D" Company. You will have heard that Tom Vance was killed in Ortona—a great shock to the family. Dick Wilson, Brigadier Wilson's son, is gone too, and that's a great loss. Ken Barton was seriously wounded some time ago; he's doing well, though, and still the same old Kenny, sitting up in bed when I saw him in hospital and smiling his quiet friendly smile and saying, "Well, you know, I've done the best I can and I've had a go at it, and now maybe I have a back-to-Canada." Davie Fulton is now with the regiment. . . . As for my present surroundings, they are pleasant. The Germans chose other roads to defend here, and so the tide of war flowed around the town. Our quarters are in a Bishop's palace, which is stripped of what glory it once possessed. We lay out our bedrolls in a series of inter-connecting rooms — wide-arched doorways, vaulted ceilings, and bare cement floors. Our place of eating is quite magnificent, formerly the residence of a wealthy Fascist, we are told: blue rooms and red rooms and fine paintings on the walls, and a huge dining room done in heavy gold and white ornamentation, yellow drapes and great crystal chandeliers. . . . Sentences to these staging camps are indefinite, but I think I'll be on my way again before the week is over. . . .

23 January, 1944 (near Fossecesia) . . . Another move and another Sunday. I am half lying on my bed with my feet thrust out through the raised tent flaps, and the warmth of the sun on my legs is luxury after the cold nights. From here I have glimpses of colour and movement—a green and white towel hung on the slant of a tent rope, stirring in a light breeze; an empty cigarette package, Capstan, blue, with edges white towards the sunlight; an assortment of fire-blackened water-tins; a green canvas bucket. Across this, from time to time, drifts a thin blue veil of woodsmoke from the next-door tent, where Lieut. Mitcheltree, an engineer officer who was at Chenoua Plage with me in North Africa, is experimenting with an improvised stove. I am getting a kink in my side. Don Colquhoun is complaining too. He is sitting on the ground outside, trying to write a letter on a Jerry-can balanced on his knees. A moment ago he was chuckling as he described to his mother the decoration we have sewn up this week.

It's called the Volunteer Medal, and it comes up with the rations, as the boys say — everybody gets one, even the men back home, though we who are over here wear it with a maple-leaf bar which is not for them. Spam and egg, we call it, Spam being an issue of tinned meat. We should get the 1939–43 Star when that comes out, and it will be more distinctive. . . . Last night Don and I went a few hundred yards along the way to a rickety village and had a late supper at an Italian house. From the road it was three short steps into a small shabby room, dimly lit, with dull brown walls and a worn wooden floor. Hanging from the ceiling were racks of dried peppers, and in the far wall was a large open fireplace in which was set a large black cauldron. The old woman of the house, *Nona*, no teeth and a face like a dried apricot, sat on a stool before the fire and prepared our macaroni. Grandpa hovered around and put out red wine on the white tablecloth. He told us he was 92 and seemed pleased about it. His eldest son is 65 and lives in America. We had a pleasant meal, joking with the old couple in awful Italian — spaghetti and tomatoes, a dish of hard-boiled eggs and meat patties. . . . Back at the tent, we lay in our beds and talked for a long time, as we often do, about the progress of the war and about what will have to be done afterwards by those who survive. . . .

30 January, 1944 (Fossecesia) . . . The days go by here and there's little to distinguish one from another. No call from the unit yet. In the mornings we are lazy and shave after breakfast since there are no parades to worry about. So when we have eaten we come back up to the tent and get a fire going under the blackened water-tin; and then we stand around and watch the shaving water heat. Fuel is quite a problem; everything loose has been gathered for quite a distance around. . . . For the remainder of the day we putter around — perhaps look in on the men's lines, inspect tents, rifles, talk a bit, do a little washing, read what little we can get our hands on. The other day we had a violent storm, with gale winds blowing in from the Adriatic and lashings of rain. The tent lines came alive as we scuttled around, miserably wet, pounding in tent pegs, weighting down flaps with stones and adjusting straining ropes. Then we stood about in a huddle inside, while the tent billowed and flapped around us. Soon there was a water-course you could sail toy boats in between our beds. . . . Last Wednesday night we saw a movie at a British billet near at hand. It was a war-film, and it depicted the Germans as barbaric fools, brutal and stupid. The boys who have fought in Ortona don't take kindly to that sort of nonsense. . . .

6 February, 1944 (near S. Vito) ... I have moved another step in the long journey forward. We are camped in a dismal spot, the remains of a brickyard, at the bottom of a deep draw not far from the sea. If it seems particularly dismal, the weather is to blame. The spirit wearies when the body lives in a state of perpetual cold and dampness. Eternal mud. We trail it into the tent, we get it on all our clothes, we eat and sleep in it. In the mornings the mess-tins we eat from are cold, and the porridge you put in one half is cold before you can eat it, and the bacon you put in the other quickly becomes a congealed lump of fat. Yet we joke and laugh, and it is always that miracle of laughter that saves the day. ... When we can, we go into S. Vito on the hill above. Here there are a few amenities, and we have become masters of the appreciation of amenities. The town has been fitted out as a rest and amusement centre for the troops, although the Germans are not far away as the shell flies. One can see a movie or an ENSA show on occasion, and there is a Beaver Club, which is sort of a men's canteen, and an Officers' Club. Don and I had dinner at the Club last night. The dining room is very plain, but the meal is presentable, and there are tablecloths and plates, and we drink our tea out of real China cups. It is a place of refuge in the evening: the lounge warm and well-lit, and the chairs comfortable. It is also our point of contact with people of the battalion, who come down here sometimes from Ortona. I expect to be called up soon, and with any luck will join Johnny's company. ... We sense the coming of a final phase, and we know that for others and for us it will be tough and may be long. "Strength to think brave thoughts and do brave deeds ... "

with love as ever,

Rob

163

III

The Hitler Line

All roads lead to Rome. For almost five months following the fall of Ortona the political and strategic necessity, as the Allies saw it, of the capture of Rome was to exert the pull of a vast magnet which shaped the tasks and movements of scores of formations and units, and amongst them, those of the Seaforths, who were to be drawn eventually across Italy from their Adriatic positions and into the very heart of the drive for Rome in a single day of ordeal on the 23rd of May. This influence in its turn rested on another influence whose roots went back to the time of the first Allied landings in Italy but whose immediate source was the decision of the British and American high command to launch operation "Overlord" against the Normandy coast early in June. In the face of the pull of the second influence Churchill's opinion of the importance of Rome had so far prevailed as to sanction the assault landing by the 6th U.S. Corps at Anzio on 22 January and the related attack by the 10th British Corps over the lower Garigliano River, south of Cassino, the week before. Had these measures been quickly successful the 1st Canadian Division would doubtless have continued to push strongly northward from Ortona towards the town of Pescara, which had been its original objective at the crossing of the Moro early in December.[1] General Montgomery's reluctance to accept the dispatch of 1st Canadian Corps Headquarters and the accompanying complement of the 5th Canadian Armoured Division to Italy late in October in part reflected the optimism of Allied commanders: there seemed little prospect of a role for an armoured division in the sector held by the Canadian infantry division on the Adriatic front.[2] But both the bridgehead at Anzio and the bridgehead over the Garigliano were contained (though at a cost to the Germans of the deployment of a second army in Italy), and Rome did not fall. The pull from east to west became measurable. The problem faced by General Alexander could be simply formulated: how to

---

[1]Pescara had in fact been the objective with which the Eighth Army had begun its assault across the Sangro River in the third week of November.

[2]For a full account of the complex series of events leading up to the establishment of a Canadian Corps in Italy, see Nicholson, *The Canadians*, p. 340 ff.

concentrate, without benefit of net increase to the strength of his armies, a maximum force at the entrance to the Liri valley below Cassino, and in the Anzio bridgehead, while containing a maximum number of Germans elsewhere in Italy, and especially in the Adriatic sector. Canadian troops were to play an important part in the meeting of both these requirements.

Such larger considerations would not of course have prevented the Canadian, Indian, British and New Zealand divisions which comprised 5th and 13th Corps in the east from driving on up the coast beyond the Ortona-Orsogna lateral if they had had the opportunity and the strength to do so. But the men of the companies and squadrons who were the fighting edge of these formations were by the end of the year tired and depleted and in no condition to maintain a hard-hitting offensive against the difficult odds of continuing bad weather and a stubborn enemy. Like most other units in their brigade and in the division, the Seaforths had fought their companies at something like 50% of their normal complement of 120 men during the action at The Gully and in Ortona; and the index of weariness had met the index of thinning ranks in the large number of cases of battle exhaustion which Major Anderson had evacuated through the R.A.P. in that period.[3] Men and officers needed rest in weeks rather than days of release from contact with the enemy — time to absorb reinforcements, time to put their house again in order. These ends the battalion achieved between the beginning of January and the end of April, in no small measure the result of the tact and skill, wonderfully suited to the circumstances, of Lt.-Col. A.J. Creighton, to whom Colonel Thomson turned over command of the Seaforths prior to his departure for England early in the new year to take senior officers' training. At the same time, however, the battalion in its corporate life felt strongly throughout the period the often irksome pressures of the pull of the general plan.

Perhaps the most trying and certainly the most pervasive task assigned to Seaforths in these first months of 1944 was the task of patrolling. The task of putting the Seaforth house in order, which was begun in Ortona almost as soon as the last Germans left the town on the 28th of December, was a task which was accepted as inevitable by the seasoned men of the

---

[3]The term "battle exhaustion" covered more than the term "shell shock", familiar to veterans of World War I. It recognized the possibility of a man's fighting capabilities being destroyed completely for a time, sometimes permanently, without his having suffered a scratch or even a near miss from a shell, but simply from prolonged exposure to the holocaust of battle.

battalion, though without relish, even with a certain amount of good-natured grumbling. By the end of the first week in January the companies were training "as per syllabus" and officers and N.C.Os. were studying, with the help of a cloth model of Ortona set up by the Intelligence Section at BHQ, the techniques of street fighting.[4] They had been paraded by the Q.M. for kit deficiencies, by the M.O. for skin inspection and inoculation, by the Paymaster for battalion muster and pay adjustments; they had been paraded for baths and for disinfestation of their clothing. They were being inspected daily by their platoon and company commanders, frequently by their C.O., and on the 5th of January they had been required to look their best on the occasion of a visit to the area by their brigade, divisional and corps commanders. Only the Padre's church parades, it seemed, were voluntary, and these, perhaps as much for affection's sake as for love of the Lord, were well attended. If all this was not quite the soldier's idea of a rest, it was at least a token of peaceful days, despite the heavy shelling of Ortona by long-range guns which persisted throughout the Seaforths' stay. And there were other compensations: the real pleasure of restoring some sort of order to the chaos of a broken town and of scrounging a few creature comforts for the furnishings of billets; poker and bridge games in the evenings, perhaps a movie after the town's theatre had been cleared of debris; and the beginnings of a programme of forty-eight hour leaves to San Vito, and, later, of week-long leaves to Bari far to the south. It was a pleasure, too, to hear the Pipe Band play in the company areas after supper, or in the town square, and, in another mood, to go on work parties to the Church of Santa Maria to help prepare a cemetery there for Seaforths who had fallen since the action at the Moro. But when the cemetery was dedicated in an impressive ceremony on the 16th, the period of rest was in any event about over. On the 19th the Seaforths moved north and west of Ortona three miles to take over positions on the southern fold of the valley of the Ricchio River. And it was here that the new regime began whose central fact was the night patrol. It was a regime which was to be continued, with only brief abatements, for the next three months — first in the coastal sector, then in two positions farther inland,

---

[4]The street battle for Ortona had attracted considerable attention and visitors to the Seaforths' BHQ were numerous in the first weeks of January. Most welcome amongst these were Seaforth officers posted elsewhere in the Italian theatre of operations, who were almost certain to show up on these occasions. The V.I.P. for 5 January was the G.O.C. 5th British Corps, Lt.-Gen. C.W. Allfrey.

north of the Ortona-Orsogna lateral and opposite the German-held town of Crecchio.

The situation which had by this time developed on the Eighth Army front was, for reasons already noted, one of largely static warfare. Two attacks in brigade strength were made against the Germans in January, but neither seems to have been launched with any serious intention of disrupting the equilibrium of the line. The first was made on the 17th of January by the 11th Brigade, the lorried infantry of the newly arrived 5th Canadian Armoured Division, and its declared intention was to move the Canadian line on its right flank over the ridge beyond the Ricchio to the south bank of the Arielli River. A second intention, not included in official orders, was to give the brigade battle experience. Two weeks later, on the 30th of January, the 1st Brigade put in another attack, again designed to secure high ground dominating the Arielli but this time on the left flank up the Villa Grande-Tollo road. Again, however, there was a second intention undeclared: to hold by pressure as many German troops as possible in the Adriatic sector and so prevent their transfer to the west during the crucial days of the Fifth Army's battles at Anzio and the Garigliano.[5] Had the transfers already been made, of course, and the German defences proved soft, the Canadians would undoubtedly have pushed to the Arielli, and perhaps beyond. But Heidrich's paratroopers, the tough defenders of The Gully and Ortona, were defenders still, and only minor redispositions of forces had been made in the sector as a whole. Both Canadian attacks failed, with heavy losses.[6] The month of January, therefore, saw the emergence of the concept of an "Adriatic barricade".[7] A good deal of the energies of staff officers at Canadian headquarters was now turned to

---

[5]The undisclosed intention in this case may have had a place alongside the undisclosed intention I have cited above in the case of the 11th Brigade; the notion of the "holding action" must have been firmly implanted in the minds of Canadian commanders from early in January. The notion was made explicit in a 5th Corps directive of 23 January, which read: "During the crux of the fighting on Fifth Army front, additional steps are to be taken to stop the enemy reinforcing from this side." (Quoted in Nicholson, *The Canadians*, p. 376.)

[6]Seaforths scoffed, and are still inclined to scoff, at the poor showing made by the 11th Brigade, recalling their cockiness as they passed through Ortona on 13 January, their spanking new equipment and blancoed webbing. Undoubtedly these regiments suffered for their greenness; but it is worth noting that the seasoned 1st Brigade did not fare much better than the 11th when it attacked later that month under similar conditions.

[7]The phrase appears in C.M.H.Q. Report No. 178, p. 19 (mimeographed), and is taken up by Nicholson in *The Canadians*, p. 379.

167

offsetting the ill effects which categoric notions of static warfare are likely to produce in the mind of the soldier.

"Recce" patrols are small and are designed to secure information without stirring up trouble. "Standing" patrols are larger and are designed to protect by means of ambush. "Fighting" patrols are larger also and are designed for penetration and attack. But for all patrols there is an over-riding purpose: to assert one's superiority over one's enemy in disputed territory and to make him nervous. The Seaforths were quite aware of this larger purpose, though the knowledge did not appreciably lighten the burden of patrolling that fell on individual shoulders. And burden it was for most, a kind of awful duty roster on which an officer, an N.C.O., a private might expect to find his name at least once and perhaps even twice a week. To accept the duty and discharge it honestly took courage and determination of a high order.

So night after wintry night Seaforths prowled the valley of the Ricchio, and later the valley of the Arielli, moving in darkness or, as it might be, by the eerie half-light of a moon, seeing trees and bushes grow to phantom shapes in the mind's eye, bodies strained and pressed against God knows what sudden and fearful eruption of the silence in the explosion of a mine or boobytrap or in a searing burst of fire. By day many of them lay up in their company areas in slit trenches or in houses on forward slopes exposed to enemy view. The demand was at first, with special urgency, for a German prisoner as a check on the timing of the expected transfer to the eastern front of the 1st Parachute Division — a division always sent for, it was said, when the going was tough. But a prisoner snatched from a weapon-pit was a good bag at any time, destructive to enemy morale, as indeed was any form of patrol activity that kept the Germans watchful. Maps and aerial photographs blossomed with code-names identifying nameless fords, junctions and farmhouses: "Daisy", "Cornflower", "Buttercup", "Cow", "Clean", "Call", "Crump", "Pan", "Pal", and "Pot"; and to and from these positions Seaforths moved in a seemingly endless round of tasks. On the 2nd of February Lieut. V.C. Moore led a patrol across the Ricchio to investigate a suspected enemy position on the far slope. On the way out he observed a 12-man German patrol making its way to a ford in the river. His own patrol reached its objective, was fired on by rifles and Schmeiser machine pistol, withdrew, heard voices in a field on the way back, was fired on by two enemy machine guns, returned to "C" Company lines. On the 4th of February Lieut. S. Lynch led a fighting patrol of "A"

Company to "Cornflower", killed one German in an observation post there, and wounded and brought back to the Seaforth R.A.P. a second who was later identified as a member of 7th Company, 2nd Battalion, 3rd Parachute Regiment. This was the first prisoner taken in more than two weeks and brought congratulations from the brigadier and authorization for an issue of rum.[8] On the 5th of February Lieut. O.H. Mace of "B" Company reported that a "recce" patrol which he had taken to a re-entrant on the far side of the river had heard voices and the sound of digging to their front, but finding the pathways leading to the area strewn with loose bamboo canes they had been unable to go farther without giving away their position. On the 7th of February a patrol from "A" Company, this time sent out by day, came upon a slit trench west of "Cornflower" occupied by two Germans. The patrol leader, Lieut. J.A. Charters, opened fire, killing the two Germans, while the remainder of the patrol threw grenades into a nearby dugout, which was then visited by German stretcher-bearers while the Seaforths withdrew in good order.[9] That night a "D" Company fighting patrol, in search of another prisoner, went out under the protection of an artillery concentration available to them on the firing of red and green flares if they were in serious trouble on their objective. Two hours later "C" Company reported a red followed by a green flare to the left of their positions, and the artillery fire was brought down. At one o'clock in the morning "D" Company's patrol returned intact. They had reached their objective, they said, and had engaged in a spirited fire-fight with the enemy, though without successful outcome in the taking of a prisoner. They had fired no flares. On the 8th of February a patrol from "C" Company investigated a position near "Daisy", where they made no contact with the enemy but found a dummy dressed in a British uniform which they believed to be booby-trapped by means

---

[8] Also, eventually, an M.C. for Lieut. Lynch for his aggressive action on this occasion and his excellent control of a difficult situation in which one of his own men was killed and a second wounded. Though much was made of the identification of the German prisoner, and of a subsequent identification made by a Carleton and York patrol on the 20th of February which established the fact that the 1st Parachute Division had been relieved, it is worth noting that the 3rd Battalion, 1st Parachute Regiment, had been identified in action on the Fifth Army front as early as 31 January. The 1st Parachute Division was not the type of division that was split up for long. The "take-a-prisoner" instruction was to an extent, undoubtedly, a device, though of course a necessary one.

[9] This patrol was sent out as a "recce" patrol (Seaforth W.D., 7 Feb., 1944), an interesting example of a proper flexibility in patrol command. Lieut. Charters was later awarded a Mentioned in Dispatches for his excellent leadership in patrolling.

of a wire attached to the dummy's arms. Thus a few (by no means all) of the patrol entries in the Seaforth War Diary for the first week of February. Later, for the weeks in the line opposite Crecchio in March and April, the names of the people and the places change, but the nature of the ground and the tasks remains essentially the same.

Though the cost to the Seaforths of this period of static warfare was not great, it was nonetheless appreciable. Good men were killed on patrol, amongst them a promising officer, Lieut. M.E. Tucker, in an ambush on the far side of the Arielli on the night of 25/26 March. Three men were killed and several wounded, including one officer, in an abortive company raid against German positions on the extreme coastal flank on the night of the 13th of February.[10] Shelling and mortaring, moreover, was persistent in all three sectors occupied by the Seaforths during these months, and the harassment took its toll. And the more violent forms of aggression against enemy outposts practised by the Seaforths could of course be turned against them: two men were taken from an "A" Company forward observation post under cover of an enemy stonk on the night of 25 January, and on the evening of 16 February, just prior to the battalion's final departure from the Arielli-Ricchio front, six men were carried off in a fierce German raid on a forward platoon of "C" Company. Yet on the whole the Seaforths unquestionably held the upper hand, and knew it, and especially so in the inland positions after the end of February when the departure of the 1st Parachute Division's remaining regiments to join the 51st Mountain Corps at Cassino left the German positions thinly manned by inferior troops of the 305th Division. As March wore on into April, the credit side could be easily tallied. There had been time for continuation of the work of reorganization begun in Ortona, time in this new type of warfare for officers and men to learn something of the nature and importance of the counter-attack role, to which until now they had given little attention, and time for a full programme of leave. There had been time also for the rounding out of the life of the battalion again in a variety of traditional and ceremonial occasions: the annual Burns Supper, observed by W.Os. and Sergeants on 26 January;[11] the presentation on 2 March by the commander

---

[10]The attack was called "Bronco" and was assigned to "D" Company. It was not to be pursued in the face of heavy losses, and when the first stages failed it was called off.

[11]As a record of names: Pipe-Major Esson proposed "The Immortal Memory"; C.Q.M.S. W.M. Marshall, "Our Guests"; C.Q.M.S. James Aitken, "The Regiment"; C.S.M. 'Jock' Gibson, "Our Fallen Comrades"; and C.Q.M.S. C.A. Jones, "The Lasses". Capt.

of the Eighth Army, General Sir Oliver Leese, of decorations recently awarded to members of the battalion; the dispatch in the third week in February of a platoon of "A" Company, with the Pipe Band, for a tour of duty as Honour Guard at Corps Headquarters.[12] On the evening of 20 April the 10th Indian Division began to relieve the 1st Canadian Division on the Adriatic front. Seaforth morale was good and the standard of training high.

On 12 May, three weeks after they had loaded their R.C.Vs. at Villa Jubatti just south of the Ortona-Orsogna lateral for the trip out of the line, the Seaforths were camped, with other units of the division, far to the west and south at Sant' Agata, near Caserta. They had travelled perhaps 150 miles in the interim, but they had done a good deal else besides travel. On the eve of the division's departure from the Adriatic front General Vokes had made it clear to his commanders that their troops were not going out for a rest. Discipline might well have become lax in the static warfare in which the units had been engaged (Seaforth eyebrows went up) and there were in any event two forms of training which it had been impossible for them to carry out during the winter months and which must now be considered mandatory: the men must be toughened up physically, and they must be thoroughly instructed in the techniques of infantry co-operation with tanks.[13] Arrived in their first training area five miles south of Campobasso on the 25th of April, the Seaforths had therefore begun, after two days' confinement to sodden tents by torrential rains, a period of vigorous activity in which route marches had played a prominent part.[14] Then on the 8th of May they had moved east again 30 miles to a second training area south of Lucera on the fringe of the Foggia plains. Here for

---

D.B. Cameron and Sgt. T.G. Gormley, two of the best caterers, I should think, in the Canadian Army, laid on an excellent dinner for the occasion.

[12]This was at Rocca San Giovanni, and the headquarters was that of 1st Canadian Corps, which relieved Headquarters 5th (British) Corps from 1 February to 7 March.

[13]Some Seaforths had of course had excellent schooling in co-operation with tanks under the most exacting of conditions. But by this time new members of the battalion far outnumbered the old — and of these, it must be said, few had received anything like the intensive training which members of the original battalion had had before they left England in 1943.

[14]The area was a familiar stamping ground for some: Vinciaturo crossroads, Cercemaggiore, above all Baranello, now peaceful in the lush green countryside; and though Baranello was placed out-of-bounds, the C.O.'s orders inevitably filled up quickly with cases of unauthorized visits to the town.

three days they had worked intensively with squadrons of the North Irish Horse of the 25th (British) Tank Brigade. They had learned the ways of tanks, observed their fire-power, inspected the new Churchills with which the North Irish were equipped, and had above all laid the foundations for practical and friendly associations which the compact of a bloody battle would fuse and strengthen into a lasting tie before the month was over. Early on the 12th, as fit as any unit could be for what the official army history was later to call perhaps the most spectacular operation of the entire Italian campaign,[15] they had set out for Sant' Agata. That day, as the Seaforths travelled through Troia and Benevento, thence to the Appian Way, then north through Airola and Moiana, the Allied offensive up the Liri valley was already in its first crucial stages.

The Liri valley is really the valley of several rivers whose names change confusingly as they merge in their southward flow to join what is finally the Garigliano in its course eastward from the mouth of the valley to the Gulf of Gaeta. From the head of the valley, where the low crest of a watershed marks the beginning of the fall of the land north towards Rome, the Sacco River establishes the main line of the water-course south towards Cassino, passing in its way through rolling country dominated to the east by the rugged barrier of the Apennines and to the west by the lower contours of the Aurunci and Ausoni Mountains. Fifteen miles above Cassino, its bed by this time shifted to the western limits of the valley floor, the river is joined from the east by its main tributary, the Liri, whose name it now assumes. Its flow is then south again to a point about opposite Cassino, where, as it swings off to the sea around the end of the Aurunci Mountains, it meets the heavy waters of the Rapido-Gari system traversing the valley mouth from the east. It was in the lower reaches of the Liri defile, over the quite flat country which lies south of the junction of the Liri and the Sacco, that the most bitter battles of these weeks were fought.

The disposition of Allied and German forces across the front of this southern approach to Rome holds few surprises. Despite the establishment by the Eighth Army of an elaborate cover plan designed to suggest the imminence of an assault landing 30 miles north of Rome, the Germans remained reasonably certain that the Allies would launch a major offensive up the Liri valley sometime in May.[16] Reserves held well to the rear where

[15]Nicholson, *The Canadians*, p. 386.
[16]The essence of the cover plan was the initiation of a carefully thought-out programme of signals traffic which the Germans might be expected to intercept and which would show

they could be shifted easily to meet emergencies in either the Anzio or the Cassino sector, they had assigned the defence of the southern front to two corps, comprising four divisions and their supporting arms. The 14th Panzer Corps was to hold the right flank from the line of the Liri River to the sea, while the 51st Mountain Corps, with the hard-hitting 1st Parachute Division under command, was made responsible for the main approaches to the valley on the left, including the key area of the town of Cassino and the monastery high on the hill above. Two lines of carefully prepared defences would ensure efficient use of the relatively small number of troops which made up the strength of the four divisions committed. The first of these, called the Gustav Line, followed the north banks of the Rapido-Gari-Garigliano system west from Cassino, its chief natural asset the deep and fast-flowing water to its front which was an effective barrier to tanks and an obstacle even to infantry. The second, though it shared the same hinge as the Gustav Line in the mountains behind Cassino, struck off at an angle which carried it across the neck of the valley seven miles to the rear. It was known most commonly as the Hitler Line, and in the scale of its fortifications it was a kind of miniature West Wall, complete with concrete bunkers, covered trenches, armoured anti-tank gun turrets and encased weapon-pits.[17] On the other side of the picture, ranged against the Germans and vastly superior to them in numbers, was the most dense concentration of Allied troops ever mustered in the Italian campaign. In

---

false locations for a variety of formations and an intention to launch soon a major assault landing. The whole operation was primarily the responsibility of the 1st Canadian Corps, and the 1st Canadian Division, known to the Germans as an experienced assault force, had an important place in the theoretical manoeuvrings involved. The net effect of the plan does not seem to have been very great. Camouflage precautions do not appear to have prevented the Germans from remaining aware that the Allies were marshalling a large force south of the Gari and Rapido Rivers. But the plan may have led them to miscalculate the date of the Allied attack in the south (they were still disposing their troops there on 11 May) and it certainly left them with a confused picture of the Eighth Army's order of battle. See Nicholson, *The Canadians*, p. 391 ff.

[17]Work on the Hitler Line over the preceding months had in fact been under the supervision of the "Organization Todt", whose experts earlier in the war had been the chief architects of the famous West Wall defences (Nicholson, *The Canadians*, p. 395). The line had been named "Führer Riegel" in December, 1943; but on 23 January, when the Anzio landings temporarily at any rate made it a bad risk, it was re-named on Hitler's orders "Senger Riegel" after the commander of the 14th Panzer Corps (*ibid.*). Some fifty miles behind the Hitler Line, beyond the head of the Liri valley and the Anzio positions, a third line, the "Caesar Line" was projected, but much of it remained uncompleted at the time of the Allied break-through in late May and early June.

the narrow coastal sector were two divisions of the 2nd U.S. Corps, and to their right, facing the Aurunci Mountains, four Moroccan and Algerian divisions of the French Expeditionary Corps. These left-flank formations were under the command of the Fifth Army. The remainder of the line east to Cassino, a distance of about seven miles, held the Eighth Army's punch for the impending attack: on the left, squared up to the lower stretches of the Gari and Rapido Rivers, the 13th (British) Corps, consisting of four divisions, with the two divisions and one tank brigade of the 1st Canadian Corps immediately behind it as a reserve striking force; on the right, facing Cassino and the mountains beyond, two divisions of the 2nd Polish Corps. In all, by the end of the first week in May, eight Allied divisions and the equivalent of at least three additional brigades stood ready to be crammed into the mouth of the Liri valley. Control of traffic under these conditions would be almost as much of a problem as the winning of the fire-fight against the Germans.

On 14 May Lt.-Col. S.W. Thomson, newly returned from England, took over command of the Seaforths from Lt.-Col. A.J. Creighton, who was to leave for Canada to assume the important post of Director of Military Training in Ottawa. By the evening of the next day the battalion was on three hours' notice to move, and on the 16th it began jockeying its way forward towards its position in the line. It was now D-day plus five, and the first stages of the Allied offensive had been completed. The results, as might be expected, were less than had been hoped for, but the tide of battle was on the whole running favourably for the Eighth Army. The 8th (Indian) Division and the 4th (British) Division, given the task of making the main breach in the Gustav Line, had crossed the Gari River late on the night of the 11th and in the forty-eight hours of stiff fighting which had ensued had established a bridgehead on the far side nourished by two substantial Bailey bridges. The F.E.C. had in the meantime begun its drive into the Aurunci Mountains on the left, initially, as in the case of 13 Corps, against stubborn resistance. On the right, Polish troops had fought their way desperately on the 12th to within a stone's throw of the monastery at Cassino but had in the end been driven back. The situation in the centre had improved, however, and with the initial bridgehead extended three miles to the Cassino-Pignataro lateral by the 15th, General Leese had ordered the 78th (British) Division to pass through the two assaulting divisions at their common boundary and veer right in a drive at maximum speed for the town of Aquino at the eastern end of the Hitler Line. Late on the 15th, in accordance with plans already made, he committed the 1st Canadian Corps on the left flank of the 13th Corps and in immediate support of the advances being made in the western sector of the valley by the 8th (Indian) Division. The 1st Brigade was in action between Pignataro and the Liri River on the morning of the 16th, and the 3rd Brigade was soon after engaged on its right.

Ten miles to the rear the Seaforths and the 2nd Brigade awaited their turn, their movements forward jerky and uncertain in the enormous flow of traffic pouring into the mouth of the valley. Highway No. 6, which the battalion convoy had followed that day to Mignano, was the main artery leading to Cassino, and eventually to Rome, and it was jammed with every kind of vehicle imaginable. Now, west and north of Mignano on secondary roads, the Seaforth companies were hard put to it to find stopping places within this thick part of the tail of eight divisions and their supporting arms. Bivouacs of other troops, gun positions, vehicle parks and scattered caches of ammunition, petrol and supplies blanketed the area, the whole camouflaged as best it could be, but mercifully protected by air cover supplied by the 2000 Allied planes flying sorties for the offensive and by a pall of dust and smoke which limited observation from Monte Cassino, at this time still in German hands. On the 17th, after a short move forward by T.C.Vs., the Seaforths marched eight miles across country to occupy positions on high ground to the left of Pignataro. The role reserved for them in the developing battle was not yet clear. To their left, in the mountains west of the Liri River, units of the F.E.C. were making excellent progress and were well abreast of the most advanced elements of the Eighth Army. To their front and right every effort was being made to rush the Hitler Line and breach it, most hopefully at Aquino and along the axis of Highway No. 6, before the Germans had a chance to settle in their new positions. Much would depend on the degree of success achieved within the next forty-eight hours. That night the battalion suffered its first casualties when 12 German planes bombed the area under cover of darkness.

By the end of the forty-eight hours it was clear that the Hitler Line had not been breached and would not be breached without a regrouping of Eighth Army forces and a set-piece attack. Both brigades, the 1st on the left and the 3rd on the right, had pushed forward with great determination on the 18th and 19th, and both had had men within sight of the low bands of wire and the minefields that were the preliminaries to the line itself. But here they had been subjected to punishing fire and had been forced to stop. The 78th Division had done no better at Aquino, though their rapid convergence on Highway No. 6 had at least resulted in the occupation by units of the 4th Division of the town of Cassino and the embattled monastery, from which the paratroopers were withdrawn by Kesselring's express order (they were still reluctant to go) on the night of the 18th. New orders were therefore quickly issued by Eighth Army Headquarters: the 1st Canadian Corps would punch a hole in the Hitler Line 2000 yards wide between Pontecorvo on the left side of the valley and a point just short of Aquino on the right where a water-course called the Forme d'Aquino crossed the German defences; they would then exploit their penetration in a rolling attack to the town of Ceprano ten miles beyond. The 78th Division and the 2nd Polish Corps would in the meantime exert pressure on the Aquino flank, while the French Expeditionary Corps in the mountains to the west would drive forward five miles to the town of Pico and there turn towards the east in an attempt to trap the enemy forces being driven back on Ceprano. The breakout of the VI (U.S.) Corps from the Anzio bridgehead would be timed to coincide with this renewed offensive.

Between the 19th and the 23rd of May, which was the date set eventually for the Canadian attack on the Hitler Line, the Seaforths' part in the general plan was subject to a number of confusing changes — most of them, it should be said, the result of commendable last-minute attempts by General Burns and General Vokes to find some way of turning the Hitler Line without resort to a set-piece attack whose cost in casualties, they well knew, would be high. Late on the afternoon of the 19th the battalion had moved forward on the left flank of the divisional sector, prepared to advance through the 48th Highlanders' positions on short notice in an attack which would take them first to a group of barrack buildings north of Pontecorvo, then to the right in a sweep designed to loosen the main German defences from the rear. By nightfall, however, the line had been judged too strong for such bold measures, and the Seaforths were moved back in darkness from the 1st Brigade front. At two o'clock the following day, the 20th, Colonel Thomson received orders to relieve the Carleton and York Regiment on the right flank of the divisional sector, but at six o'clock the order was cancelled and replaced by a more general instruction for an attack by the 2nd Brigade at a point between the 1st and the 3rd, with the Seaforths entering the battle on the left and the Patricias on the right. Then on the 21st, when the front for the proposed attack was enlarged to make room for two brigades up rather than one as before, Seaforth responsibilities were restricted and shifted slightly to the right as the Carleton and Yorks assumed an attacking role on their left.[18] These changes, moreover, had scarcely been absorbed when the picture was further complicated by an important alternative plan. Impressed by the apparent softness of the line in the vicinity of Pontecorvo, where reconnaissance troops of the 4th Princess Louise Dragoon Guards serving with the 48th Highlanders had identified members of the inferior 44th Ersatz Battalion in action, General Vokes had laid on a 1st Brigade attack for the 22nd, through which, if it were successful, he would pass the Seaforths and the remaining units of the 2nd Brigade. Throughout the whole of that day, therefore, on the eve of the main battle, Colonel Thomson was forced to hold the battalion well back from its starting position, occupied at the time by the West Nova Scotia Regiment, in a state of uncertainty as to its final commitments. News that the 1st Brigade's attack at Pontecorvo had not been successful reached BHQ at 4 p.m. on the 22nd. The Seaforths closed quickly with the Hitler Line and settled down to a tense night of waiting.

Four o'clock reveille and a cold breakfast finished by four-thirty, the leading companies moved to their start-lines, where liaison with their tanks began at five. Less than a mile in front of them, hidden at the moment by belts of woodland and a light morning mist, lay the Pontecorvo-Aquino lateral which they must reach, then put behind them in a further advance after an hour's pause at the road for re-grouping. At three minutes to six the open-throated roar of Allied artillery began, some 400 guns firing to the Seaforths' immediate front, partly barrage lifting at a rate of 100 yards in five minutes, partly counter-battery fire on which the men pinned the few flickering hopes they had for an easy advance. At six o'clock "A" and "D" Company, left and right respectively, moved off, followed closely by "B" and "C", each pair of companies supported by a squadron of the North Irish Horse.

Thereafter, no accounting can be given of the actions of companies or platoons, squadrons or troops. Enemy fire from guns and mortars, more intense than anything the battalion had known, worse by far than the fire in front of Ortona, enveloped the attacking formations, shattering their ranks

---

[18]The change from a one-brigade to a two-brigade assault was made on the advice of General Leese, who was dissatisfied with the original Canadian plan. But the additional brigade, which was to be the 3rd, would have only one battalion up. The West Nova Scotia Regiment would support the Carleton and Yorks, and the Royal 22me would be held in divisional reserve.

and dispersing their force. Tanks of the North Irish emerging from the cover of the woods were knocked out like clay figures in a shooting gallery, six within minutes, and others in rapid succession as they tried desperately to push forward with the infantry. Two company commanders, Major J.F. McLean of "A" Company and Captain J.J. Conway of "C" Company,[19] were early casualties in the battle, and as the toll of platoon officers and N.C.Os. mounted at an alarming rate the advance became almost wholly a matter of the initiative of individual survivors who in woods and grainfields blasted with fire and shrouded in smoke kept their wills bent on the lateral road and pressed on towards it by gathering about them whatever handfuls of men they could muster. Shortly after eight-thirty Major J.C. Allan of "B" Company reported Seaforths astride the road. With him were Lieutenants T.E. Wolley and W.R. Artindale, and about 100 Seaforths of all companies. Major L.M. McBride of "D" Company had been seriously wounded.[20] Major Allan thought that the force he now commanded could hold its positions if it could be given protection from enemy tanks. Few P.I.A.Ts. had survived the advance into the main line of defences, and ammunition was running low. Could support be sent immediately? But with the minefields still not breached and German 75 mm. guns still in action in well-concealed turrets on the flanks, neither the tanks of the North Irish nor the guns of the 90th Anti-Tank Regiment could be got forward quickly to answer the call. Back at the farm building which was BHQ, now clogged with streams of wounded pouring into the R.A.P. but fortunately untouched by the shellfire which fell thickly around it, Colonel Thomson tried by every means possible to raise the help needed. Anxious men came and went in an endless round of errands. The Patricias on the right, stopped at the wire or very little beyond, had been cut up beyond immediate repair, and the Edmontons, prematurely committed in support, had been caught in the same murderous trap as the Patricias. There were no reserves. As morning gave way to afternoon a composite force of North Irish tanks, the remnants of two squadrons, was organized and sent to the lateral road, but it did not reach the Seaforths' positions.[21] Carrying

---

[19]Command of "A" Company passed to C.S.M. F.D. McMullen, who was subsequently wounded and taken prisoner. Command of "C" Company passed to C.S.M. J. McP. Duddle. C.S.M. Duddle was awarded the D.C.M. for his outstanding contribution to the day's action.

[20]Lieut. Wooley, who had been wounded at the start-line, was sent back. Major McBride and Lieut. Artindale were both taken prisoner later in the day.

[21]This composite force, under the command of Capt. C.M. Thomas, reported later in the

parties for ammunition disappeared into the inferno between BHQ and the objective and were not heard from again. For almost eight hours wireless communication had been maintained intermittently with Major Allan, but at four-thirty contact failed completely. Fifteen minutes later (so it was learned when the story was told) the positions were overrun by German armour, which shot up the ditches along the road, killing and wounding many Seaforths and taking the remainder prisoner.[22] Desperately in need of first-hand information, Colonel Thomson had by this time turned over the task of consolidating the rear positions of the battalion to the 2 i/c, Major D.M. Clark, and had gone forward himself to the objective. Finding it unoccupied, he returned to BHQ. As evening drew in, such strength as remained to the battalion was grouped close to the start-lines from which the companies had begun their attack twelve hours before. In the midst of great hurt and frustration, this much only was clear; the Hitler Line was broken; the Germans had gone.

The ordeal of the 23rd of May, 1944, was thus for the Seaforths a strange mixture of triumph and defeat. The Germans had indeed gone, urged partly on their way, undoubtedly, by the dogged stand of the battalion on its objective throughout the greater part of the day, but more conclusively by the success of the 3rd Brigade, whose attack on the left had put all three of its battalions beyond the lateral road by the time Colonel Thomson reached the Seaforths' objective to find it unoccupied. The placing of fresh squadrons of the 12th (Three Rivers) Armoured Regiment under command of the 3rd Brigade that afternoon had provided the stiffening necessary to keep open the hole which the Carleton and Yorks and their British tanks had been able to make in the line during the morning and through which the West Novas and the Royal 22me had subsequently driven almost a mile to report "Caporetto", which was the code name for the division's final objective in the attack. While the Seaforths, therefore, experienced the bitter taste of failure, German transport, screened by low rain clouds and failing light, was

---

afternoon (time unspecified) that it had reached the objective, "but was unable to find any trace of the Seaforths." The group was working under difficult conditions and from a mosaic aerial photograph, and it may have been deflected to the right of its advance. It was a valiant attempt to bring help, and the North Irish paid dearly for it. Ten tanks were lost in the action. See *The North Irish Horse Battle Report: North Africa and Italy* (Belfast: W. & G. Baird, 1946) p. 34.

[22]Major Allan escaped capture by playing dead in the ditch. He was wounded but returned safely to BHQ that evening. For the gallantry and determination he had shown during the crucial hours of the battle he was awarded the D.S.O.

already streaming north, breaking first from the weaker Pontecorvo end of the line but beginning also their inevitable withdrawal from the mountain hinge at Aquino and Highway No. 6, where the Polish and 78th British divisions had maintained pressure throughout the day. Deeper in enemy territory the breakout from the Anzio bridgehead had achieved complete surprise, and in the Ausoni Mountains to the west the F.E.C. was far enough forward to constitute a decisive threat to the Germans' right flank in the Liri valley.[23] In the valley itself the 5th Canadian and the 6th British divisions, both armoured, were ready momentarily to roll through the breaches in the Hitler Line in pursuit of a badly damaged and demoralized foe. Of the estimated 800-odd defenders opposite the Canadians on the 23rd all but a handful had been either killed, wounded or taken prisoner.[24] Within this larger picture the loss of the greater part of the fighting strength of a brigade, the 2nd, could be counted as a drastic but acceptable price to pay for success. The Seaforths, the Edmontons and the Patricias had had to face the stiffer end of the Hitler Line defences, and in so doing had had to cope again, as the units of the 3rd Brigade had not, with the skilful soldiering and fanatical spirit of Heidrich's 1st Division paratroopers.[25] That was the fortune of war. Total Canadian casualties in the day's action numbered 879 all ranks, of which almost two-thirds were suffered by the 2nd Brigade. The Seaforths lost 215 men: 3 officers and 49 other ranks killed; 7 officers and 102 other ranks wounded; and 2 officers and 52 other ranks taken

---

[23]The decisive influence of the advance of the F.E.C. was later corroborated by Maj.-Gen. Fritz Wentzell, Chief of Staff, Tenth Army: "As seen by the German staff, the French Expeditionary Corps made the decisive contribution to the breakthrough in the Gustav Line and the Senger position (Hitler Line). This statement is not an attempt to evaluate the capacities and performances of the French troops, for the French Expeditionary Corps attacked the weakest part of the German defensive front." Quoted in C.M.H.Q. Report No. 179, p. 65 (mimeographed). General Wentzell noted also, of course, that the breakthrough at Anzio prevented the transfer of a much-needed reserve division to the Cassino front.

[24]The figure of 800 is for infantry only, of which the Germans were conspicuously short at this time. See Nicholson, *The Canadians*, p. 416.

[25]General Heidrich's division had originally faced the Poles at Cassino, and, a little later, 13 Corps at Aquino; but a shift of all German troops 300 metres to the southwest on the night of 22/23 May had put a company of II/3 Parachute Regiment into a position facing the extreme right of the Canadian front (C.M.H.Q. Report No. 179, p. 62, mimeographed).

prisoner.[26] It was by long odds the battalion's most costly day in World War II.[27]

The postlude to the 23rd of May was a small but brisk and completely successful engagement on the 31st which did much to restore the fighting spirit of the Seaforths. This action took place some twenty miles up the valley from the Hitler Line at a Y-junction on the far side of Frosinone where an important secondary road, later to become the axis for 13 Corps, strikes northeast from Highway No. 6 towards the towns of Alatri and Subiaco in the hills. On the 24th the battalion had got on with the grim work of collecting and burying the dead, and on the 25th, while the 5th Canadian Division fought its way across the Melfa River six miles ahead, and on towards Ceprano, the rifle companies were reorganized and brought up to strength following the arrival at BHQ that morning of reinforcements numbering 8 officers and 208 other ranks. On the morning of the 26th Seaforths attended a dedication service at a hastily constructed brigade cemetery which was a cemetery also, in tribute to comradeship, for men of the North Irish

---

[26]These figures, which differ slightly from totals compiled from C.M.H.Q. Casualty Cards dated 23 May, include what are probably delayed returns of 4 other ranks D.O.W. and 15 other ranks wounded for 24 May. C.M.H.Q. totals are 12 officers and 189 other ranks killed, wounded or missing. See C.M.H.Q. Report No. 179, fn., p. 61 (mimeographed).

[27]I see little point in entering into a discussion of how the cost might have been reduced. In the light of after events it seems doubtful that further reconnaissance would have improved the Seaforths' lot on the 23rd of May. Aerial photographs of the German line opposite the Seaforths had shown a number of "unidentified objects" which later turned out to be 75 mm. anti-tank gun emplacements, and these became a prime source of trouble to the North Irish Horse. Further reconnaissance might have led to specific action against such strongpoints, and their destruction — hence to improved tank support for the infantry. But the lethal shell and mortar fire which the Seaforths faced would have made this type of specific action extremely difficult. The lack of time for reconnaissance was one of two reasons advanced by General Burns for the heavy losses sustained by the 2nd Brigade (C.M.H.Q. Report No. 179, p. 64, mimeographed). The second reason given was that the allotted frontage of 2000 yards was too narrow for an attack by three battalions. One point can be safely made: in a frontal assault within narrow boundaries and against positions as well prepared as those of the Hitler Line there is only one thing for good soldiers to do, and that is to get up and go and keep going until the objective is overrun. This, to their lasting honour, the Seaforths did.

Horse,[28] and in the afternoon the battalion moved up through Pontecorvo to a position near the banks of the Liri River a mile and a half beyond the town. Here, it was said, they would lie up for a week. A training syllabus was laid on, and the men washed and swam in the river. "It was a muddy, fast-flowing stream," the War Diary records, "and an occasional dead German went floating by."

The seven days' respite, however, did not materialize. On the night of the 29th the Seaforth companies were on their way north by T.C.V. to Ceprano, thence to a point just west of Pofi, six miles short of Frosinone. The sideroads which wound through the heavily wooded terrain were jammed with vehicles. On the battalion's left flank a strong mobile force made up of Carleton Yorks and troops of the 4th Canadian Reconnaissance Regiment were pressing forward to establish contact with elements of the French Expeditionary Corps at Ceccano on the Sacco River. Beyond Pofi the 11th Infantry Brigade of the 5th Division was closing the gap to Frosinone. The 2nd Brigade was to pass through the 11th and capture the town and the road junction beyond.

The following night, 30/31 May, the Seaforths moved up again, abandoning both their T.C.Vs. and "F" Echelon vehicles after three miles at snail's pace on clogged roads, and proceeding on foot, with complete wireless equipment, to a position under the shadow of the Frosinone heights. On the morning of the 31st the Edmontons were into the town and engaged in a light action against a German rearguard. With the Edmontons and the Patricias established as a firm base in Frosinone, the Seaforths were to attack the road junction in a flanking movement to the left. At noon Colonel Thomson began committing the battalion in two sweeps designed to bring all four companies progressively to bear upon the objective. On the inner arc, close to the town, "D" Company secured a bridge across a small stream over which "C" Company passed later in the afternoon to occupy a position dominating the road junction. On the outer arc, with a starting time two-and-one-half hours after that of "D" Company, "B" Company moved deeper into enemy territory, reached a disused railway-bed which the Germans had developed as a tank route, and followed this line of advance to come in upon the road junction from the rear. "A" Company, in a similar deep hook to the left, closed with the objective slightly to

---

[28] As a result of the close and honourable associations of the 23rd of May the North Irish Horse requested and received permission to wear the Maple Leaf as part of their regimental insignia.

the right of "B" Company. The whole operation moved like clockwork. The road junction was held by German tanks and machine-gun positions, and opposition from these, together with some brief but intense fire from mortars, caused a number of Seaforth casualties. But "A" and "B" Company moved vigorously against the strongpoint, and the enemy, obviously surprised at the speed and force of the attack, was soon routed. Later, in positions astride the crossroads, the companies had the satisfaction of ambushing German transport attempting to gain access to Highway No. 6 by way of the road from Alatri. Four German jeeps were destroyed, two trucks and one motorcycle. In the day's action, at a cost to themselves of 3 killed and 16 wounded, the Seaforths killed 4 Germans, wounded at least 3 others, and took 17 prisoners. That night the Patricias came forward to consolidate positions beyond the road junction.

For the Seaforths, as it turned out, the battle of the Liri valley was over. Drawn back to Frosinone, they watched crowded convoys of the 1st Brigade and the 4th Reconnaissance Regiment pass through them in a rapid exploitation towards Ferentino and Anagni. But Anagni, forty miles north of Cassino and the Hitler Line, was the end of commitment for the 1st Canadian Corps.[29] The Allied Fifth and Eighth armies now formed a continuous front from the head of the Liri valley to the Alban Hills. On the 3rd of June the 6th South African Armoured Division resumed the advance on the 1st Division's front and with other divisions of 13 Corps drove off to the right through the hills to the east of Rome. American units had by this time cut Highway No. 6 at Valmontone.[30] Other elements of the Fifth Army, turning sharply left, were speeding towards their promised prize, and these entered Rome on the 4th. On the 6th of June came the electrifying news, heard first by Seaforths as the relay of a German broadcast, of the opening of the second front on the coasts of Normandy. It was heartening news, and it gave rise to speculation. Perhaps now the 1st Division, which had been in action almost continuously for eleven months, would return to

---

[29]Though the commander of the Eighth Army paid glowing tribute to the work of the 1st and 5th divisions in the battle of the Liri valley, he was sharply critical of the functioning of 1st Canadians Corps Headquarters. Both General Leese and General Alexander, indeed, suggested the Corps be broken up. For a discussion of the "political" aspects of the situation, see Nicholson, *The Canadians*, pp. 450–51.

[30]Valmontone was to have been a key point in the Caesar Line defences. But the emplacements were never completed for this last-ditch position south of Rome, and the Germans were by this time in any event in no condition to man this or any other defensive line in the area.

England with the 5th and the rest of the 1st Corps to rejoin the Canadian Army. Allied commanders, however, had other plans. The Seaforths were to fight again in Italy — and in battles quite as tough as any they had experienced to date.

<hr/>

Extracts from Letters from Lieut. R.L. McDougall to Mrs. R.I. McDougall, 512–15th Street East, North Vancouver, B.C.

27 February, 1944 (Rocca San Giovanni) ... It is wonderful to be with Johnny McLean again, and with a fine company that combines happiness with efficiency to a marvellous degree. The guard of honour that I told you about in my last letter continues but will end shortly, no doubt, and then back we go again to the real job. This is a luxury job of the kind that is so good that one squirms a bit and feels like going out of one's way to make it tougher. There are some out here who have become almost fond of punishment. ... In this strange and varied existence I find the realization of place difficult. I look out through the glassless window now and see the tops of bare brown trees, and a few other trees ragged with dead leaf, and across the gully to a hillside dabbed in grey and brown, and a skyline of scrub growth. And I say to myself this is such-and-such a spot in Italy, but I'm not really convinced. Sometimes I put my finger on a map and say "There I am," but that's not much help either. Jack Conway and I spoke of this last night. He turned up recently in the neighbourhood to begin a new job at 1st Division Headquarters. He came over about six o'clock yesterday — too late for supper, but we scrounged two eggs which the cook fried up for him, and all was well. Then we sat around with a drink and talked, as the custom is. A headlight hooked to a battery shone on the white ceiling to give us light, and a make-shift kerosene stove whirred and popped softly to give us heat, and it was all quite cosy. When Jack left I walked with him out to the main road to light him on his way, and it was then that I thought, well, this is a bit unreal and might be any place and any time. The small core of light from the torch wobbled along over the shiny, light-brown mud of the cart-track, and the toes of our boots came forward rhythmically into the arc of light and then withdrew. It all seemed familiar somehow, and the stars were familiar too — the Dipper and Orion, and Castor and Pollux — and the black masses of bushes and buildings.

We must have talked for nearly an hour, standing there on that spot in Italy where a certain cart-track joins the main road north.

This assignment being what it is, we are on display, and the result is a good deal of polishing, everybody neatly turned out and very regimental. This is not very difficult since we Seaforths are so regimentally proud these days that we almost choke ourselves. As icing to the cake we have attached to us for the moment the Pipe Band. The Band is virtually intact, the result of deliberate policy, and a very wise one since in the pipes and drums is caught up practically the sole continuity of a changing regiment. They make a wonderful sight, colourful in this strange setting, just as they were when they played retreat every night on the shores of the loch at Inverary. At four o'clock one afternoon last week they played retreat in the town here, and a crowd gathered, soldiers and civilians, from goodness knows where before the bugles had blown their first measures. The Italians looked quite amazed, which is natural enough, I suppose — all except one old duffer in a ragged coat and twisted boots who stolidly wheeled a barrow across the square, oblivious to everything. It was an impressive show, however, and when Johnny took the salute from Pipes at the end there was a great hubbub of clapping and cheering. . . .

19 March, 1944 (the Crecchio positions) . . . We are back in the line again, after a short spell of rest for the battalion behind San Vito. I had meant to write you from there but went to church parade instead, which is perhaps a fair exchange. The service was held outside in a grove of olive trees beside BHQ, and the Padre's pulpit was a rickety wooden table with a Union Jack spread across it. It was a voluntary service, but the turnout was good, and I could see that Roy was happy to see so many standing around. He is a gem, an old-timer with the battalion since the days of the landings in Sicily — much before, in fact, because he was with the Seaforths when I first joined them at Stonecross in England. He has learned the subtle art of preaching successfully to men in the field, which is no mean achievement. He is a great soul — wise and kind, humorous and humane. He should be proud of the place he has won here. . . . The two weeks that have passed since then have been busy. For a time I was understudying the Adjutant, possibly with prospects, possibly not. At the moment I am back with "A" Company, happy with my platoon, re-discovering the good things that come with directing and sharing the life of a group of men. We occupy a place called "Cat", which is an Italian farmhouse far out on a limb overlooking a valley and in plain view of the Germans. It was a three-storey building when first we came here, but already the top floor has been demolished by systematic shelling. Two more to go. But when BHQ gave us the option of moving out to a less exposed position the boys said no, they thought they'd stay. At night we sally forth on patrols into the valley. . . .

9 April, 1944 (near Lanciano) . . . This past week I have been back at helping Bill Reid with the adjutancy, this time at one of our rear echelons several miles behind the line where a paper tangle had developed that had to be unravelled. Hence the writing of this letter on a typewriter. George, our one and only crusty and beloved Paymaster, is sitting at his little desk here in the orderly room, he also writing home. From time to time we both gaze in silent fixity out of the open window, thoughts tumbling round and then being drawn together. There follows the brief chatter of the typewriter and the scrape of a pen. There are also interruptions. C.S.M. Elaschuk has just been in, and I have been distracted because he's a great talker. We have wonderful times together; he was one of my section commanders when we touched down in Sicily. The salt of the earth. Momentarily, I am expecting another interruption in the form of Colin Tarbuck. He came in on a draft to the regiment a few minutes ago, piled his kit at the foot of the stairs and made off for the kitchen to have a bite of supper. I think Colin was the first Seaforth officer I saw when we arrived in England in the summer of '42. I remember the night well. It was very dark when we pulled into the station at Milford, dark enough on its own account but doubly dark because that was our first real taste of a blacked-out countryside. We piled out of the trucks onto the pavement beside the transport garage at Whitley Camp, and the person who met us was Colin, who was at the time commanding the Seaforth Company there. I remember him leading us over to the Mess, the torch he was carrying throwing light on the bottoms of his neatly pressed trews and on the shiny blackness of his shoes. Some who trooped across the parade ground that night are gone now — Dickie Wilson with the Seaforths, Dunc Grant and Bill McLellan with other units. There has been much suffered, much learned since then. . . .

Today, after a night of rain, has been splendid with sunshine. We are beginning to be aware of the greenness of things, and soon, I suppose, it will be hot and we shall grumble about that. The almond trees are in full blossom, the most gorgeous and somehow ethereal pink. There is some white blossom about too, and the white and the pink are delightful puffs of colour in the valleys and on the slopes of the hills. . . . Did you by any chance hear Churchill speak last week? I had gone downstairs to have a word about something with Sgt. Hamilton, who is our orderly-room sergeant and who with his partner Cpl. Westwell knows more about the paper work of the battalion than I am likely to learn in a lifetime, and I was sidetracked, as is so easy, into conversation before the fire. We had had an issue of beer that day, and we sipped as we talked. John LeClaire was there — ex-Brigadier LeClaire who for obscure reasons reverted to a private a year or so ago and is now our Transport Officer. Quite a character, but a good soldier as far as we are concerned. Came nine o'clock and news time, we rigged up one of the signals sets and tuned in on the B.B.C. We put the earphones in a mess-tin to make a loudspeaker, and we gathered around. When Churchill came on we thought his speech a bit disappointing. He sounded tired, as well he might be. It was a very political speech, but I suppose that is as good a sign as any that the end of the war is in sight. . . .

Extract from a Letter Written by Padre Durnford to Mrs. John Tait, President of the Seaforth Women's Auxiliary, and Published in the Christmas Issue of "The Pibroch", 1944.

Dear Mrs. Tait:

It was at the spring of the year when I sent my last dispatch to you, telling you of my visits to the hospitals and the distribution of Christmas parcels among our sick and wounded boys. . . . [31]

The month of April, 1944, found us north of Lanciano, a little town west of Ortona. A gully of 200 yards or so lay between us and the Germans, who had taken up their position in the devastated village of

---

[31] As a result of the tireless and dedicated work of the Women's Auxiliary, an unusually large shipment of food and creature comforts had reached the battalion early in the new year, and at the suggestion of Major Clark the Padre had set out immediately with a truck-load of gifts to be shared amongst Seaforths in hospitals and reinforcement depots scattered over the length and breadth of Italy. In a letter of acknowledgement to Mrs. Tait, Major Durnford had described his preparations for the trip: "First I got the boys of the Pipe Band to assist me in parcelling and tying. I had made a careful allotment of every item sent from Vancouver, so that each man should get his fair share of the good things in his parcel. Four were employed in assembling the individual parcels. Six did the wrapping up and two did the tying. We were able to tie up 225 parcels in this manner in three hours" (*The Pibroch*, May, 1944).

Crecchio. During the day neither the Germans nor we dared move, for the country was open except for shallow creeks and coulees. This no-man's-land was being watched by keen-eyed snipers from both sides. Every shell hole, every bit of jagged masonry, every vine and olive tree was suspect. The slightest movement brought machine-gun fire, and mortars fell with shattering concussion. The rains were mostly over, and the hot Italian sun beat down upon this eerie stretch of territory; only the occasional crack of a sniper's rifle broke the brooding silence and gave a hint of the lurking menace of no-man's-land.

As often as I could escape the eagle eyes of my old friends Colonel Creighton and Major Clark I would steal away from BHQ and wander up the linc to visit our outposts and forward companies. As long as I did not encourage the unwelcome attention of enemy fire by exposing myself, I was always well received. . . .

The trail between forward BHQ and our outposts and companies had been marked out by our mine-sweepers. There in the village overlooking Jerry from our side of the valley was one of our companies. They were in fact distributed over a front of about half a mile. If you saw a battered house that supported at least two walls, you could be sure that some of our boys would be there too. I would make my rounds, detouring every position exposed to enemy curiosity. But my first call was always through this village or hamlet. It had all the atmosphere of what is familiarly known as a "ghost town". Once it had been a thriving little community, but now it was in ruins and deserted. A dejected cat and her kittens and a few pet rabbits, with a lost air about them, alone remained of a population that had fled our artillery bombardment of some weeks earlier. The mangled remains of things precious to little cottage homes lay everywhere about us where the shells had blasted them. Some flower-pots had managed to survive the ordeal and were doing their best to nurture a few sickly geraniums and carnations in window sills that could no longer boast a window.

There was a strange almost furtive atmosphere about this deserted village. The silence was the more intense because the sweltering heat kept activity down to a minimum and drove our boys into the cool shade of the cellars. In one house I would find the boys fast asleep. It had been their turn the night before to patrol no-man's-land in search of information and prisoners. Most of them had returned just before dawn. In another partial ruin I would find them shaving or taking a bath in a barrel. At company headquarters there was always a wakeful alertness. Here the stillness would be broken from time to time by the peremptory buzz of the field telephone, and perhaps by the tap of a typewriter, for the company clerk was usually on the job. The Scout Officer would be poring over maps and aerial photographs of Jerry territory just across the valley. I would pass around a few cigarettes, retell the news of the day received earlier, and I think I can safely say that I never disappointed the lads when asked for the latest rumours. These, incidentally, if regarded as such and if they are sufficiently highly coloured as to appear improbable, are always enjoyed and quite exhilarating — as for instance the one I told (confidentially, of course) of the 1st Division being about to be returned to Canada to make a picture in Hollywood with Ann Sheridan and Dorothy Lamour.

The spirit of the lads in this section, as indeed on all parts of our front, was splendid. Here they were planning a night patrol into enemy lines, always a hazardous undertaking for a variety of reasons which I cannot go into here. Suffice to say that all those who go out on night patrols need nerves of steel, a knowledge of the Germans' devilish tricks and surprises, and a great resolution of purpose.

On Easter Day, the 9th of April, I held four services, one of which was attended by the lads from the front line who came out for an hour to take their Easter Communion. It was an unforgettable sight and one which I know would have gone straight to your hearts if you could have seen those boys of yours kneeling there among the deserted ruins of a farmhouse and in the presence of Him Who blessed them there. For some it was indeed the Last Supper. They now drink of a new cup in their Father's kingdom. . . .

Extract from the Diary of a Paratrooper of the 3rd Regiment, 1st Parachute Division, Captured by a Seaforth Patrol on 4 February, 1944.[32]

. . . I have changed a good deal; I cannot smile now. Here one must run for one's life. . . . We squat day and night in our anti-tank ditch. Listening posts are put forward and patrols with grenades and machine pistols. One cannot feel safe here. . . .

---

[32]Quoted in Nicholson, *The Canadians*, p. 381.

A Narrative of War

Extracts from an Interview with Lieut. W.F.J. Gildersleeve, dated 20 July, 1960, at Vancouver, B.C.

McDougall: I suppose it wasn't often in your experience with the battalion that you had the opportunity for the kind of full signals layout you had opposite Crecchio?

Gildersleeve: That's true, though of course there were difficulties there too.

McDougall: Tell me something about the netting in of sets. Radio communications so often failed. What were the problems?

Gildersleeve: Well, we had a daily assignment of call signs issued by the R.C.C.S. and brigade. We had our own frequency allotted to us, and it was simply a case of calling the companies up after we had given out the call signs and getting them to adjust their sets so they were all on the same wavelength.

McDougall: Didn't they tend to get off rather easily?

Gildersleeve: Yes, the sets might wander off if the signaller had to get up and down continually or start crawling.

McDougall: This was mechanical, because of the shaking?

Gildersleeve: It was the shaking. The dial would come loose, even though it was supposedly locked in position with the screw. Sometimes, of course, there would be intervening ground and the transmission would be blocked off. Then the batteries might run down and the signallers would not have the spares they were supposed to carry with them. We tried to keep them supplied with spares, but batteries were not always available in the numbers we needed. Or the antenna might be hit — that was a wonderful target — or a tube might go out. But chiefly it was the dial wandering off.

McDougall: How long would a set of batteries last?

Gildersleeve: A battery would last about eight hours.

McDougall: At what point did you consider it feasible to run out wire?

Gildersleeve: We would get out wire just as soon as the CO thought we would be there, in one place, for 48 hours. And of course we would save batteries right away, and there would be the chance that we could turn over our system to an incoming battalion which would repay us with a couple of reels of wire. But we had to be pretty skimpy with wire because it was hard to get. In fact sometimes I had to go out and scrounge from other divisions; we used to get the odd bit of cable from the 5th Armoured Division.

McDougall: We're using the terms "wire" and "cable" interchangeably. Was there any difference?

Gildersleeve: No. There was an assault cable, which had a light plastic cover, but we didn't use it. It was on a very light reel which could be carried quite easily by a man and unwound as he ran forward. But it was very fragile and would last only a short while. The insulation would be scraped or blown off. All our cable was earth return, a single line which the signaller took out and hooked up to his Don 5 telephone, and the other terminal was plugged into the ground with a spike.

McDougall: These worked pretty well?

Gildersleeve: Very well indeed.

McDougall: Until somebody took the wire up for a clothesline?

Gildersleeve: Yes, or until they were shelled out.

McDougall: Would you have used more wiring and Don 5s if you'd been able to get them?

Gildersleeve: I think we were taken care of all right. We were always able to get what we required eventually. We picked up quite a bit of German stuff, which was just as good as ours, sometimes better. Their telephones were certainly better, and we took quite a few of them. They were hand generator affairs which made beautiful test-phones for linesmen to go out with. The Don 5 had no generator handle; it was just a buzzer telephone.

McDougall: I suppose you had quite a complicated layout in a place like, say, the Crecchio position?

Gildersleeve: That's right. We had two ten-line boards, and both were full. We had one trunk line to 2 C.I.B. Headquarters, two direct alternate routes, routed through the artillery, and three indirect alternate routes. Six routes to get back to brigade by line.

McDougall: What would be the difference between the direct and the indirect?

Gildersleeve: Simply that in the case of the direct we would be answered by the brigade operator when we turned the generator handle; in the case of the alternate route we would be answered by the artillery operator, and we'd then ask for brigade. Then in the case of the indirect alternate route we would have to go through one of the artillery representatives with the companies, who would have his own means of communication with his senior formation, and, by this means, with brigade. All this was of course supported by radio.

Extracts from the Diary of H/Capt. Roy Durnford, Regimental Chaplain to the Seaforth Highlanders of Canada, dated 21–23 May, 1944.

21 May We did not go up the line last night after all. We go up tonight and will mill about and then go into a brigade attack on Tuesday morning. Our artillery fire and air strafing is heavy and constant. The Carleton and Yorks are having a bad time of it, I gather. Ernie McQuarrie is with their R.A.P. about 1000 yards forward from here; they are being shelled heavily, and seventeen were killed yesterday. Some of our officers have been looking at these forward positions and do not like the undulating terrain, which they think can conceal surprises for them later. It is a grand day and I can see Monastery Hill to the front of my slit trench and facing east. The Hitler Line runs to the west across the valley. Through my field glasses the monastery appears huge and in ruins. St. Benedict is buried there, and it was the cradle of the order 900 years ago. . . . We get all set to move up at 9:30 p.m., but once again the move is cancelled at the last minute.

22 May I sleep in the hovel occupied by Danny Clark, Syd Thomson and Robbie McDougall. I would have been asleep more quickly if I had been in my old slitty. The daily readings of the scriptures are very blest to me these days: "Thy word is sweet unto my mouth." As I go about among the lads I am able to sow a little here and there. God grant me a rich harvest. . . . Our artillery barrage is simply terrific. Kitty Hawks bomb and machine-gun ahead of us. German shells are dropping close by. My boys move in tonight. I see them off. How can one ever forget the scene? New boys with fears hidden under quick smiles and quick seriousness; old campaigners with a faraway look in their eyes. It is the hardest thing to watch without breaking into tears. I go up first thing tomorrow morning. The attack is at dawn. Danny Clark and I try to play checkers. . . .

23 May Wednesday morning. As I write it is 8:30 a.m. and a roaring barrage has been going on for almost four hours. Danny and I go up the line and stay there. The R.A.P., which is an old barn attached to a house, begins to fill with wounded. Incredible suffering and unbelievable bravery. Cliff Preece[33] and the M.O. of the North Irish Horse work ceaselessly throughout the day with a marvellous staff of uncomplaining helpers. The battlefield is very near. The house is a BHQ as well as a hospital, and it is a hive of activity: intelligence staff, signallers, anxious officers and battered and war-weary men weave about everywhere. Shells dropping all around the area frequently wound German prisoners who stand near the R.A.P. These Germans are either dull with shock or nervous and excitable; pale, dirty and utterly exhausted, they stagger down the line. I make tea endlessly, and soup. The boys keep coming in — some bomb-happy, some terribly broken and shell-shocked, some with limbs torn off, some almost gleefully with light wounds. . . . Johnny McLean has been wounded. Lieut. Whiting got up to the barbed wire, I'm told; he is reported killed, with others. The men of the North Irish Horse who are with us have been wonderful. Their casualties have been heavy. Ours are extremely severe. Syd Thomson is feeling the strain but has been marvellous all day. Who has not? "How are things going, Syd?" I asked him. "I don't know, Pad," he said, "but I think I've got about 100 men left in all the rifle companies, and three officers." I can't begin to tell all I have seen, but it has been our best and our worst day.

———————

Statement by K52573 Pte. L.B. Poppel of "A" Company, Taken Following the Battle of the Hitler Line, 23 May, 1944.

At 0600 hours 23 May, 1944, "A" Company crossed the start line on the left. We advanced quickly at first, meeting virtually no opposition and a minimum of shell and mortar fire. It was exceptionally misty, and the enemy added to the poor visibility by firing a bevy of smoke bombs. Moving towards the wire, No. 5 Section encountered two machine-gun posts which were hastily silenced, resulting in the capture of 4 prisoners and 4 Germans killed. It was immediately after this that Major McLean was wounded when a mortar bomb fell amongst company headquarters. With

---

[33]Captain C.G. Preece had joined the Seaforths as Medical Officer on the 25th of March, 1944, vice Major E.H. Anderson, D.S.O., who had served the battalion through the difficult period of the Moro-Ortona battles.

the aid of another man I carried Major McLean to a partly demolished house on our left and dressed his wounds. Due to the morphine and exhaustion he fell asleep, and taking this opportunity I returned to our position where I found that C.S.M. McMullen had taken command of the company, which was by now considerably depleted as a result of the devastating effect of enemy shell, mortar, and machine-gun fire — so depleted, in fact, that organization into platoons was impossible, and the remnants had formed one group. The men had moved through the wire in extended line and were now in dug-in positions along the road. Of my section there remained but two other men, and we were on the extreme right flank of the company, with the sergeant-major as the right-hand man.

It was now getting on into the afternoon, and visibility was almost perfect, though it was raining heavily. Our tank support, which was trying to move up behind us, became perfect targets for the concealed 75 mm. guns on the right and left.[34] This crossfire proved extremely effective, and within ten seconds three tanks had been kayoed. We remained in our position, waiting for further developments. This came in the form of three enemy tanks, against which we were powerless, having no P.I.A.Ts. at our position. Rolling forward, they commenced to shoot us up with machine-guns, stopping at several slit trenches and taking prisoners. I lay low where I was until 3 a.m., the night being punctuated by bursts of fire, movement of tracked vehicles, and shouting. All apparently enemy. When it became quiet I moved down the road towards the 3rd Brigade area, passing through the Royal 22me lines, and arrived back at our BHQ at 0915 hours, 24 May, 1944.

Statement by K50302 Pte. H.F. Dore, Taken Following the Battle of the Hitler Line.

My role in the battle was as part of a special assault section made up of Sgt. Storch, Cpl. Moore, two engineer personnel, three riflemen and myself — all carrying bangalore torpedoes and beehives for the purpose of blowing wire and dugouts.

We moved onto the start line behind "D" Company headquarters. At zero-hour (0600) we moved off, advancing 100 yards, then going to ground

----

[34]The tanks referred to here may have been part of the composite force from the North Irish dispatched that afternoon to support the Seaforth positions on the road.

in a ditch due to heavy enemy mortar and shell fire. I saw a Seaforth walking back, his arm bloody and apparently suffering from severe shock. We pulled him into the ditch and told him to remain there until it was possible for him to go to the rear. We spent fifteen minutes in this ditch, then moved forward.

There was much smoke and mist, and in this poor visibility our sergeant, the Pioneer and one man were separated from the rest of the party. Myself and the remainder advanced past a house which was, I believe, later used as our advanced battalion dressing station. There were six or seven German bodies around this house. We then went into a hollow, at the bottom of which was a ditch partly covered by bushes and grain on either side. It ran in line with our line of advance to the enemy wire. We proceeded up the ditch. I noticed two of our tanks burning, one on either side of the ditch, then saw two wounded men lying on the right edge of the hollow, just in front of the wire. They were Clarke and Lipsey of "D" Company, and we got them into cover. We approached the wire and found it to be low and quite damaged by shell fire, so that bangalore torpedoes were not needed. We crossed the wire under heavy machine-gun fire, enfilade and frontal, then saw Pte. F. Wilkin of "D" Company returning with four prisoners at the point of a Bren Gun which he had picked up when the gunner was killed. We directed him to the rear. We also saw a German dying just beyond the wire, near a machine-gun post.

From the wire we cut over to the right, moving to the left of a 75 mm. gun mounted on a tank turret set in concrete. To our left was a German wheeled anti-tank gun. We moved to the road, our first objective, when our own artillery came down behind it. This barrage was terrific, so we drew back to a dugout a few yards behind the 75 mm. emplacement (a lot of the shells were dropping short). Finding the entrance to the dugout booby-trapped by a beehive, and wires, we entered by the other end, near the road, to shelter from the shell and mortar fire. From here we saw a Seaforth, Pte. Wedge, walking in from the right flank without weapons. He was suffering from severe shock and had to be kept in the dugout for safety. Then Pte. Stewart passed the dugout with three prisoners.

I left the dugout to assist Stewart, and we went to the 75 mm. emplacement, looked into the dugout beneath it and saw enemy therein. When ordered, they began to file out, then dashed in again. I fired a shot into the entrance, and three of the Jerries came out; then I threatened to throw a No. 36 grenade into the dugout, and two more came out. Three of the prisoners were paratroopers, one of them an officer. They were in a state of terror. We took them to the spot where earlier I had crossed the wire, and up the ditch and over the bank past the dressing station, where we met a Provost Major and some of his men, and turned the prisoners over to them. One Provost was killed by shell fire, and another wounded, as we did so. On the way in we had noticed many dead lying about, and seven tanks burning in a small area on either side of the ditch. By this time visibility had improved slightly, but enemy fire was heavy and continuous.

After turning over the prisoners, we started back to the first objective. On the way we stopped in at the Edmontons' advanced dressing station and were advised to remain there until a then particularly heavy shelling had abated. While we were there a shell fell beside the house, killing one man and seriously wounding an Edmonton officer and a signaller. Ferguson, Kerr and I then resumed our return forward. We went across to a house where Seaforth, P.P.C.L.I. and Edmonton wounded were sheltering. We stayed there half an hour, then went forward to the gully on our front. We were half way down the hill when machine-guns from the other side of the gully, and to the left, began sniping at us, so we returned to the house. Three tanks were burning and exploding on the edge of the gully. We tried to cross again an hour later, but we were unable to do so. We took up positions in slit trenches to the right of this house. Then Stave, a runner, gave us a message to return to BHQ, which we did and were ordered to dig in there on the left. We were digging in when we were ordered to return to the front. We went up in single file to our advanced dressing station and awaited further orders. By 9 p.m. we were soaked from the rain. We stayed in these positions all night, our tanks firing from time to time and enemy tanks firing back, wounding three of the men here. Our wounded were coming in from forward areas. We returned to BHQ the next morning as a body.

Statement by Company Sergeant-Major J.M. Duddle of "C" Company, Taken Following the Battle of the Hitler Line.

... As we went forward, No. 13 Platoon struck off in the wrong direction, and although I went after them to divert their line of approach I could not contact them due to the heavy smoke pall that was now hanging over the front. Returning, I contacted No. 14 Platoon and continued the advance with it. After advancing approximately 300 yards we came under an intense artillery concentration. Mr. Robertson, the platoon commander, was badly wounded; three men were killed and six others wounded. The tanks, in support, were coming up now, and we attempted to gather information as to the situation forward from the squadron commander, but to no avail. Moving forward some distance with Cpl. Mountford, I encountered Pte. Campbell, who said that "A" and "B" companies were pinned down by fire a slight distance ahead. Heavy artillery and Nebelwerfer fire was still coming down, and three of our tanks had by this time been knocked out by anti-tank fire. Our group moved forward again, and after 50 yards advance captured five Germans and sent them to the rear. Eventually, about fifteen strong, we reached a building where we attempted to consolidate, digging in and awaiting further information.

We were informed that we were now almost 200 yards beyond our first objective and were to withdraw to the lateral road, where the remnants of "C" Company were posted. On our arrival, we found Major Allan and C.S.M. Moss, with the remaining men of "B" and "D" companies in position. Major Allan's orders were to hold the position. Snipers were active, and artillery and mortar fire was still heavy. Communication had been established by wireless with BHQ. Two men, Pte. Gustafson and Pte. Richardson, and myself went forward with a P.I.A.T. to stop a tank about 200 yards to our right. We approached to within 30 yards of a tank which was not the tank previously seen, and we moved into a fire position. Pte. Gustafson was informed of the direction and the range of the target, and very calmly removed his glasses and commenced to polish them. Resting the P.I.A.T. tripod on Richardson's back in order to get sufficient elevation to clear the tall grass, he fired two bombs, both of which exploded against the tank. Immediately, machine-gun fire opened up from another tank, and we withdrew to our previous position. We then fired with rifles on any enemy to be seen around the tanks. About five minutes later the tanks moved away.

About this time Cpl. Jenkins of No. 15 Platoon contacted me with information that there were still men of "C" Company out in front of us. Sgt. Game, Cpl. Jenkins and myself went forward to a position where we found three badly wounded men, in addition to six others. I decided we would have to improvise stretchers to remove them, and on Pte. Henderson's suggestion we went up to a house a little way ahead and returned with a few pieces of railing, which, with the aid of our tunics, webbing and shirts, was fashioned into two rude stretchers. Returning to the wounded, we were forced to go to ground by the re-appearance of three German tanks which cut forward to Major Allan's position and opened fire. By now it had started to rain, and we were extremely cold. Cpl. Jenkins worked his way back to the road, and on returning said that some prisoners had been taken away on tanks and quite a number killed.

We decided that this was the time to get out with the wounded. As we got up I noticed a German standing about 100 yards to our left. I waved for him to come over, but he did the same and eventually turned and walked towards a tank. We headed back towards BHQ under heavy artillery fire. Encountering a stretcher party after about 400 yards, we gave our wounded to them. A few minutes later we discovered lying beside his tank a very badly wounded lieutenant of the North Irish Horse, who told us there was a stretcher in the third tank away. There was no stretcher there, but beneath the tank were two badly burned troopers with one man in attendance. They said they would try to walk back, but one, who was practically blind, had to be half carried out. We arrived at BHQ at 1930 hours.

Having given the Adjutant my report, I remained at BHQ until 2100 hours, when, at the Adjutant's request, I guided a stretcher party made up of members of the Protection Group in an attempt to find some of our wounded. It was dark by now and very difficult to locate any particular spot. However, we found a Seaforth lying in a slit trench, and he was removed. We also found a wounded officer in a Churchill tank, and an additional man burnt around the body. The officer told me that the enemy had set up a machine-gun post on the ridge, and I could hear German voices in addition to the movement of vehicles. We carried the two wounded back to BHQ, arriving about 0100 hours, 24 May.

I would like to say that every man with me displayed magnificent courage at all times. Sgt. Game, Cpl. Jenkins, Ptes. Gustafson, Richardson and Henderson,[35] and Cpl. Kalinauskas, all performed miracles, showing great determination and bravery above the call of duty.

---

[35]Cpl. W. Henderson was subsequently awarded the M.M. But it is clear that there could not possibly be enough medals available to match all the bravery shown on the 23rd of May.

Statement by H17393 Cpl. B.C. Garrioch of "B" Company, Taken Follow-
ing the Battle of the Hitler Line.

Almost immediately after we crossed the start line we ran into heavy shell and mortar fire, and within the first ten seconds the platoon had suffered two casualties. Lieut. Artindale moved our platoon forward into a gully before the wire. Here we found Cpl. Cameron of "C" Company wounded, and two others killed. Moving on again, we were stopped by the wire, and it became obvious we were not in our battalion area. Cpl. Beard and Cpl. Cromb left the platoon and crossed to the right in an attempt to find the company. After a short time, however, the platoon commander decided that we were by now quite a way behind the forward troops, and so without waiting for the two corporals to return we pushed on through the wire, where we found a Carleton and York company digging in. Swinging right along the wire, we ran into a small gully, which proved a haven in the hail of Nebelwerfer fire which was coming down. Here we contacted three men of "A" Company.

From this point we turned onto the road, gaining same and without further casualties and with five prisoners removed from a dugout as prize. However, since there was a terrific amount of fire coming down on the road, Mr. Artindale decided to head for a small house about 200 yards beyond. Half of us made the house, the remainder stayed on the road. Around the house were a series of German trenches, and we inhabited these. Around the trenches were a few "A" Company men. Firing was still very heavy, but Cpl. MacDonald left the position and contacted an approaching tank, which in turn informed BHQ by wireless of our position and asked for instructions. It developed that we were on the startline of a new barrage which was about to commence. Fifteen men returned to the first objective to dig in, while Pte. Barkase and Pte. Dupuis and myself remained in the slit trenches around the house. Within a few minutes three German tanks approached from the right and commenced to shoot up the men in the road position and take the remainder away on their backs. Meanwhile, a few feet from my own position were two dug-in 8.1 cm. mortars, which Dupuis and myself destroyed by dropping grenades into the barrels. The explosions drew the attention of the tanks, and they fired five armour-piercing rounds at the house, smashing the remaining wall.

About 1700 hours Dupuis went back to the lateral road but found no one but a wounded "A" Company man, Pte. Russel, whom he brought back to our own trench. We patched his wounds to the best of our ability, but it couldn't have been too effective because he died during the night. About half an hour later Dupuis went out again to contact aid and get a stretcher for Russel. He did not return. From 2000 hours to 2200 hours a German tank machine-gunned us intermittently but made no attempt to come and get us. We went to sleep about 2300 hours. At first light we were awakened by the noise of tracked vehicles, which were tanks of the 5th Division.

I buried Russell, and Barkase and myself started back, coming under fire from a tank or self-propelled gun. I arrived at BHQ at approximately 0730 hours, 24 May.

———————

Extracts from an Interview with Brigadier S.W. Thomson, dated 15 July, 1961, at Victoria, B.C.

McDougall: Have you any after-thoughts about the Hitler Line?

Thomson: Not very deep ones. Because it was probably our most disastrous engagement, we tried to analyze where we had gone wrong. It was very much a set-piece attack: tape start-line and boundaries and everything. I think most of us felt that more smoke should have been used locally.

McDougall: I was reading the account at Army and Corps level this morning, and certainly smoke was laid on — and in quite heavy concentrations.

Thomson: Where? On the flanks?

McDougall: It doesn't say exactly.

Thomson: Well, I mean local smoke, on the objective, because of the anti-tank guns in the emplacements. If we'd had local smoke we might have been able to get in amongst them. There was plenty of smoke on our side of the wire, of course, but that doesn't seem to have done much good. Any way you look at it, the crux of the matter was the silencing of those anti-tank guns. While I think of it, I recall we were criticized for having our headquarters too far forward in the battle. I don't understand it, because at no time was my headquarters affected by enemy action.

McDougall: The stuff was falling all around, but not on BHQ.

Thomson: Do you recall it falling behind?

McDougall: I think some of it was hitting troops formed up ready to come through.

Thomson: Anyway, I couldn't have controlled the battle from farther back.

McDougall: No, it wasn't all that far forward. It turned out to be an excellent BHQ.

Thomson: But when we got 300 yards forward from there we were in trouble every time. I tried three times to go up. I thought at first I was going to ride up on a Honey Tank, but it hit a mine. I finally made it on foot. . . .

McDougall: Was the Honey Tank standing by for your use?

Thomson: Yes. You remember, it was a tank they used in the desert, and they took the turrets off. It was for command use in getting from here to there when the shells were falling.

McDougall: How were your communications with the North Irish Horse?

Thomson: Very poor. I believe Colonel Strickland himself went up to take command of the squadrons, but I never saw him, never talked to him after the battle started.

McDougall: You don't remember the North Irish any farther forward than the fringe of the wood?

Thomson: As far as I'm concerned, they never were. A few of them went forward later; certainly during the main battle they never got beyond the fringe of the wood, which was not very far from the start-line. But of course it wasn't their fault.

McDougall: Have you any thoughts about the problem of command in a battle like this one?

Thomson: I have no answer for it. Technical people have always done the best they could to get the answer. It's just that war is difficult. We lost touch eventually with Jim Allan on the objective. I remember the last thing I told him on the set while it was running was that I was coming up to spend the night with him. I started out with the I.O., Bobbie Swinton, and Wilf Gildersleeve, I think it was, and we got up to the positions, found the weapons, the slit trenches, but no personnel. We found some Germans in a dugout. . . .

McDougall: Where was Jim then?

Thomson: He'd come back with a handful of men. He'd been hit in the backside. But you ask about command. I think that given the basic training a commander needs, there's only one thing that matters from then on in, and that's what they call leadership. My experience was that you never really had any opportunity to use tactics as tactics was taught. There were exceptions, and the show at Frosinone may have been one of them. But in most cases the task was laid down, tied often to a start line. You somehow didn't have much choice for the use of ground, or seldom. From then on, all you could do was exercise a kind of personal force. . . .

McDougall: Then there's the crucial period, following the commitment to attack, when you almost lose control; it passes out of your hands temporarily into the hands of the companies. You have to find out what they're doing in order to resume control.

Thomson: But even then the influence you have, the opportunity to influence, is very small. Because you're often told exactly how you are to approach the task. For instance, the Hitler Line — two companies up and two behind. We had no reserve. Even if we had success there was nothing we could do except report it. . . . The picture that sticks in my mind is the way the Edmontons became involved behind the Patricias when they should never have gone in at all. It was a stereotyped scheme; they would go in, they did go in, when I'm sure they never should have when we knew how little success the Patricias were having. . . .

McDougall: I have a picture of the good work that so many did that day. I remember Don Colquhoun organizing the carriers with stretchers and going out again and again after wounded. This was when the Support Company people, who were mostly out of it, felt so terribly about the battalion being cut up. . . .

———————

Extract from a Letter from Captain R.L. McDougall to Mrs. R.I. Mc-Dougall, 512–15th Street East, North Vancouver, B.C., dated 8 June, 1944.

Dearest mother:

You must worry as the days draw out and no letter comes, and you know that the time grows longer, longer since you last heard. I'm sorry for that, but I have had little choice because of the swift flow of events. Now I draw a breath, and into our shiny new typewriter, recently liberated, I roll this letter form, liking the clearness of the print and the firmness of the table and the crisp clack-clack of the keys. The typewriter becomes a symbol of stability.

We have had a rough time of it these last two weeks. But the job was done, and I think done well. There was a price; you will perhaps have seen the casualty lists. I believe some stories on the Seaforths have been released to the Press now, and you will get some sort of picture from these when you read them. For once, over-writing will match the event. It was Jimmy Parish who told me that the Seaforth stories were being released.[36] He breezed into our BHQ a few days ago, brown-tanned and merry, and the seven months since I had seen him last seemed hardly to exist. That was quite a BHQ. The wave of fighting had been rolling forward, and for a while we rode the crest of it. And then suddenly we lost the movement and the lift of it, and the crest was gone. On up the valley it went, seen sometimes in the smoke-dust burst of shells and the white clouds rising from the churn of columns moving up the road, and heard in the sounds of battle receding. We found ourselves left high and dry like a chip of wood on the top of a hill, or rather on the spine of a ridge, with BHQ set up in an enormous white-walled mansion and the companies clustered around. The history of the mansion was uncertain. Some said it was one of Mussolini's numerous country estates, others that it was a girls' school in the piping days of peace. For a few days, in any event, it was ours. It was an enormous establishment, and when we had spaced ourselves out in it almost to the point of loneliness there must still have been about thirty rooms left over. No luxury, of course, for the place had been stripped of everything, absolutely everything—not a piece of furniture of any kind, no pictures, no chandeliers, no carpets, no beds, no tables, no chairs. Nothing that could be taken was left. Just a lot of rooms,

---

[36]Captain James Parish, English dramatist and free-lance writer, was a Press Relations Officer with the Eighth Army.

bare, high-ceilinged, frescoed, blank walls showing only the marks where tapestries and pictures had hung. Long corridors, innumerable stairways and landings, a few rooms with straw covering the floors on which the Germans had slept such a few hours before, great kitchens and fouled bathrooms. But even the army's touch is human, and beneath our hands the dead building, or at least a part of it, came again to life. It was a lovely setting, with the hills near at hand and a valley of lavish beauty laid out below.

It was here that Jimmy caught up with me, and we had a good talk that took me back to the days of convalescence at Chenoua Plage and Algiers. After supper we listened to the Pipe Band play Retreat on the sweep of driveway before the house, and then I drove Jimmy back to his headquarters. We skimmed along Highway No. 6, fought for not many hours before, now serene and silvered in the moonlight. By night only the craters and the blown bridges remind one of what has passed. . . .

I am very busy cleaning up work that has accumulated during the battle. I have still no word from brother Dick; I suppose he will be caught up in one way or another in the great events taking place now in the west. These are momentous days. In a short time we shall know whether the road is near its end or whether there are long stretches still ahead.

Much love,

Rob.

• Cap-Saint-Ignace
• Sainte-Marie (Beauce)
Québec, Canada
1996